HARDY
PLANTS
and
ALPINES

HARDY
PERENNIAL
PLANTS

including ALPINES

ALAN BLOOM

PREFACE

In this completely new edition, the two sections of perennial plants, which have been published separately in earlier editions, have been brought together into one book. As author, I welcome the innovation. Whenever I have been asked to classify them separately, I am hampered by the fact that there is no clear distinction to be drawn. So many so-called alpine or rock garden plants are adaptable and suitable for growing in front of taller plants, or as edging groups. The only section of perennials which requires the true alpine conditions, i.e. of very gritty or porous soil, are those which come from high altitudes or very low rainfall areas of the world.

Advice on cultivation begins on page 10.

Alan Bloom

Alan Bloom

First edition published 1990 in the U.K. by Burall + Floraprint Ltd, Wisbech, PE13 2TH

British Library Cataloguing in Publication Data
Bloom, Alan 1906-
    Hardy perennial including alpines.
    1. Gardens. Hardy perennial plants
    I. Title
    635.9'32

    ISBN 0-903001-62-4

(Above) *Pyrethrum* or *Chrysanthemum* Coccineum-hybrids (this one is 'Brenda') always like sunny spots.

(Page 1) *Tradescantia* andersoniana-hybrid 'Purewell Giant'.

(Page 2) The white gardens at Sissinghurst Castle with, among other plants, *Artemisia stelleriana*, and the beautiful ornamental pear *Pyrus salicifolia* with its greyish branches.

(Page 3) *Coreopsis verticillata* 'Grandiflora' provides a bright welcome to everybody on this entrance path.

Picture sources: I.G.A., Liechtenstein (the Floraprint picture library)
Back cover: Blooms of Bressingham

The publisher cannot be held responsible for possible consequences of inaccuracies occurring in spite of all care taken in publication.

Index compiled by Richard Raper of Indexing Specialists.
Printed in Holland.

CONTENTS

* With the advent of wider European interest, extra plant groups have been included in addition to Alan Bloom's own selection. These are marked throughout by an asterisk*. All text for these extra groups, the colour panels and the picture captions are by the publisher.

ADAPTABILITY

Veronica teucrium, now called *V. austriaca* ssp. *teucrium*, is a species which belongs to lightly shadowed woodland margins on loamy or slightly limy soils. The variety 'Royal Blue' does very well in this border near the Dutch castle Walenburg.

Above: Festuca glauca prefers rather dry sites such as here between rocks and stones in full sun.

'Edelweiss', *Leontopodium alpinum*, needs sun and good drainage. Unlike a lot of other alpine species it adapts very well to our climate.

Adaptability

Other than the true alpine subjects demanding special conditions, one other group of perennials also has a narrow limit of adaptability: these are those which in nature grow in the shade of tall trees or rock cliffs on north-facing slopes. A much smaller range requires permanently moist conditions, but the vast majority of subjects outside these special groups have a quite wide adaptability even if they prefer mainly open sunny positions, as in their native habitat. It is worth remembering that plants took millions of years to become adapted to certain conditions of life, and it follows that they grow best 'in captivity', as it were, where grown in a more-or-less similar environment.

Hardiness

This factor is also determined largely in the climate in which plants grow in the wild. In a general way, all species other than tropical should be hardy in the temperate zones of Europe and North America. But there are such variations of climate within the temperate zones – such as California and Vermont, or Sicily and Sweden – that no rules can be applied. There is also the matter of snow cover in Winter: some plants will survive in Montreal or Moscow with reliable snow cover which would perish from soil-penetrating frost in Britain. Another factor in the matter of hardiness is drainage. In soils which become soggy and sticky in Winter, frost is likely to be more damaging than in free-draining soil. But again, it must be stressed that the great majority of perennials will survive even if frozen solid for several weeks.

Salvia superba 'May Night' and *Helenium* 'Moerheim Beauty'.

Left: South-American pampas grass may rot away during our wet winters, if not protected properly.

Sedum acre will withstand most conditions if undisturbed.

FASCINATION

This plant lover's garden is filled with a great number of perennial and herbal plants to provide a spectacular vista.

The Fascination of Variety

In recent years there has been a decided swing in popularity towards perennials. This has come about not only because they are such good value in terms of garden worthiness, but because of the immense range in existence. Many erstwhile 'Cinderella' species have been introduced; and to search for, prove and distribute them has given me intense pleasure over the past 50 years or more.

Now that the trend towards variety is well and truly begun, it will yield many more useful, beautiful plants for the enthusiast.
And it can be safely said that once a person becomes interested in growing a wide variety, a new dimension is added to the pleasure of gardening.

Ways and Means

It is also safe to say that scarcely a garden exists which would be an unsuitable site for perennials. This statement must of course be qualified by adding that some gardens might require a special selection to be made. The 'adaptability factor' needs to be observed, and the lists of kinds for special purposes or conditions on pages 229-245 will be helpful. But one may be assured that whatever conditions prevail — shade or sun, wet or dry, stony and clay soil, alkaline or acid, as well as climatic extremer — a suitable collection of perennials can be made. Furthermore, perennials can be grown in one-sided or island beds as edging plants, on banks or as ground coverers. Those in the category of alpines need not be grown in a rockery or rock garden. They will in fact grow better in raised beds without rocks, whilst the peat bed can hold many treasures which prefer acid and humus-rich soil, whether for sun or partial shade.

A display of *Campanula*, *Lavandula* and *Tunica*.

Though rather short flowering, *Delphinium* is appealing.

Garden-worthiness

This is a factor which must make allowance for individual taste and appreciation. In a general way, and in my personal opinion, reliability as perennials ranks No. 1. Long flowering, complementary foliage, tidy habit and overall grace are equally as important as brilliance in flower. But some subjects, such as *Iris* and paeonies for example, have appeal for some people even if they have a relatively brief flowering period. Much the same applies to *Delphinium* and oriental poppies; but if they are more troublesome to grow, it is a matter of personal choice — as long as one is prepared for the extra care required in staking, dead-heading or whatever.

GUIDELINES

A summer garden.

A modern border.

Guidelines for Success

One must of course begin with basics. Plants need reasonably good soil in which to grow; they need enough but not too much moisture; and they need light and air. Most kinds in nature also need sunshine and it makes sense that the greatest success comes from providing conditions of soil and situation as near as possible to those in nature. But since different subjects also have varying habits and rates of growth, planning for position is important, taking these factors into account. Light and air make for sturdy growth, and overcrowding should be avoided. This can be achieved with planning so that taller subjects do not overshadow those of lowlier height.

These are the broad outlines, applicable both to the so-called 'border perennials' and to those mostly classed as alpine or rock garden plants. More specific and detailed advice is given under the various headings which follow. These indicate, in fact, the many ways in which perennials of all heights and habits can be grown, with the widely varying garden conditions, including those of climate, which are likely to occur.

Perennial Beds or Borders: the Choice

Where the options are open as to the type of bed or border one chooses, the most pleasing and least demanding of maintenance comes down firmly on the side of island formation. All-round access also provides all-round vision. Naturally, the tallest subjects are placed in the centre parts, and heights are then graded down towards the outside, where quite dwarf kinds can be used.

Except where space is very limited, or where the maximum variety takes precedence over effect, each kind should be in groups of three or more plants. Grouping enhances the overall effect, makes planning simpler, and enables easy access for weeding, if a little more space is given between each group than between the plants comprising the group. Given adequate light and air, which is a strong feature in favour of island beds, the amount of staking or supporting will be far less than for a one-sided herbaceous border.

The Height/Width factor

The most common fault with the older, conventional one-sided perennial border is lack of width in relation to the height of subjects grown. The backing hedge, fence or wall has the effect of increasing the heights because the plants are competing for sun, light or air. The tendency is to lean away from the backing and so the tall kinds loll forward over the shorter ones in front, which makes staking necessary for the majority. In addition, the overall effect is spoiled by excessive height when in full growth, and access for maintenance is extremely difficult.

A quite simple rule to observe when planning and planting is to avoid tall subjects for any but the widest of beds. If the effective width for a bed or border is, say, eight feet (2.5 m), restrict the selection to subjects which do not exceed four feet high (120 cm), when in flower. This guide applies both to one-sided and islands beds: the difference between the two is that tall kinds are placed at the rear of one-sided beds, and in the centre parts of the island formation.

Sites, Shapes and Sizes

No-one can dispute a garden owner's right to change or develop it as he or she thinks fit. Nevertheless, a sense of fitness will appeal to most people as a vital ingredient to harmony. Compromises may have to be made, for so often one's garden plot is hemmed in by fixed environmental features in which true harmony has no place. Such a situation — for instance an oblong garden plot surrounded by the formality of boundaries and other buildings — does not suggest informality within. Yet it can be achieved if, when introducing a space in which to grow perennials, one concentrates on the latent harmony between the various subjects used.

One should not, of course, have a free-form bed or border or imitation mountain scenery in a suburban garden. Whenever formal outlines prevail, the shape of a bed or border should conform to them, but within it the informality of the plants themselves will become the focus in which harmony is to be found or achieved. Perennials have such wide variations of habit, form, height, season and colour that even a small selection offers scope for creativity.

Above: A brilliant example of a well balanced height/width relationship in the white garden at Sissinghurst Castle.

This rather modern house suits straight and strongly lined plants like *Kniphofia*.

ONE-SIDED BORDER

This border at Killerton Gardens, arranged close to the house, leaves plenty of path space.

Making the best of a one-sided Border

Although island beds are now accepted as the rational and most effective means of growing perennials, many gardeners feel they have no alternative to the one-sided border. The backing is often that of a boundary fence, hedge or wall. The centre lawn is where a degree of privacy is valued, but a mixture of perennials and shrubs as a screen is not likely to be a great source of interest if this is their main purpose.

Shrubs and perennials do not cohabit well; and wherever planting is crowded or indiscriminate, the incongruity as well as the problem of maintenance can only become steadily worse.
A decision may be hard to take, but where a feature is neither one thing nor the other, it is likely to be a hotch-potch or an eyesore. For those who

shy at converting part of a central lawn into an oblong garden plot, a fair compromise is possible. At the far end of the lawn is often a place where a few vegetables or fruits are grown. Here a small island bed can be made, fronted by the lawn, with just a narrow path behind. Beside the latter, dwarf early-flowering perennials can be grown, allowing ample space for taller, summer and autumn-flowering subjects to take over. Viewed from afar, such a bed becomes a focal point, drawing one's attention more closely to the interesting variety it contains for much of the year.

Perennials in Shade

Primulas and *Lamium maculatum* 'Silver Dollar' do well in shade.

A well shaded garden in the city with ferns and *Hosta sieboldiana* 'Elegans'.

The shade factor varies all the way from passing shadows made by trees or buildings, to the dense low shade of evergreens. The latter is the most difficult to fill because so often the soil is starved as well. Although the selection of subjects which will tolerate dry low shade is relatively small, the range of those that prefer some shade along with humus-rich soil is both wide and fascinating. So much so that some keen gardeners contrive these conditions in order to grow what they regard as special treasures, perhaps a peat bed in which calcifuge (lime-hating) plants especially will flourish. Such beds, with dappled or partial shade, or north facing, can be on the flat or raised, or as a terrace. But peat by itself is not enough. A little good soil and sharp sand and perhaps bark or leaf mould should form 30-40% of the mix and should not be allowed to become parched in a dry time. The range of plants preferring such cool moist conditions is quite entrancing. But then, much the same thing can be said of a bed specially prepared with gritty soil in full sun for the fascinating range of true alpines.

RENOVATION

Above: A beautiful, one-sided border, in yellow and white, needing regular attention to avoid weed infestation.

A so-called 'rough garden' in Kent. Another solution to the border problem. The oast houses, originally used for drying hops, have been converted.

Renovating an old Border

Since island beds are a relatively modern development (which the author has pioneered), almost all unthrifty herbaceous borders are those with a backing. A fence or wall is less of a disability than a hedge if only because a hedge has voracious roots as well as an encroaching habit of growth. As previously emphasised, it is unfair to expect perennials to compete for sustenance, light and air, and so often plants grow spindly if deprived of these essentials.

If the backing hedge is a necessary feature for a screen or windbreak, any border restoration plan should allow adequate space between the plants and the hedge. It is a case of having to give in to the demands made by a hedge.

This space of about 2 feet (60 cm) is necessary even for a newly-planted hedge and more than that for, say, a well-established evergreen such as yew, laurel, leylandii and privet.

Old one-sided borders are almost always too narrow in relation to the height of plants they contain. It is also more than likely that some are weedy by nature and this applies especially to golden rod (*Solidago*) and some of the *Aster* (Michaelmas daisy) tribe. One may have to be ruthless, for there are probably pernicious perennial weeds lurking there as well. Creeping thistle, couch, bindweed, ground elder, call for drastic treatment; for, unless a site is cleared of such weeds at the outset, disappointing losses will occur. A systemic weedkiller may well be needed but should be used with the utmost care. In any event, a thorough digging and shaking-out with a fork of all unwanted growth is essential to provide good soil conditions, adding humus where soil is poor, or sharp sand where it is heavy clay or liable to pan.

In my experience, it involves more risks and troublesome work to restore a derelict border than to begin again from scratch. Ground coverers may well be the answer to an old border which has become an eyesore.

Dividing an old *Geum* plant with a spade.

Replanting the divided parts.

A plant-lover's nursery-plot.

Sedums and sempervivums are easy to grow and dividable in Spring.

Next to growing from seeds and cuttings, dividing is the most common propagation system for perennials, though not usable for all. This can be done in late autumn or early spring. Lift the plant and divide the clump. Generally, active growth is mainly restricted to the outer ring, so discard the old central section. Replant the divided pieces of the outer ring. Plant at the same depth as the original clump.

SELECTIONS

Above: Part of the exclusive monastry gardens of Han Njio in the south of Holland, showing all kinds of shades of *Sedum* and *Sempervivum*.
Below: A harmonious border with *Lysimachia nummularia*, ('Creeping Jenny'), and *Geranium platypetalum* in front.

Making Selections

Profound changes have taken place in gardening habits over the past 30 years or so. The proliferation of garden centres has been largely the result of a more mobile public. But there has also been a great upsurge in interest in gardening due to the spread of housing estates as opposed to old-type terraces where individual gardens could not exist.

But few things in life, including improved amenities, are without their snags, and one of these is the effect of impulse buying of nursery products. People have in general become less discriminating in what they buy on sight — or how they stock up a new garden. So many plants, trees or shrubs are now on offer, grown in containers, that gardens tend to become stocked piecemeal fashion with little or no regard to anything but immediate effect. Such effect is often fleeting or transient simply through lack of reliable information on what is the plant's potential or requirement for good growth.

Finally, a word about quality is in order. It is a fact that good quality but higher-priced plants are, in the long run, less expensive than those that are cheap but of poor quality. What prospective buyers should do is to study the subject of quality if they are inexperienced. Compare the quality of different garden centres, and conclusions will come down against rubbishy cheap stock. Another comparison is worth while: that of service. Almost invariably the sales centre which offers reliable and knowledgeable help will be a sign that both service and quality go together.

Below: A smooth link between path and raised borders.

Winter Protection for Tender Plants

Throughout the alphabetical lists, any doubts upon the hardiness of certain subjects are given in the light of the author's experience of them.

Wherever snow cover (which is a protector) is not reliable, artifical cover needs to be applied, or plants should be lifted in Autumn and kept in a frost-free frame or greenhouse. Some, such as *Cosmos* and certain varieties of *Crocosmia* (the *Montbretia* type) may be be lifted and stored in peat until safe to plant in Spring.

Other tender plants fall roughly into three groups:
1. Alpines, such as *Raoulia* and *Frankenia,* which form dense evergreen mats, need only be covered with glass, if left outside.
2. Tender plants which lose all foliage in Winter, i.e. the truly herbaceous, should be covered before hard frosts arrive with material which will stay fairly dry. Coarse bark, or polystyrene packing material, up to four inches deep (10 cm), are effective. So are beech or oak leaves and hedge clippings; but leaves need twigs on top, or some other means of preventing them from blowing away. Any leaves or foliage, peat or material which soaks up rain, or rots away, should be avoided.
3. With plants which do not lose foliage entirely, or semi-shrubby plants such as *Kniphofia* and *Penstemon*, straw, bracken or the material mentioned above, should be placed on the soil around the plants, mounding up to protect leaves and stems in a pyramid fashion. *Kniphofia* and other such leaves are best tied up to prevent rain, snow or slush from penetrating the otherwise open centre of the plant. As a general rule, tender perennials should retain what foliage they have, and not be cut back or trimmed until new growth is about to begin. This practice can also be applied to fully-hardy plants.

Treading between plants on wet or heavy soil in Winter is best avoided, even if old growth is not cut off. Well into the new year, or when new growth is about to begin, is also a good time to fork over the soil, mixing in any fertiliser deemed necessary. Generally, a low nitrogen organic fertiliser is to be preferred, and should be scattered between the plants at a rate of no more than two ounces per square yard (70 grams per square metre.)

Above: *Gunnera* is not hardy, and needs protection over Winter in cold districts.

Right: A sheet of glass over alpines will protect them against winter rain.

Below: Putting a winter covering over perennials.

HARDY PERENNIAL PLANTS

including

ALPINES

A - Z

Anaphalis triplinervis 'Schwefellicht', *Liatris*, and *Campanula*.

ACAENA

Acaena microphylla 'Kupferteppich' ('Copper Carpet') showing the red burrs that make this species very good value for money.

Acanthus
The inflorescence of Acanthus remains decorative for a long time after the plant has finished flowering. In fact, the decorative value lies much more in the purple bracts than in the flowers themselves.
The Acanthus motif was used as a decoration of Greek columns centuries before Christ.
Acanthus combines very nicely with for instance Echinacea purpurea, Lavatera olbia and Salvia superba.

ACAENA

'New Zealand Burr'
These are semi-evergreen creeping plants with a fairly rapid spread. Small spiny burrs by way of flowers are dull, except in A. microphylla, which has red burrs above close bronzy foliage in late Summer.
Other species are only suitable for ground cover and paving.

A. buchananii has dense pea-green foliage.
A. 'Pulchella' has more of a coppery tint in leaf and flowers.
A. adsurgens is taller at 15 cm with arching stems of grey-green leaves and reddish burrs. Neither this nor the hybrid 'Blue Haze' are tidy, compact growers. All best in sun.

ACANTHOLIMON

These are somewhat prickly mat-forming plants, thereabouts evergreen.
A. glumaceum is the easiest to grow, but sometimes shy with its short clear-pink spikes 7 cm high.
A. venustum is slow growing but free, needing gritty soil and is 10 cm high.

Acantholimon glumaceum is a mat-forming evergreen plant with pink flowers.

ACANTHUS

These deep-rooting, long-lived perennials have handsome, jagged and sometimes prickly leaves. They should be sited where they can remain undisturbed, having good overall appearance; and though not evergreen, they will form large imposing clumps with abundant glossy foliage. They are not fussy about soil, given good drainage; and, though best in sun, do not object to a little shade.
Roots inadvertently left in the ground will sprout again.
A. spinosus is the most spectacular, with hooded flowers on 90 cm spikes, each flower being protected with a sharp thorn.
A. mollis prefers a warm situation to encourage free flowering.
A. hungaricus (syn. A. longifolius) has leaves up to 60 cm long and purplish flowers.
A. perringii is dwarf, forming greyish rosetted foliage and has 12 in. spikes of lilac pink, also best in full sun.

ACHILLEA

There is a wide variation in height here, but all flower on flattish heads. In general they are very adaptable and easy to grow in full sun, and only the dwarfest — 15 cm or less — should be classed as alpines. Several in the 15-30 cm height range are excellent for frontal border groups and most kinds have finely dissected leaves with a somewhat astringent odour when crushed.

The dwarfest alpine types such as the primrose-yellow *A. x lewisii* (often listed as 'King Edward'), and the few species with silvery foliage and white flowers, are best divided and replanted frequently.
A. aurea (syn. *A. chrysocoma*) and *A. tomentosa* are bright yellow with foliage green in the latter and greyish in the others. All make a good show either as frontal border subjects or as alpines, being about 15 cm tall. In this range are also silver-leaved, white-flowered species such as *A. argentea* and *A. x wilczekii*.
All flower May to July.

Achillea ptarmica 'Pearl' can be rather invasive, but are good for cut flowers.

Achillea filipendulina varieties are some of the tallest of achilleas.

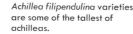

Taller species and varieties
Some first-class kinds come in the 25-50 cm range. The most popular is the silver-leaved lemon-yellow hybrid 'Moonshine'.
A. taygetea is also good but lacks foliage effect, whilst *A. clypeolata* has greyer leaves and deeper-yellow flowers.
Heads of white above green foliage come on *A. sibrica* 'W.B. Child', but the double white button-flowered *A. ptarmica* 'Perry's White' and the similar *A. ptarmica* 'Pearl' are invasive. They also need supporting but are good for cutting at 80-90 cm.
A. millefolium has produced some brilliant colours in the 'Galaxy' range which supercedes the old 'Cerise Queen' and 'Fire King'. This type makes a vigorous spread of deep-green filigree foliage with quite wide, semi-branching flower heads at about 90 cm tall, June to August.
'Apple Blossom' light pink, 'Great Expectations' a tawny yellow, 'The Beacon' crimson, along with 'Lilac Beauty' and 'Salmon Beauty', make up this range.
A. 'Coronation Gold' at about 100 cm produces masses of deep-yellow heads, whilst *A. filipendulina* 'Gold Plate' is a stately 150 cm. 'Moonbeam' at about 120 cm is a clear light yellow.
Two excellent additions to the 45-60cm range have appeared. One is 'Schwellenburg', which is

Achillea millefolium 'Red Beauty' is one of many brightly coloured varieties within this species.

an improvement on *A. clypeolata*, with long silvery leaves and heads of deep yellow flowers. The other, named after my daughter, is 'Anthea'. It has an upright habit, clothed in soft silvery leaves and the erectly branching stems carry glistening canary yellow heads which fade to a primrose shade. It has a long flowering period from late May onwards.
All these are good for cutting and will hold colour if dried for Winter decoration. All achilleas are increased by division or basal cuttings.

ACONITUM

Acorus gramineus, a variegated form.

Top: Aconitum napellus varieties often show strong colours.

Bottom: Aconitum fischeri (syn. A.carmichaelii) 'Arendsii'.

Acorus
The sweet flag, Acorus calamus is a naturalized water-side plant in Europe. It is very rampant and in particular the rhizomes have been used medicinally (for instance for gastric and intestinal troubles). 'Variegatus' with variegated foliage is smaller and less rampant. Combines very well with for instance Primula rosea.

ACONITUM

The monkshoods show obvious relationship to delphiniums, and include some very good garden plants. They are easy to grow, in sun or partial shade, but respond to good treatment by flowering freely where not starved. A mulching when dormant, of fertilised peat or compost, is helpful, but it pays to lift and replant every few years. All unwanted roots should be dug in deeply or composted.

A. napellus has several variations of which A. 'Bicolor' is one of the best, with slender branching spikes 90-110 cm tall from June to August.

A. napellus 'Newry Blue' is an earlier deep blue, growing to 120 cm tall. The shapely A. napellus 'Bressingham Spire' is outstanding for its symmetrical spikes to 90 cm, furnished with pretty glossy leaves. The flowers are violet-blue, from July to September, and

A. napellus 'Blue Sceptre' is of similar habit, but a little dwarfer and has blue and white bicolor flowers. For Autumn flowering, A. fischeri (syn. A. carmichaelii) is attractive, and both this and its variety 'Arendsii' prefer some shade where not too dry. The latter is superb, with amethyst-blue flowers topping strong 110 cm stems, August to October.

A. septentrionale 'Ivorine' is distinctive on three counts: not only has it a profusion of ivory-white flowers on erect 90 cm spikes, but it flowers early from May to July. It has a compact clumpy rootstock which promotes a shapely, well-foliaged, bushy habit; and in a position not too dry, it can be left for several years.

A. orientale is also worth mentioning because it is of similar habit and colour, though a little taller, and flowers from June to August.

A. japonicum grows sturdily to 100 cm with clusters of deep blue flowers June-August.

A. vilmorianum is twice this height, but with willowy stems carrying amethyst-blue flowers on terminal sprays.

ACORUS

A. gramineus
Neither the green-leaved nor the variegated form of this somewhat grassy-leaved plant is of value except for ground cover.

They form mats with narrow bladed leaves and flowers are seldom visible. Flowers are, however, not needed to enhance the bright golden foliage of A. 'Wogon' which remains colourful even in Winter. It forms a slowly expanding clump with leaves 15 cm long.

Above: The white berries of *Actaea erythrocarpa* 'Alba'.

Right: Several forms of *Adiantum*

ACTAEA

Interesting, but not spectacular, these shade loving plants have small heads of whitish flowers above delicate foliage.

Their charm is the pearl-like berries which follow, and there are white, red and black forms in, respectively, *A. erythrocarpa* 'Alba', (formerly called *A. spicata* fructo-alba), *A. rubra* and *A.* 'Nigra'. All are about 80 cm high.

ADENOPHORA

Very few species of these are in cultivation. They much resemble campanulas but have a more compact habit. *A. tashiroi* is well worth growing for its sprays of sky-blue bells on 30-40 cm stems, June-August. It roots deeply and needs light soil. Increase is by seed.

ADIANTUM

The maidenhair fern is available in several distinctive forms all preferring cool, shady conditions and light humus soil.

A. pedatum makes clumpy plants with a canopy of attractive leafage on wiry stems about 25 cm. A dwarfer (15 cm) form exists in *A. p.* 'Minor', and *A. p.* 'Aleuticum' is another small cultivar.

A. venustum has a creeping habit with shorter, smaller-leaved fronds.

They will grow in deep shade where not too dry, but do not relish heavy damp soil and should be replanted in Spring.

ADONIS

Aethionema
This genus, related to *Iberis*, comprises about 60 species and many more hybrids which are very difficult to distinguish from each other. The species all originate from Western Asia and the Mediterranean. Although some are yellow flowering, the colours are mainly pink, red and white. In practice many plants offered are of undetermined or wrongly named hybrids.
The only species that does not like a position in the full sun is the pink-white flowering *A. oppositifolium*.

Top: *Adonis vernalis*.

Below: *Aethionema armenum* 'Warley Rose' is one of the best of these sun-lovers.

ADONIS

The earliest perennial to flower along with *Helleborus niger* is *A. amurensis*. These are choice slow-growing plants, with the one fault that some have a long dormant period. They need good but well-drained soil, but take well to peat beds.
A. amurensis 'Pleniflora' flowers February to April, with fine double, greenish-yellow flowers 15 cm tall.
Both are increased by division in early Autumn when the clumpy plant is large enough, but *A. vernalis* is slower to increase. Its charming yellow flowers come on ferny-leaved bushy growth, March to May, 30-35 cm tall where happy.
A. volgensis is similar to the latter, but a week or two earlier to flower. So long as the adonis are not smothered, ajugas are attractive in association.

Adonis amurensis 'Pleniflora'.

AEGOPODIUM

Aegopodium podagraria (ground elder) has become a plague since the 16th century. It is so fruitful in its increase, that 'where it hath once taken root, it will hardly be gotten out again'. The leaves are very like those of the true elder (*Sambucus nigra*). However, the variegated form *A. podagraria* 'Variegatum' is cultivated.
The plant (30-60 cm in height) flowers abundantly May-July.

AETHIONEMA

These sun-lovers are best in poor or stony soil, and are excellent wall plants.
A. grandiflorum (syn. *A. pulchellum*) are much alike with a low twiggy habit and bluish foliage, to 25 cm, smothered in rounded spikes of clear, light-pink flowers in early Summer. They may be raised from seed, but the *A. armenum* cultivars, 'Warley Rose' and the slightly deeper pink 'Warley Ruber', can only be increased from Summer cuttings under glass. Both have intense-pink flowers above the blue-grey foliage on compact 15 cm bushy growth.

AGAPANTHUS

These are excellent perennials for all but coldest districts where Winter protection should be given with a covering of litter to prevent deep frost penetration. Generally speaking, those with the broadest strap-like leaves are less hardy than those with narrow leaves. Most modern varieties are in the latter category. Colours range from white to deep blue, of trumpet-shaped flowers clustered at the top of smooth, leafless stems. The most important species is *A. africanus*. At least 20 named varieties exist varying in height from 75 – 100 cm and flowering in later Summer. A miniature 'Tom Thumb' is only 25 cm tall. 'Headbourne Hybrids' are a mixture, which can be raised from seed, taking 2-3 years to flower. Otherwise named varieties to colour can be divided in Spring. They respond to rich soil and ample Summer moisture.

* AGRIMONIA

Agrimony is common in the fields and alongside roads and hedgerows. The flower stems are upright, unbranched and hairy.
Flies and bees are attracted to it. It grows up to 60 cm in two species: *A. eupatoria* and *A. procera* which is cultivated as well for the natural garden.

AGROSTEMMA – see LYCHNIS

Above: *Agapanthus* are generally grown in pots for ease of over wintering. The broader the leaves, the less hardy they are.

Right: *Agapanthus africanus* 'Albus' is an attractive white form.

Left: *Agrimonia* attracts many flying insects. Another fascinating aspect of gardening.

AJUGA

This *Ajuga reptans* mat shows the blue spikes, typical of most of the species.

AJUGA

This genus makes attractive leafy mats of real value when not too dry, all having short flower spikes in Spring and early Summer. All form rosettes of shiny leaves, rooting as they spread, making for rapid increase. They are useful under deciduous shrubs and pleasant in association with silver or gold foliage.

A. reptans has several cultivars, including white and pink-flowered, as distinct from the basic blue type. *A. reptans* 'Burgundy Glow' has crinkled, shiny foliage variegated pink, bronze and cream with *A. reptans* 'Multicolor' (syn. 'Rainbow') having many shades; both have blue spikes in Spring.

'Pink Elf' is a dwarf form, and *A. reptans* 'Variegata' spreads quickly by runners, with creamy-marked leaves.

A. pyramidalis 'Metallica Crispa' has dense, shiny, crinkled leaves of deepest blue and *A. pyramidalis* is best for flowering with spikes of gentian blue to 20 cm but needs a damp soil.

Ajuga

The creeping *Ajuga reptans* of this genus is practically the only available species. However, there are more species worth growing. *A. genevensis*, for instance, makes tall spikes of a beautiful violet-blue colour from April till August. The cultivar 'Robusta' has spikes up to 60 cm tall. *A. brockbankii* is a hybrid with a dark blue inflorescence. The flowers are excellent for cutting.

Ajuga reptans 'Multicolor' is the most colourful variety with leaves in many shades.

ALCEA

As the hollyhock (*Alcea rosea*), this has continuing appeal, but is scarcely to be recommended owing to its short life span. *A. rugosa* and *A. ficifolia* are species with single lemon-yellow flowers on strong 200 cm stems which are more reliable. As with hollyhocks, they can only be raised from seed.

Right: *Alcea ficifolia* has fig-like leaves.

Left: *Ajuga reptans* 'Burgundy Glow' has crinkled, shiny, variegated foliage and intense blue flowering spikes in late Spring.

Above: *Alchemilla alpina* is a good ground-covering species.

Right: Flowering garden with *Alchemilla mollis* near a pond.

Below: *Alchemilla mollis* in a border.

ALCHEMILLA

A. mollis is a splendid ground cover or space filler for any but the driest, starved conditions. The rounded glaucous leaves mound up to 30-40 cm and above, then from June to August come loose sprays of sulphur yellow, to give a hazy effect. There is a lushness about this very adaptable plant, and it can be relied on to smother weeds without itself being a nuisance. It can be increased by seed or division and is reliably hardy.
Smaller and scarcely less attractive species exist which deserve recognition.
A. alpina grows only 15 cm making good ground cover, with yellow flowers just above, and *A. splendens* with its hybrids are more grey-green with similar flowers, both growing about 25 cm high.
The sprays of *A. mollis* are very effective as a foil in floral arrangements.
A. ellenbeckii quickly forms a close evergreen carpet for ground cover but green-buff flowers are insignificant.
A. erythropoda grows neatly as a silvery-grey carpet, 8 cm high, with tiny greenish flower heads.

Over the years *Allium cernuum* forms clumpy plants.

Allium christophii (syn. *A. albopilosum*) is one of the many alliums with starry flowers that lose foliage after flowering.

ALLIUM

This is a vast genus, which includes leeks and onions as well as some good garden plants. Some of the taller bulbous ones are faulted because they lose foliage after flowering, but others are more or less evergreen. Only the shorter non-invasive are recommended. All have starry or bell-shaped flowers dangling in clusters on smooth stems. All are easy to grow.

A. cernuum forms clumpy plants and has mauve-lilac flowers on 35 cm stems.

A. carinatum ssp. *pulchellum* has pinkish flowers, 25 cm.

A. pyrenaicum gives a long succession of purple-blue flowers above deep green foliage.

A. senescens has silvery foliage and yellow flowers, as does *A. splendens* at 25 cm. (syn. *A. stellerianum.*)

A. schoenoprasum is the culinary chives, of which there is a very ornamental hybrid named 'Forescate' which makes a good display of near-red flowers in early Summer.

Only the smallest, non-invasive species can be recommended as members of the bulbous onion family. All have heads, sometimes dangling with small, brightly coloured flowers. Some have a long period of dormancy, but all are readily increased by division when dormant.

A. cyaneum and *A. beesianum* are both excellent for their sheaves of blue flowers on 12 cm stems.

A. oreophilum (syn. *A. ostrowskianum*) has tufts of narrow leaves with umbels of broad carmine-red flowers.

A. moly, a yellow species, should be avoided, being invasive, but *A. cyathophorum* var. *farreri* is recommended for its heads of purple flowers, 15 cm.

A. narcissiflorum is only 10 cm with nodding bells of wine-red.

All these alliums are Summer flowering, and are best combined with plants of a mounded or cushion habit, such as the dwarf *Dianthus*.

Alopecurus pratensis 'Aureo-variegatus' shows golden-variegated leaves.

Right: Alstroemeria Ligtu hybrids give a splendid display.

Alstroemeria
These will only start flowering a few years after they have been planted. They need time to settle. Provided they are covered in Winter, they will get through this difficult period easily.
Alstroemeria may seed itself spontaneously. Plants from seed may flower in many difficult colours.
Besides A. aurantiaca, there is also A. hoemantha with narrow foliage and A. ligtu with round leaves. The first has deep yellow flowers and its height does not exceed 50 cm. A. ligtu may reach a height of a metre and the inflorescence is yellow with purple stripes.

ALOPECURUS

Alopecurus pratensis (meadow foxtail) is rather similar to timothy (Phleum pratense) but more refined. The flower-heads of this grassy species appear in April-June. It is good for the natural garden.

ALSTROEMERIA

The strain known as 'Ligtu Hybrids' give a splendid display where happy, but are difficult to establish. One has to begin with seed or year-old pot-grown seedlings, which need to be planted 15-18 cm deep in good light soil. Though not easy to fit in as perennials, the flowers in shades of pink, salmon-orange, etc., on 15 cm stems, are known as Peruvian lily.
The species A. aurantiaca (syn. A. aurea), with several varieties, is more robust with deep-yellow flowers.

A. pulchella (syn. A. psittacina) is easier to grow though not fully hardy. It is tuberous rooted, 10 cm deep, and has orange-brown flowers on leafy stems 60 cm. All flower June — August.

ALTHEA – see ALCEA

ALYSSUM

Alyssum saxatile 'Dudley Nevill' displays primrose yellow flowers in spring.

Alyssum saxatile varieties are the most showy amongst alyssums.

as is the cultivar 'Gold Ball'. Both are bright yellow but *A. s.* 'Citrinum' is a lemon yellow, and 'Dudley Neville' a primrose yellow, of which there is a form with variegated leaves.

The double-flowered *A. s.* 'Plenum' is very showy with fuller flowers, but is less vigorous. All the above need sun, like lime and good drainage. Of the true species, the mat-forming *A. serpyllifolium* with yellow flowers in Spring is the best.

AMSONIA

A. tabernaemontana var. *salicifolia* is a reliable, unusual plant, though not spectacular. It makes a strong clump and sends up willowy leafy stems carrying small light-blue periwinkle-type flowers June — August, 100 cm.

A slight improvement with larger flowers is seen in the cultivar 'Ilustra'. Both are easy to grow and may be increased by division.

There is another less important species *A. angustifolia*.

Amsonia tabernaemontana is an unusual plant.

Anacyclus

The upper sides of the flowers of *A. depressus* are white and crimson-red underneath. When it is rainy weather or where there is not much light (such as in the evening) the flowers close, to give a red impression all of a sudden.

The plant cannot stand wet conditions in Winter and needs to be covered, such as with a sheet of glass, so that no rain will fall on the plant, but still leaving sufficient air around it.

ALYSSUM

Although this genus contains a number of species, very few are good garden plants. They have a somewhat sprawling habit and almost all are yellow flowered.

The best come under *A. saxatile* and its variations. They are showy and deservedly popular for Spring display. They form robust mounded to spreading growth above ground from a single non-spreading root system with sprays of small flowers in yellow shades, covering the greyish foliage. The yellow species are easily raised from seed, but variations come from framed cuttings in late Summer or Autumn. *A. saxatile* is offered in *A. s.* 'Compactum', but is not really compact when old

ANACYCLUS

A. depressus is not long-lived and needs sharp drainage or scree soil. It forms flat rosettes of finely cut leaves producing large white daisy flowers which are crimson underneath. About 8 cm high, flowering in early Summer, it can only be increased by seed.

Left: *Anacyclus depressus* does not like wet conditions.

* ANAGALLIS

These *Primula*-related plants are known as weeds in *A. arvensis*. Good garden forms are *A. linifolia* (syn. *A. monellii*) with the varieties 'Pacific Blue' and 'Phillipsii' (red). They grow up to 30 cm and flower all Summer. Another good variety is *A. tenella* 'Studland' (but is less hardy).

Anagallis linifolia (syn. *A. monellii*) is available in several good garden forms in different shades.

ANAPHALIS

These are useful plants with silvery foliage and white near-everlasting flowers, carried on loose heads. They are very adaptable, with dwarfer kinds able to give ground cover even in poor soil and in fairly shady places. They divide easily in Spring and resent only wet conditions. *A. margaritacea* var. *yedoensis* has silvery leaves on 70cm stems carrying papery white heads in late Summer to make it a useful subject for dry cut flowers. *A. nubigena* is neat growing with long-lasting white flowers.

A. triplinervis and cultivars are adaptable to some shade and are mat-forming, the creamy-white flowers coming on 25 cm heads. All are everlasting if cut and dried.

Below: *Anaphalis margaritacea.*

Right: *Anaphalis triplinervis* 'Summer Snow'.

ANCHUSA

ANCHUSA

Anchusa azurea 'Loddon Royalist' is brilliant and useful for early flowering, though this and similar anchusas may need supporting. They also tend to leave a bare patch once flowering is over by late June and should be cut to promote fresh basal leaves. They grow from 90-150 cm high from brittle fleshy roots, and as they resent wet soil in Winter should be in a well-drained spot.

Other varieties include the deep blue *A.a.* 'Morning Glory', and the sky-blue *A.a.* 'Opal', but both these are tall.

A.a. 'Little John' is only 50 cm, but though flowering for longer, is less spectacular.

Full marks go to *A. angustissima* both for brightness and continuity in flower. Sprays spread out and up to 40 cm, set with brightest blue flowers from early June to September, but unfortunately plants exhaust themselves after 2-3 seasons. It sets occasional seeds, but basal cuttings in early Spring can be taken, whereas the taller anchusas can only be increased from root cuttings.

The true *A. caespitosa* is a charming rarity for gritty soil with intense blue 10 cm sprays. The species *A. sempervirens* (named *Pentaglottis sempervirens* nowadays), has small blue flowers above leafy clumps and is not choice, but will often fill an odd corner or spaces amongst shrubs. It flowers on and off all Summer, 75 cm.

ANDROSACE

These *truly* alpine plants are widely distributed in nature. Most of them form hummocks of rosettes, some grey-green, and are easy in very-well-drained soil. Rounded heads of mostly pink flowers come in early Summer. *A. sarmentosa* (syn. *A. primuloides*) is the best known of this type, growing 5-10 cm tall, having rosy-red flowers.

The species includes the former variety 'Watkinsii' as well.

A. sempervivoides is also attractive.

A. microphylla is smaller, safest in scree conditions, but *A. lanuginosa* and its cultivars are distinct. They have silvery trailing stems carrying heads of pink or near-white flowers in later Summer. These are good subjects for a sunny wall. They are best increased from cuttings, but the rosette-forming kinds will divide with care, and pieces detached with sufficient root should survive.

A. villosa is a compact white-flowered species.

Above: *Anchusa azurea* 'Loddon Royalist' is one of the best known cultivars of this genus.

Androsace sarmentosa shows rosy-red flowers in rounded heads.

ANDRYALA

Andryala agarhdii needs a warm place and very good drainage to show off its silvery tufts of foliage set with vivid yellow flowers for several weeks of Summer. It grows to 15-20 cm and can be increased from late Summer cuttings or seed.

ANEMONE

This is a genus with wide varations in habit and height. The earliest to flower grow from brittle, twiggy rhizomes, and although they give a fine display, they are best regarded as one does winter aconites and snowdrops, not to be included with perennials. Some are quite invasive.

A. nemorosa is the wood anemone in white and blue shades, 10-15 cm.

A. ranunculoides is yellow in both single and double-flowered forms, whilst *A. apennina* and *A. blanda* are on similar lines in various colours, and all are best considered along with Spring bulbs.

A. pulsatilla see under *PULSATILLA*.

The most valued border perennials come under *A. japonica* (syn. *A. x hybrida*) and (*A. hupehensis*). Under this name are some first rate subjects for flowering in late Summer and Autumn. They are long lived and trouble free in well-drained soil, flowering for weeks on end.

In Winter they die back to both woody and fibrous roots which penetrate deeply, and from these increase is made whether left alone or lifted to use as root cuttings. Old plants however do not divide well and young pot-grown stock gives best results.

A. hupehensis 'Profusion' is one of the dwarfer varieties with small double flowers, but not quite so deeply coloured as *A. x hybrida* 'Bressingham Glow'. Both grow under 60 cm.

A. hupehensis 'September Charm', is a clear single pink, 50 cm, while *A. x. hybrida* 'Lady Gilmour' is almost double, and a little taller. *A. x hybrida* 'Krimhilde' is one of the best taller pinks, reaching 75-90 cm. The two best whites with large flowers are *A. x hybrida* 'Luise Uhink' and 'White Giant', both attaining 90-120 cm and both with telling effect.

'Hadspen Abundance' is a recent introduction, having glowing deep pink single flowers at about 40 cm.

A. x lesseri is a charming hybrid with almost blood-red flowers on erect 30-40 cm stems in early Summer and often later also. It grows from compact lacy-leaved plants and is best in light soil.

A. magellanica has creamy-white flowers of somewhat similar habit, June-August, 40 cm in the larger and better of the two forms existing.

A. rivularis is undeservedly neglected for it has a long succession of pure-white cups in branching 40-50 stems, needing no special culture in good light soil.

The single-borne flowers of *Anemone sylvestris* appear above fern-like foliage.

A. sylvestris has somewhat ferny foliage on clumpy growth and dainty white bowl-shaped flowers, singly borne, becoming fluffy as seed heads.

Anemone x hybrida 'Max Vogel' is one of many good cultivars of this species.

Anemone

There are about 70 wild species in very different areas. These vary from cool deciduous woods to sunbaked Mediterranean regions. In practice mainly 3 groups are of importance for the garden:
- the species which flower early in the Spring, many of which originate from the woods. The alpine anemones also belong to the early flowering kinds.
- the summer- and autumn-flowering kinds, often characterised by very attractive fluffy seeds, which are formed after the rich inflorescence.
- the Mediterranean species which only grow well in warm places and are, in fact, mainly cultivated for cut flowers.

ANEMONOPSIS

ANEMONOPSIS

Anemonopsis macrophylla is a choice subject for cool humus soil. It flourishes best in damp Atlantic coast regions or in northern valleys. The leaves are deeply divided, freshly green where suited, and slender arching stems carry nodding cup-shaped violet-mauve flowers, 70 cm, flowering June-August.

* ANGELICA

Angelica archangelica is a beautiful flowering herb which grows up to 150 cms. The flower-heads are situated at the ends of stalks sprouting from the angle between stem and leaf. White flowers appear in July-August.

ANTENNARIA

This small genus consists of grey-leaved carpeters, having fluffy petal-less flowers. *A. dioica* is the best known, with whitish flower heads on 15 cm stems in early Summer, but more showy is the pink form 'Rosea', and even deeper pink one 'Rubra', both 10-12 cm.

The form 'Minima' is half the height, and pink-flowered. A taller 50 cm faster-spreading species exists in the white-flowered *A. parvifolia* (syn. *aprica*). All are easy to grow and readily divide, but need to be in full sun and well-drained soil.

Left: *Angelica archangelica* is an impressive flowering herb with great ornamental value.

Antennaria
The silvery white carpets of *Antennaria* are not only beautiful as a ground cover for poor soil, but the plants are also very suitable for boxes and troughs. They combine well with other grey foliaged plants such as *Marrubium, Raoulia, Alyssum saxatile, Achillea* species and *Onosma*.

Below: *Antennaria dioica* is available in white and pink shades.

ANTHEMIS

These are easy in any well-drained soil, but the white-flowered *A. cupaniana*, though showy and long flowering, spreads too quickly for small beds. It has finely divided leaves, as has the less rampant *A. triumfettii* and *A. pedunculata. A. tuberculata*, also white flowered to 20 cm, is grey-leaved with clumpy growth. The most valuable as an alpine plant is the silvery-leaved *A. rudolphiana* (syn. *A. biebersteiniana* and *A. marschalliana*) with deep-golden flowers. These are borne erectly to 15 cm and make a fine show in early Summer. All the above can be divided or raised from seed.

A. nobilis is the herb chamomile with aromatic deep green foliage. It grows close to the surface with a fairly rapid spread; and though the double white-flowered *A. nobilis* 'Plena' is of limited value as a garden plant, only 10 cm tall, the non-flowering *A. nobilis* 'Treneague' is used for lawns or as a walk-upon carpeter.

The taller species of *Anthemis* are showy plants, but short-lived unless cut hard back, as flowering tends to encourage new basal growth. The most reliable is *A. x hybrida* 'E.C. Buxton' with lemon-yellow daisies on twiggy 80 cm stems, June-August. 'Wargrave' is similar but slightly paler, whilst 'Grallagh Gold' is rich orange. It tends to flower itself to death, as does the more compact deep-yellow *A. sancti-johannis*.

Some stocks of *A. x hybrida* are more reliable than others. All anthemis are increased from basal cuttings or division.

Above: *Anthemis rudolphiana* (syn. *A. biebersteiniana*) with warm-yellow flowers.

ANTHERICUM

These and the closely related *Paradisea (q.v. below)* are charming, easily-grown plants for early Summer. They form compact clumps with grassy basal leaves, and send up a profusion of slender stems carrying small lily-like white flowers to 80 cm. *A. liliago* (St. Bernard's lily) is the best known. *A. ramosum* is also white-flowered, but if the flowers are smaller, more are carried on each stem, 80 cm.

A. liliastrum (now correctly *Paradisea*) is included here for simplicity. This St. Bruno's lily is of similar clumpy habit but the white flowers are more lily-like and the stems barely 60 cm tall. *Paradisea liliastrum* 'Major' is a slightly larger-flowered form, as is 'Gigantea'.

Right: *Anthericum* species and cultivars produce lots of lily-like flowers on slender stems.

Above: *Anthyllis montana* is reminiscent of clover. The silvery leaves cover the ground.

Right: The pink-flowered *Aquilegia* 'Biedermeier' is one of the best varieties to come true from seed.

Aquilegia

Columbine species are very common in the northern hemisphere. There are about 120 wild species most of which grow in the light shade of trees and shrubs. Many species naturalize easily. The production of seeds is often abundant. Small species are attractive in rock gardens. Many varieties provide excellent cut flowers which are long lasting in a vase. *Aquilegia* makes a good combination with grasses or autumn-flowering anemones, in the latter case because they flower after each other and attention is drawn away from the *Aquilegia*, which does not look so attractive once it has flowered.

ANTHYLLIS

This is a long-lived, sub-shrubby plant of value in well-drained sunny places, including walls.
A. hermanniae makes a dense twiggy mound of greyish hue, with an abundance of small yellow pea-shaped flowers in Summer, height 20 cm.
A. montana is best in the deep-pink to red (*A. m.* 'Rubra'). It makes a surface spread of silvery leaves covered in early Summer with clover-like heads to make a bright display 8 cm high. Seed increase is possible as is careful division in Spring.

A. vulneraria 'Rubra' makes a brilliant display of deep orange-red over trailing fingery light-greenery in early Summer. 8 cm.

AQUILEGIA

Aquilegia 'McKana Hybrids' have the largest flowers and the best colour range of these garden favourites, growing to about 90 cm high, with long spurs. Although easy and adaptable, all aquilegias tend to be short-lived, but are easily raised from seed. Plants should, however, be a year old to flower freely and should be grown on, to plant in Autumn for the next season. Apart from such mixed strains as 'McKana Hybrids', there are a few species in cultivation in blue, white, purple, red and yellow, varying in height from 10-90 cm (4 inches to 3 feet), but these are usually obtainable only from a specialist, and from seed do not always come fully true to name and colour; although the red variety *A.* 'Crimson Star' is fairly reliable in this respect, along with the pink shades of *A.* 'Biedermeier', both growing about 45 cm high.
'Columbine' or 'Granny's bonnet' applies to *A. vulgaris*. It has produced natural hybrids in a variety of colours and a few are fully double. These will reproduce from seed if isolated, and the pinkish *A. v.* 'Nora Barlow' has proved very popular, growing about 75 cm.

The columbines have a wide range in nature. Some of the dwarfest are best in scree soil, others prefer some damp and shade, but unfortunately few are long-lived.
They can only be increased from seed and this does not invariably produce plants true to name, except in the dwarfest kinds. These include *A. bertolonii* with large blue flowers on 12 cm stems and *A. discolor* blue and white only 8 cm. *A. scopulorum* has soft-blue flowers and silvery foliage, 12 cm. These three are best in scree or rock crevices.
A. flabellata 'Nana', is available in both blue and white. 'Nana Alba' is most robust at 20 cm as is

Left: *Aquilegia vulgaris* 'Nora Barlow' is a rather tall growing (75 cm) pink-flowered variety.

the charming blue-and-white *A. glandulosa*. These both like a cool position with peaty soil. All flower in early Summer, and seed should be sown outdoors when ripe.

ARABIS

Although there are several quite tiny alpine species existing, few are widely cultivated and almost all are white. The best known is the somewhat rampant *A. caucasica* (syn. *A. albida*) of which the double- flowered pure white is still a favourite Spring plant. The flowers come on 15 cm sprays. There is a deep-pink single named 'Corfe Castle' which has proved more reliable and much more compact, flowering March-May at 10-12 cm; also an older light pink *A. c.*'Rosabella' of similar

Right: *Arabis caucasica* (here a pink-flowered variety) may produce rather rampant growth.

height, much like an *Aubrieta* in growth. *Arabis* species reproduce from seed or Autumn cuttings and are not at all fussy given a sunny place.

Below: *Arenaria nevadensis* is a very attractive cushion-forming species, sought by collectors.

ARENARIA

These are easy, close-growing plants for early Summer, nearly all white-flowered.
A. balearica is the only exception to a general preference for sun. It grows as a mere film of bright green, dotted with white flowers only 5 cm above. It needs a dampish, half-shady place, is quick to spread, but is not hardy in coldest districts.
A. caespitosa 'Aurea' (named *Minuartia verna* ssp. *caespitosa* 'Aurea' nowadays) is somewhat similar but needs sun; it has permanently golden foliage and sparse white flowers. It needs to be frequently divided and replanted to retain colour and compactness.
A. ledebouriana has close grassy foliage and small white flowers, but the brightest is *A. montana* whose somewhat trailing deep-green foliage is smothered in larger, pure white flowers in Summer. Both are about 10 cm. *A. pinifolia* is also attractive, with a mounded-leaved growth.
A. nevadensis (and. *A. tetraquetra*) make curiously attractive cushions but is best in scree conditions. Both rank as collectors' items.

ARISAEMA

ARISAEMA

These are *Arum*-like plants, but though of considerable attraction are rarely offered and sometimes difficult to establish. They need good light soil and are not averse to some shade. Some tuberous roots have a long dormancy and need to be planted 10 cm deep. Arums and their kin flower as spathes, a kind of sheath with a pokery centre-piece.

A. candidissimum sends up white spathes in June, 30 cm tall, after its long dormancy, somewhat hooded, and with faint pink stripes followed by lush green divided leaves.

A. consanguineum needs a warm place. The 'flowers' are greenish-brown striped, up to 80 cm, with umbrella-like leaves.

ARISARUM

Arisarum proboscideum is included here as a close relative. The typical leaves are small, only 10 cm high, and the curious 'mouse tails' at flowering time in early Summer make it an attractive curiosity.

Above: *Arisaema candidissimum*, with white spathes in June, grows from tuberous roots in light soil and shade.

Below: *Arisarum proboscideum* is another *Arum* related species with a peculiar flower form.

Above: *Aristolochia clematitis* has bright-yellow flowers in the early summer months (May-July).

* *ARISTOLOCHIA*

Aristolochia clematitis is a native of S.W.Europe and Near-Asia. 30-100 cm in height and with upper parts of the stem bending. Flowering May-July, the bright-yellow plant likes limy soils.

ARMERIA

The thrifts are mostly evergreen with grassy foliage, growing compactly in any position and are very adaptable as to soil and position as border or alpine plants.

They are first rate, the choicest and slowest to grow being *Armeria caespitosa* with clear pink flowers only 5 cm tall, for well-drained soil or scree.

A. maritima is a variable, easily-grown species. The brightest and nearest to red is 'Dusseldorf Pride', 15-20 cm. 'Vindictive' is pink and 'Alba' pure white, 12-15 cm, flowering in early Summer.

A. corsica is distinctive for its heads of brick-red colour on 25 cm stems.

Armeria caespitosa are rather slow growing, but beautifully flowering plants.

Armeria

Around 50 *Armeria* species occur in the whole northern hemisphere as well as in the Andes mountains in South America. Wild species are hardly cultivated, and not all of them are very attractive either. There are many short-lived species with an inconspicuous inflorescence.

Armeria varieties are inclined to push themselves up on their roots, very often as a consequence of frost. It is therefore recommended to replant them regularly. *Armeria maritima* is very suitable for salty areas, but the plant will grow anywhere provided it gets full sun.

Left: *Armeria maritima* 'Dusseldorf Pride' is one of the best cultivars of this species, almost red and very bright.

All are easy to divide in Spring or Autumn, except *A. caespitosa* which is best from seed or base cuttings.

A few hybrids are somewhat taller and make good frontal groups in beds and borders. *A. m.*'Ruby Glow' flowers at 20 cm, along with the slightly deeper 'Bloodstone'. The brightest, glistening pink, is *A.* 'Bee's Ruby', with rounded heads to 30 cm, but this does not readily divide nor are cuttings easy to root.

There is also a range of a seed-raised mixture 'Giant Hybrids' which includes red, salmon, pink and white shades, growing to 30-40 cm, but these are not so long-lived.

All armerias are sun loving and prefer light, well-drained soil.

ARNEBIA

Arnebia echioides shows its spotted yellow flowers in April.

* ARNICA

The most important of the 32 known species is *Arnica montana*, a native on mountainous areas in all Europe.

Its yellow flowers remind one of asters and indeed it belongs to the *Asteraceae*. The flowers can measure 8 cm in diameter, the leaves forming a rosette. Height 30-50 cm, it is a special plant for lovers of the natural and environmental garden. Flowering time is May — July.

Arnica montana is a European native, but garden worthy because of its fine, yellow flowers during summer.

* ARRHENATHERUM

Arrhenatherum elatius ssp. *bulbosum* is a grassy-looking plant with yellow female flowers on top and male flowers underneath. The flower stems can reach up to 1.2 m, the leaves up to 60 cm.
Good as a bedding plant with special features, this plant also does well in heather gardens. Acid soil is preferred. They are increased by division.

Below: *Arrhenatherum elatius* is very well suited for natural and heather gardens.

ARNEBIA

Arnebia echioides, the prophet's flower, holds a legend. Mahomet once stumbled in a rocky place and would have bruised his hand but for the flower of this plant which cushioned his hand as he fell.

The maroon spots on the bright-yellow flowers are the imprints of the prophet's fingers; but though these fade in a few days, it makes little difference to the value of this unusual hardy plant. It grows only 25 cm high from a tuft of tongue-shaped leaves, the sprays opening in April and lasting for a few weeks. Plants are fleshy-rooted, prefer light open soil, and can be divided when old in early Autumn — when occasionally a few late flowers are seen.

ARTEMISIA

With the one exception of *Artemisia lactiflora,* all are grey or silver-leaved plants grown for foliage effect, having flowers of no significance.
They are also best where dry and sunny.
Artemisia abrotanum is shrubby with aromatic leaves growing up to 80 cm, with 'Lambrook Silver' the best form. The hybrid 'Powys Castle' is also outstanding, but both are best pruned back in Spring to encourage shapeliness and vigour.
A. canescens (splendens) and *A. nutans* are much dwarfer with fine silver filigree foliage.
A. stelleriana has broader silver-white leaves, having a modest spread, but *A. ludoviciana, A. l.* 'Silver Queen' and *A. pontica* are non-shrubby.
They form vigorous mats and send up leafy stems with silvery or grey leaves tipped with nondescript flowers to 60-70 cm.
The smallest species is *A. schmidtiana* 'Nana' (rather similar to *A. pedemontana*) and has very

Above: *Artemisia ludoviciana* 'Silver Queen' is a mat-forming variety, good to combine with other plants because of its silver leaf colour.

silvery divided leaves and a mounded habit, about 15 cm high.

A. lactiflora is distinct from all the rest for having handsome plumes of beady creamy-white flowers in Autumn. The leaves on the strong 150 cm stems are lacy and green and it grows best in good soil in sun of partial shade, disliking the dry soil preferred by the rest.

All are increased by cuttings or division.

Right: *Arum italicum* is easy to establish if left undisturbed. The evergreen leaves and whitish spathes (in Spring) make it worth growing if you have a good, slightly shaded spot for it in rather moist soil.

Arum
The 12 known *Arum* species grow wild in Europe and around the Mediterranean. They practically all like moist to wet soil and often shady positions.
They grow from corms, on which they form bulbils which can be used for propagation. They can also be multiplied from seed. Drought in Summer is no problem, so this is a plant which you do not have to worry about during your holidays.

ARUM

As with the related *Arisaema*, very few species are listed in catalogues. The one most likely to be found is for naturalising rather than planting in a cultivated bed. It is *Arum italicum* 'Pictum' and has pretty marbled leaves of broadly arrow shape — like the wild 'lords and ladies', giving winter greenery and greenish-white spathes in Spring. This will naturalise if required or allowed to do so.

A. creticum is choice and best in full sun. Shiny green leaves and yellow flowers make this a very attractive species.
See also *Zantedeschia*.

ARUNCUS

Above: *Aruncus dioicus* is very impressive with tall white plumes in summer.

ARUNCUS

Name-changing has brought the best-known species to be termed *Aruncus dioicus* from the form *A. sylvester*. Given ample space in soil not dry with some shade, it is quite majestic with its very white plumes up to 250 cm, June-July. It makes a hefty, tough root and is best left alone. Less tall, but equally spectacular, is *A.plumosus* and the cultivar 'Glasnevin'. Both are 120-150 cm, flowering June-July.

A. x kneiffii is a hybrid with lacy, deep-green foliage and wiry stems carrying somewhat arching plumes up to 100 cm, June-July. It is a refined, beautiful plant for a good soil and some shade. Although it has a short flowering period, *A. aethusifolius* has become popular. It is only 15-20 cm tall with creamy-white flowers but the delicate foliage is very attractive.

Aruncus dioicus comes from seed if both male and female plants are grown — not distinguishable when dormant. Division of the others is possible but difficult, due to their tough, woody roots.

ARUNDO

Arundo donax is a giant grass growing erectly with sheeted stem blades up to 300 cm, but seldom flowering. It needs a warm sunny place and light soil, forming slow-spreading clumps.

ASARINA

Asarina procumbens (formerly known as *Antirrhinum asarina*), resents being sun-baked, but in a cool place spreads between rocks or walls to give a long succession of creamy-coloured, snapdragon-like flowers, 10 cm. Division is in Spring.

Left: *Arundo donax* seldom flowers, but the ornamental value of the tall, elegantly leaved stems make it a worthy contribution to any sunny garden.

Right: *Asarina procumbens* needs a rather cool place to show its snapdragon-like flowers at their best.

Asarum europaeum is one of the best evergreen ground covering plants for even heavily shaded sites under trees and shrubs, provided that the soil is slightly moist.

Asclepias

Most Asclepias species (there are at least 120) can only be found in botanic gardens. Wild species occur in the United States and other American areas and in the middle of the South African continent, and in South Africa. Asclepias species are good plants for bees and other insects. Not only are the flowers very attractive, but so also are the silvery-white hairy seeds.

Right: A very beautiful variety of Asclepias incarnata is this 'Cinderella'.

Below: Asperula suberosa with bright pink flowers is perhaps the most beautiful of all Asperula species.

ASARUM

These are good evergreen ground coverers for shady places not bone dry. The best-known with shiny, rounded leaves is A. europaeum, but for the connoisseur a few others are occasionally to be had. Flowers are insignificant.

ASCLEPIAS

Asclepias tuberosa. If this plant, with its startling colour, were more adaptable, it would be seen in every garden. But it is unfortunately rather faddy, disliking clay and chalky soils and needing light, sandy soil with perfect drainage and a sunny position. Its tap roots have a small terminal crown from which shoots appear in May, and the crowns are easily damaged when dormant. Stems reach 40-50 cm, branching at the top into a glistening orange head from July to September.
A much easier species exists in A. incarnata. This makes stout and leafy bushes up to 120 cm high with waxy heads of deep rose pink. It will grow in ordinary soil and can be divided in Spring.

ASPARAGUS

It is not generally known that Asparagus as a genus includes a few subjects which are for decorative purposes, apart from the much-favoured A. officinalis for eating.
In Germany the decorative cultivar 'Spitzenschleier' is to be seen, but the pretty 45 cm A. filicinus has an upright deep-green ferny appearance as a foliage plant.
A. tenuifolius is twice as tall, but I have not found them very robust, needing as they do ample summer warmth.

ASPERULA

This includes some choice diminutive species, but A. capitata is easy to grow, forming slow-spreading hummocks with tiny, shell-pink flowers in early Summer, 5 cm.
A. lilaciflora (syn. A. caespitosa) makes a prostrate, deep-green mat, set with clear-pink flowers for many weeks, only 3 cm.
A. nitida makes a dense green cushion studded with pink flowers, 8 cm.
A. suberosa is a treasure, having more upright, grey-leaved stems to 6 cm with clusters of clear-pink, tubular flowers in late Spring. Both are best in scree-type soil and resent winter wet. Careful division is carried out in early Spring.
A. odorata (syn. Galium odoratum) is the native 'woodruff'. It has rather floppy light-green leaves and small heads of white flowers to 30 cm, June-August. The odour comes from drying or dried growth.

ASPHODELINE

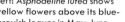

Left: *Asphodeline lutea* shows yellow flowers above its blue-greyish leaves in May-June.

Above: *Asplenium trichomanes* is an evergreen, rosette-forming fern for a cool position.

ASPHODELINE

The two genuses have so much in common that they may be joined here.

Asphodeline liburnica is a graceful member of the lily family, with narrow silvery leaves and slender spikes of starry light-yellow flowers, to 90 cm, June-August.

A. lutea is a little more robust and earlier, with deeper-yellow flowers. The narrow basal leaves are of a blue-grey hue. Flowers are slightly fragrant and the spikes are imposing in any well-drained soil. 'Gelbkerze' is an improvement on *A. lutea*, having bolder spikes of larger, brighter flowers. 100 cm.

ASPHODELUS

Closely related to the above and the only species likely to be available, *Asphodelus cerasiferus* (syn. *A. ramosus*) has white flowers with brownish markings. Strong spikes to 130 cm come in early Summer followed by cherry-size seed capsules, but early dormancy is a fault of an otherwise pleasing subject.

ASPLENIUM

The 'spleenwort fern' is well suited for cool positions and dwarf enough as alpines. Two species of ferns are suitable for shady nooks and crevices, one being the dainty, grey-leaved *Asplenium ruta-muraria* with deeply-cut rosette leaves, and the other *A. trichomanes* which is also evergreen and rosette-forming with fingered bright-green fronds.

The well-loved 'hart's tongue fern' now comes under *Asplenium*.

As evergreens they are deservedly popular and are easy to grow in cool, shady places. The type is *A. scolopendrium* and it has several variations of the broad, leathery, bright-green leaves. 'Undulatum' has wavy edges to the 30-40 cm leaves and some forms have crested tips.

Asphodelus cerasiferus with white flowers most of the time is the only species of this genus offered.

Aster amellus is just one of the many *Aster* species that have proven their value for the garden over many years.

Aster thomsonii 'Nana' makes a nice little bush studded with light-blue flowers.

ASTER

To some the name may denote only the annual 'China aster', but this genus includes an inmense range of plants in which differences of height, habit and size of flower are very marked. Many of the species are worthless from a garden point of view; but as with so many, popularity of some has led to a great deal of breeding so that now an original species bears little comparison with modern hybrids. This is particularly marked in the case of Michaelmas daisies; but just because these have become so popular since breeding begin 80 years ago, there is no excuse for neglecting species which have definite claims to garden worthiness. One of the objects of this book is to bring some of the lesser-known plants to the notice of keen gardeners at a time when their attention is mostly drawn to popular hybrids. Michaelmas daisies have lost some popularity in recent years, largely due to the diseases wilt and mildew, resulting no doubt from over-intensive hybridising. Happily, some have stood the test of time, but there are several trouble-free species still awaiting recognition as good garden plants. Whilst the majority of asters are easy and reliable border plants, a few are adaptable as alpines. These come first below.

Aster alpinus forms clumpy plants and sends up ray-petalled flowers in May, June, 20-30 cm tall.

Colours range from white to lilac and shades of blue.
A. natalensis, (also known as *Feticia rosulata*), has green rosettes and creeps a little. Intense-blue flowers on 10 cm stems appear in early Summer, but it needs frequent replanting.
A. sativus atrocaeruleus is a rare little beauty. Forming neat clumpy light green plants, it has 12 cm sprays of small sky-blue flowers for much of the Summer.
A. souliei also grows neatly with erect 15 cm stems carrying mauve-blue flowers.
A. spectabilis is outstanding for its bright-blue daisies in Autumn above rounded leathery leaves and a slow spread.

Dwarf species and varieties

Dwarf enough to be adaptable as border or alpine plants are a few mat-forming species with yellow centred, ray-petalled blue flowers. *A. farreri*, *A. himalaicus*, *A. subcaerculeus* (syn. *A. tongolensis*), and *A. yunnanensis* all come in this category, along with cultivars such as 'Napsbury' and 'Berggarten'. All flower in early Summer in the 25-40 cm height range.
There are also two pretty flowered hybrids under 35 cm in *A.alpellus* 'Triumph' blue and the lilac 'Summer Greeting'. All the above divide easily in early Autumn, except *A.spectabilis* which replants best in Spring.

ASTER

Above: *Aster cordifolius* varieties, not often seen, are graceful late flowering plants.

Below: *Aster natalensis* has green rosettes and intense blue flowers in early summer.

Aster

This enormous genus comprises at least 600 species amongst which there are many annuals and biennials. They have flowers in any colour, and the earliest kinds flower in late Spring whereas others flower in very late Autumn. They can be used anywhere, and there is hardly any type of garden for which there is not some suitable *Aster* species.

Wild species occur in Europe, Asia, North and South America and South Africa. Most varieties (especially the tall ones) must be replanted every 2-3 years in order to maintain their rich flowering, but others can stay in the same place for years without any visible deterioration. You will find out for yourself.

For convenience sake *Aster* is divided in 2 groups which makes recognition easier:

1. Spring-flowering varieties, practically always with single flower stems.
2. Autumn-flowering varieties with branched upper stems.

Plants which show rich flowering for many years in the same place are often less sensitive to pests and diseases.

The dwarf Michaelmas daisies, *A. x dumosus,* are indispensable for frontal positions and are less prone to disease. Some have quite a vigorous spread and are not to be recommended as alpines. The colour range includes the white 'Kristina' or 'Snowsprite'; light blue 'Kippenburg' or 'Lady in Blue'; pink 'Little Pink Beauty' and reddish 'Jenny', all 25-40 cm tall in Autumn.

Taller michaelmas daisies

For the taller Michaelmas daisies, choice must be a matter of taste, but less tall varieties are less troublesome. Some are little more than 60 cm high and ample variety of colour is available. Both dwarf and tall are best divided and replanted in Spring.

The *amellus* asters are first-rate for long flowering and freedom from trouble. This is an important but rather neglected group. No doubt this is due to their being slower-growing, but this is in their favour and they do not suffer from the troubles of wilt and mildew which affect the more unusual Michaelmas daisies.

A. amellus flower from August to October, growing quite erectly with soft grey-green foliage from a somewhat woody rootstock, and carry wide heads of single flowers. They vary in height from 30-90 cm, and unless pot grown, are much safer to plant in Spring, which is the correct time for division. They are not fussy as to soil so long as it is well drained and in an open position.

The best old variety, 'King George', is a lavender-violet colour, but 'Violet Queen' is superior, a rich glowing violet and very free flowering. Pink shades in *A. amellus* tend to be less strong growing, but 'Lady Hindlip' and 'Sonia' are both of proven worth, the latter being the lighter colour, as is Pink Zenith'. 'Nocturne' has a distinctive rosy-lavender shading.

A hybrid between *A. amellus* and *A. thompsonii* has stood the test of time as a very fine plant: it is *A. frikartii* 'Wonda von Stafa', with open branching habit and large lavender-blue flowers at 90 cm high, from July to October. Another, named 'Monch', is worth growing. This is less branching in habit and has a long season of rich-blue, yellow-centred flowers.

A. 'Flora's Delight' comes from the same cross but is less tall and needs very-well-drained soil. The flowers are lilac-blue on 60 cm stems for many weeks.

The charming *A. thomsonii* 'Nana' makes a shapely bush 40 cm high studded with light-blue flowers for many weeks. The hybrid 'Little Carlow' is distinctive for its 120 cm sprays of fairly small but very bright blue, yellow centred flowers.

Akin to the *A. novi-belgii* Michaelmas daisies are the *novae-angliae* varieties. These too are late flowering with terminal heads of rayed flowers from stout, trouble-free clumps, although some taller kinds may need supporting. The light-pink

Aster novae-angliae 'Alma Potschke' displays warm salmon-pink flowers.

Astilbe

These plants originate from the Far East, some of the 30 species even occur in tropical areas.
The species are hardly ever offered. You will mainly find plants from the groups of hybrids of which the Astilbe Arendsii hybrids are the most important. These hybrids are divided in groups according to the flowering period:
July flowering, July-August and August-September flowering.
Always ask for the flowering time when you buy them. The plants are often not completely hardy and might freeze. This does not affect the flowering, because new growth develops easily. Propagation from seed — especially of wild species — is difficult, as the seed rapidly goes stale, leading to poor germination. Division in Autumn is best when the pieces can then spend the Winter under glass. They should be replanted in Spring.

'Harrington's Pink' is an old favourite, but the most effective colour is 'Alma Potschke', a warm salmon-pink. 'September Ruby' is close to red and 'Lye End Beauty' and 'Treasure' are deep lilac. 'Autumn Snow' is white. All these are 120-150 cm tall. Several other types, mostly species, are worth while. A. acris (syn. A. sedifolius) is somewhat floppy but has myriads of small blue flowers June – August at 80 cm, but a dwarfer form at 50 cm is available.

A. cordifolius is not often seen but is a graceful late plant, small-flowered, blue or white, at 100-120 cm.
A. ericoides is also small-flowered but has a strong bushy habit and is trouble free. Colours are subdued but worthwhile for late flowering. 'Starshower' and 'Delight' are whitish, 'Brimstone' and 'Golden Spray' are yellowish and 'Cinderella' is pale blue. All are 80-100 cm in height.
A. harveyi is seldom offered but it has sizeable blue flowers on 100 cm stems in later Summer.
A. lateriflorus and A. f. 'Horizontalis' have arching slender stems with attractive lateral branches carrying small lilac-blue flowers in abundance, September-October, 100 cm.
A. linosyris is known as 'goldilocks'. Slender, narrow-leaved stems to 75 cm carry terminal heads of deep-yellow fluffy flowers July-September. The variety 'Gold Dust' is best.
A. tradescantii is dwarf and bushy with clusters of off-white flowers giving good ground cover. 30 cm. August-October. In general, all late-flowering asters are best divided and replanted in Spring, but the dwarfer early-flowering kinds are best in late Summer or early Autumn.

Astilbe sinensis 'Pumila' is the most vigorous dwarf of all Astilbe varieties and hybrids.

ASTILBE

Astilbes are so colourful, so perfect in form, with pretty foliage fully complementary to the flowers, that it would be worth a little trouble to contrive the right growing conditions in a garden where they do not naturally exist.
The plants themselves in all cases are tough and hardy; but, without moisture, and preferably some shade as well, they fall well short of the display of which they are capable. Moisture is more important than shade, yet this does not mean they should be treated as bog plants, but merely that they should not be allowed to dry out.
Rich soil — plenty of peat and compost, with an annual mulch when dormant — will go a long way to making good any moisture deficiency, and some shade or shelter from strong winds holds them longer in flower.
To enrich the soil is no problem, and a fairly simple method of providing extra moisture is easy to arrange as well. Tin cans — about quart size with a few holes punched in the side and bottom — can be inserted unobtrusively here and there between plants, to within an inch or less of the surface. One can, or a 30 cm — long drainpipe, will irrigate at least three plants, and all one has to do is to fill this up with water during droughty weather every other day, and moisture will percolate to the thirsty roots more effectively than overhead watering. The same method can of course be applied for the other moisture-loving plants mentioned in this book.

Astilbes in rich variety

Astilbes vary in height from 10-180 cm (4 inches to 6 feet), and even the tallest need no staking. They go completely dormant in Winter and from April onwards the leaves appear and develop, all deeply-cut and often purplish or bronzy-green. Flowering begins in June and for several weeks they are very colourful indeed.
In the middle-height range of 60-90 cm, A. 'Fire' is aptly named, with even deeper reds in A. 'Glow' and A. 'Red Sentinel'.
A. 'Cologne' is bright pink, 60 cm tall, whilst A. 'Bressingham Beauty' is a little softer shade, growing to 90 cm.
A. 'Amethyst' is lilac purple, and A. 'Ostrich Plume' has pendant spikes of bright pink. These and several more, including the 60-75 cm white A. 'Deutschland' and the dark-leaved white A. 'Irrlicht', are extensively used for forcing as pot plants. But in the garden, where height variations are important, there should be room for such beauties as A. taquetii 'Superba'. This grows to a stately 150 cm with dark outspanning foliage and noble spikes of bright rosy-purple with a long season in flower.
Also tall, and excellent as waterside subjects, there are the rosy-lavender A. davidii and the pale pink A. 'Venus'. The recently introduced 'Elizabeth

ASTILBE

Astilbe taquetii 'Superba' grows easily to a stately 150 cm with dark foliage and long-flowering spikes in a rosy-purple hue.

Below: Astragalus angustifolius is a dwarf species with creamy-white flowers in May-June.

Bloom' bears sumptuous plumes of rich pink on 70 cm stems. 'Rosemary Bloom' is later flowering and less tall at 45 cm with an abundance of bright pink plumes and a habit which reveals its A. chinensis parentage.

Even more striking is A. 'Purple Lance', a reddish-purple shade on 150 cm spikes above handsome foliage. A. grandis is equally handsome with creamy plumes at 120 cm. So is A. rivularis, having attractive deeply-divided foliage and arching white plumes at 200 cm. It has roots which spread in most soil.

Many hybrids are of German origin — notably those raised by Georg Arends — sometimes listed as x. arendsii. The varieties 'Fanal' and 'Etna' are much alike, with deep-rosy-red plumes at 40 cm and 'Federsee' is bright-pink at 50 cm. This is more adaptable than the salmon-red 'Dunkelachs' of similar height, but the most vigorous dwarf is A. sinensis 'Pumila'. This is late-flowering and spreads well in sun or part shade with stumpy lilac-pink spikes 25 cm high. A new, brighter and slightly taller hybrid is 'Rosemary Bloom', July-September. A few very dwarf astilbes are excellent as dual-purpose plants, given moist, rich soil or a peat bed. A. x crispa has dark, crinkled, lacy foliage and stiff pokery spikes to 20 cm in the best-known A. x crispa 'Perkes'.

A. simplicifolia and its variants are more airy with lighter-green basal foliage, but dark-green in the splendid little 'Sprite'. This has a profusion of pearly-pink spikes for many weeks, July-September, at 25 cm. As a type or species, A. simplicifolia varies from 15-30 cm, light pink, the dwarfest being 'Nana'. 'Bronze Elegance' flowers profusely on 20 cm sprays, but the colour is shell pink rather than bronze.

A. simplicifolia 'Atrorosea' has sumptuous plumes on 30 cm stems of deep flesh-pink. An even dwarfer one is A. glaberrima 'Saxosa', pale pink, deep green filigree foliage, and only 10 cm tall. There is also a creamy-white hybrid named 'Wm. Buchanan', 15 cm, and the species A. microphyllus is somewhat similar.

When replanting old clumps of the larger astilbes, the old woody growth under the plant should be cut or broken off and discarded.

* ASTRAGALUS

This is a genus rich in low and numerous tiny species. They grow — except for Australia — all over the world. Good perennials among them (most are annuals or biennials) are:
Astragalus alpinus from the European mountains

with white violet – spotted flowers, height up to 25 cm.

A. angustifolius from S.E.Europe with creamy-white flowers from May-June.

A. danicus, which grows as a native from the S.W. Alps up to Scandinavia, height 35 cm with bluish-violet flowers with a yellow base, May-June.

A. purshii from N.W.America, height 20 cm as a maximum – just one of the many fine American species, most offered in seed-packets, flowering June-July, white or creamy-white.

ASTRANTIA

For all their lack of brilliance, the 'masterworts' have an attraction of their own. They are long-lived perennials for sun or part shade, their only dislike being that of dry or starved soil. The taller ones are excellent for cut-flower arrangements. They are safely divided or replanted in Spring or early Autumn; and although most of them flower from June to September, they continue more freely if faded stems are removed.

The most colourful is *Astrantia maxima* with loose heads on slender 90 cm stems of glistening pink, with just a hint of green. In good soil, plants spread quite quickly with leaves not unlike the pernicious weed ground elder. Several varieties of the creamy green-flowered *A. major* – sometimes wrongly listed as *A. carniolica* – are coming to the fore. These are all in the 70-90 cm range in shades of pink, and are more colourful than *A. major* 'Rosea'.

'Rubra' may be ascribed to *A. major* but is dwarfer and less vigorous, with somewhat drooping plum-red flowers.

A. m. involucrata is profuse with its greenish-white flowers; as is 'Margery Fish', which that famous plantswoman first named 'Shaggy' as an apt description.

These too grow strongly to about 80 cm.

The variegated-leaved form of *A. major*, sometimes listed as 'Sunningdale', is bright with yellow markings on the deeply-divided leaves. The colour fades as the flowers of greenish-white begin.

A seldom-seen dwarf species exists in *A. minor* which is not very exciting.

ATHYRIUM

These include the well known 'lady fern' *Athyrium filix-femina*. It is now evergreen but has many variations on the theme of lacy fronds in light-green shades. They prefer shade which is not too dry, and, where suited, expand into quite large clumps.

A. filix-femina itself grows to about 30 cm but the form 'Minuta' is little more than half that height.

Astrantia
Astrantia maxima and *Astrantia major* form splendid combinations with a number of other shade-loving plants for moist positions.
Beautiful are combinations with e.g.:
Aruncus dioicus, Asarum europaeum and *Saxifraga rotundifolia.*

Above: *Astrantia major* varieties are tall, (up to 90 cm), attractive plants, with pink flowers in various shades.

Athyrium filix-femina is the well-known lady fern. An evergreen fern for shaded places. It spreads easily.

ATHYRIUM

Above: *Aubrieta* varieties spread over wide areas, filling them with breath-taking colour.

Below: *Avena candida* is an attractive evergreen grass, often listed under *Helictotrichon*.

Avena

Strictly speaking, according to the latest rules of nomenclature, only annuals and biennials belong to the genus of *Avena*. All *Avena* perennials have been added to the *Helictotrichon* or the *Avenula* genus. In practice, however, the name *Avena* is still commonly used. *Avenula planiculmis* is a kind of grass with smooth foliage which can reach a height of 1 m. The leaves are bluish-green. The plant likes a sunny position and has purplish-brown flower spikes. *Helictotrichon* comprises, besides *H. sempervirens* (syn. *Avena candida*), two other species: *H. parlatorei* is a practically evergreen species, up to 40 cm high, which occurs mainly in chalky mountain areas in Europe; and *H. sedenense*, a kind of grass with bluish-grey foliage up to 20 cm high.

Other athyriums worth collecting should include *A. f.* 'Plumosum' with elegant fronds up to 90 cm. *A. regale* has interesting features including crested tips to the fronds of about 80 cm, and *A. vernoniae* has a crispy texture growing to 100 cm.
A. victoriae makes fine specimens with narrow lance-shaped fronds up to 80 cm.
Though not for cold districts, *A. niponicum* 'Pictum' (formerly *A. goeringianum*) has a low outward spread of greenery flecked with silver, 25 cm. Even the all-green type is attractive.

* ATROPA

Atropa belladonna is a member of the *solanaceae*. It grows from a thick tuber and reaches up to 150 cm. The flowers are purplish blue, the poisonous fruits purple-black. The leaves are used for medical purposes. It is a European native, and flowers June-August.
The rare variety 'Lutea' has greenish-yellow flowers and berries.

AUBRIETA

These stand high amongst the indispensables for the bright display they make in Spring. Their only requirement is for sun and good drainage and any excessive growth can be sheared back after flowering. Evergreen foliage adds to their value for smothering annual weeds, and they will drape over walls and banks or may be used for edging beds and borders.

Although seed-raised plants are cheaper to rear or purchase, their specific colours can only be from cuttings, best taken in Autumn. The full range of colour is available as named varieties from pale-pink and mauve-blue and lilac, to violet-purple and red, a few having semi-double flowers. They flower the better for being trimmed with shears after flowering, but one would hesitate to do this to the one or two having golden variegated foliage. Old plants are not difficult to divide and all are best in soil not deficient in lime.

AVENA

Avena candida (syn. *A. sempervirens*). The older name is preferable to the new *Helictotrichon* for this attractive evergreen grass. It has silver grey blades 30 cm long from clumpy plants and sprays of oat-like flowers on arching 80 cm stems.

AZORELLA – see BOLAX

BALLOTA

Ballota pseudodictamnus. This plant has charm for its greyish felted leaves on a mounded habit, more or less evergreen, in a warm sunny place. Plants bush up to 40 cm or so with white, purple – flecked flowers above during Summer. It is not a plant for wet, cold districts, and is increased by cuttings or divisions.

Ballota pseudodictamnus has more or less evergreen greyish felted leaves. It only thrives in warm, sunny places.

BAPTISIA

Baptisia australis. This blue-flowered legume makes stout, long-lived clumps and has no fads. Given a sunny place it forms dense green bushes of summer growth to 120 cm, with a bluish tinge. The lupin-like flowers of indigo-blue come on short spikes in early Summer.
A slightly taller variant exists in *B. australis* var. 'Exaltata' Both are sturdy but the latter needs supporting if soil is rich or moist.

Left: Baptisia australis 'Exaltata' produces blue-flowered, long-lived clumps, but may need supporting.

BEGONIA

Begonia grandis (syn. *B. evansiana*) is hardy in warm areas and easily protected elsewhere given a warm spot. Roots became matted if the heart-shaped leaves are late to reappear. The small bright pink flowers, on 30-40 cm sprays, keep coming from July through to October. It is seldom offered and increased by division or bulbils in Spring.

Below: Begonia grandis is a rather rare, pink-flowering perennial for warm places.

* BELAMCANDA

Belamcanda chinensis (syn. *Pardanthus chinensis*) looks like an iris. Height is 60 cm, with spotted, remarkable yellow-brownish flowers. The shining blade fruits do very well in dried bouquets. Some cross-breeds are available under the name *Pardancanda norisii. Belamcanda* loves sunny sites and is not hardy.

BELLIS

BELLIS

Bellis perennis. The weedy daisy is a pest in lawns. From it have been bred larger-flowered doubles in white, pink and red, named 'Montrosa', which come freely from seed but are unworthy except for bedding.

There are, however, daintier doubles in such old favourites as the pink 'Dresden China', and 'White Pearl', which are only 8-10 cm tall, and the red 'Rob Roy' 12 cm. Another, called 'Hen and Chickens', has tiny flowers radiating from the main ones like a ruff. All these, and the bluish *B. rotundifolia* 'Caerulescens', need to be replanted at least every other year.

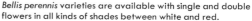

Bellis perennis varieties are available with single and double flowers in all kinds of shades between white and red.

BERGENIA

These very adaptable plants have become popular in recent years. They are shallow-rooted and have large, shiny, mostly evergreen leaves to make good ground cover in sun or shade in almost any but boggy soil. In Spring come spikes of waxy bell-shaped flowers in pink, red and white, after which new leaves develop. Although those below are fully hardy, severe spring frosts will sometimes damage the flowers. Bergenias can be divided or replanted at almost any time when not in flower; but, with a tendency to grow out of the ground, they should be set in almost up to the leaves, laying the pieces horizontally just below the surface.
B. cordifolia has somewhat heart-shaped leaves which remain green over Winter better than some. The most colourful is *B. cordifolia* 'Purpurea'. Both have flowers at about 45 cm in Spring.
B. crassifolia has leaves somewhat spoon-shaped or oval, is of compact habit with stems and flowers 30 cm. tall, and leaves fairly erect which colour well during Winter.
B. purpurescens var. *delavayi* has reddish stems and flowers 30 cm tall, leaves fairly erect which also colour well during Winter.
B. stracheyi has quite small leaves and 20 cm spikes of pale pink. There is also a white form but neither are fully evergreen.
The above species have yielded a number of hybrids. Amongst the best are 'Abendglut', dwarf

Bergenia
Of these remarkable plants with their striking inflorescence and mainly evergreen foliage some 8 species are known, which all occur wild in the Far East. They make beautiful combinations with grasses and ferns. They also grow well under trees, and are very suitable for the rock garden.
All bergenias grow from thick, creeping rhizomes. The species are hardly ever offered as you will mostly find the hybrids available.

Bergenia cordifolia 'Purpurea' is the most colourful of the *B. cordifolia* varieties.

at 20 cm with crimson flowers, 'Bressingham Salmon' is an unusual shade, and 'Bressingham White' grows more compactly than the rather untidy white 'Silberlicht'. 'Ballawley' is a tall, handsome plant with red stems and flowers, but this too lacks neatness. Spikes grow to 60 cm. 'Marjery Fish' has 45 cm spikes of magenta purple and a compact habit. 'Morgenrote' is a good deep pink and produces a second crop of 45 cm spikes in Summer. 'Pugsley's Purple' is also distinctive at 50 cm, and x. *schmidtii* is outstanding for earliness and being profuse in leaf and flower. Leaves are shiny green with toothed edges and the pink flower spikes are 30 cm tall.

Above: *Blechnum spicant* is a nicely leaved evergreen fern which will grow in sunny but moist sites.

The orchid *Bletilla striata* does very well in rather acid soil and will survive our winters with a little protection.

BERKHEYA

Berkheya macrocephala has a somewhat thistly appearance with yellow flowers on branching spikes to 100 cm for several weeks in Summer. It is not often seen but has some appeal.

BETONICA – see STACHYS

BIDENS – see COSMOS

BLECHNUM

Blechnum penna-marina is another diminutive creeping fern of bronzy green for crevices or shaded walls, with leathery fronds.
B. spicant is larger with centre fronds to 30 cm, deeply divided, above a green rosette formation. Both are evergreen, but *B. spicant* will grow in sun where not dry. Division of all ferns is best in Spring and Summer.

BLETILLA

A near-hardy orchid for peaty or humus soil and part shade, the species *B. striata* has rosy purple flowers in later Summer on 30 cm stems.

BOLAX

B. glebaria (syn. Azorella trifurcata) makes a spreading, brightly-coloured evergreen cushion of crusty rosettes whose tiny yellow flowers are stemless. It is best in sharp draining soil and sun but fully hardy.

BOLTONIA

These Michaelmas daisy relatives are also Autumn flowering but, though easy to grow, suffer from being too tall for most beds or borders.
B. asteroides runs up to 230 cm with small lilac-white flowers in abundance.
B. latisquama is a little lower in height, and the flowers are more lilac in colour.

BORAGO

Borago laxiflora is a pretty little plant, but though short-lived it usually self-seeds. The 30 cm sprays of small intense-blue flowers continue for many weeks above deep-green waxy leaves in rosette formation.

Above: Boltonia asteroides is a close relative of the Michaelmas daisy, producing many lilac-white flowers.

Right: Borago laxiflora may also be listed as B. pygmaea.

Borago
Of the 3 species belonging to this genus B. laxiflora (syn. B. pygmaea) is the most distinct perennial. All species originate from the Mediterranean.
Their flowers are totally adapted to pollination by bees. The best known is the annual B. officinalis, which is used both as a herb and medicinally. Borago laxiflora seeds itself abundantly too. Therefore, although the plant is not very hardy, you will always have new plants at your disposal, even after severe frost.

Bouteloua species are ideally suited for the natural garden.

* BOUTELOUA

This is a grass from the prairies of North-America. They are sun-lovers and do very well in the natural garden.
B. curtipendula is the less important with flower spikes about 80 cm high.
B. gracilis is the most offered with bending brownish-green narrow leaves and characteristic flowering stalks, 30-40 cm high.

BOYKINIA

This is a small seldom-seen genus akin to *Heuchera* and *Tiarella* with rounded near-evergreen leaves. The species *B. major*, *B. occidentalis* and *B. rotundifolia* are all somewhat similar, having delicate sprays 25-35 cm long of whitish flowers in early Summer, best in light shade.

BRACHYCOME

Brachycome rigidula makes a 12 cm dark-green mound, carrying lavender-blue, daisy flowers for many weeks. It comes from seed or will divide.

BRIZA

These grasses cannot be rated highly for tidiness and longevity. *B. media* is the 'quaking grass', having about 60 cm stems carrying nodding locket-shaped flowers of value for flower arrangements. The base foliage is soft but not attractively evergreen. Much the same applies to the somewhat taller species *B. maxima*.

Above: *Briza maxima* is ideal for elegant flower arrangements.

Below: *Brunnera macrophylla* looks like a forget-me-not at first sight.

Above: *Brachycome* species — most are annuals — form daisy-like flowers from July onwards, mainly in bluish hues.

BRUNNERA

Brunnera macrophylla was formerly *Anchusa myosotidiflora* and the flowers have indeed a close resemblance to forget-me-nots.

The sprays are, however, longer and more widely branched, developing up to 45 cm or so, by which time the 15-cm-wide rounded leaves are forming a sturdy, mounded plant; and when flowering has ended in June, fresh leaves continue all Summer. It is an easy and adaptable plant for both sun and shade, not fussy over soil and readily divided. *B. macrophylla* 'Langtrees' has silvery speckles on the leaves, whilst 'Hadspen Cream', a newer variety, has decidedly creamy-yellow borderings. Both are strong growers but the brightest for leaf colour, *B. macrophylla* 'Variegata', is best in some shade. At least half the leaf is a light primrose yellow. It grows less strongly than the type, and flowers just as pleasingly, but the variegation is perpetuated only by true divisions. This means that if dividing, a detached root may sprout leaves and these will be green.

BULBINELLA

Above: *Bulbinella hookeri* grows from semi-bulbous roots and forms poker-like spikes of yellow flowers.

Bupleurum falcatum is an interesting, rather rare, plant, that self-seeds easily.

Bupleurum
This widespread genus comprises about 150 annual and perennial species. They occur in totally different regions. Practically all species originate from mountain areas and make a good combination with *Aster, Artemisia, Leontopodium, Linum, Saxifraga, Festuca, Draba, Sempervivum* species. Besides *B. falcatum* and (a lime lover) sometimes species such as *B. petraeum* (also lime lover) and *B. stellatum* (hates lime) are offered.

BULBINELLA

Bulbinella hookeri has narrow, bronzy-tinted leaves from a semi-bulbous root and throws up pokery 50 cm spikes of deep-yellow starry flowers in early Summer. This is an uncommon plant for good, humus, well-drained soil, increased by seed or division, though it is of rather slow growth.

BUPLEURUM

Bupleurum falcatum is neither choice nor often offered, but it has some charm. Branching stems to 100 cm carry little umbels of deep sulphur-yellow flowers for several weeks, June-September. The foliage is narrow, glaucous green; and although plants are liable to die out after 2-3 years, it usually replenishes by self seeding and needs no special treatment.

BUPHTHALMUM – see INULA

* CALAMAGROSTIS

Calamagrostis x *acutiflora* 'Karl Foerster' is the only variety of this genus worth growing.
It reaches up to 1.8 m when flowering and makes a tremendous impression in each garden. The flowering stalks stay all the year and do a lovely job, especially in Winter. It can be increased by division, and is a very gracious subject.

Above: *Calamintha nepetoides* displays its light-blue flowers in late summer.

Right: *Calamagrostis* x *acutiflora* 'Karl Foerster' is the most impressive variety of this species.

CALAMINTHA

One alpine and two taller species are worth including. C. *alpina* makes a fairly neat mound of closely branching 15 cm stems, having whorls of purple-blue flowers May-August.
C. *grandiflora* grows more robustly to 20 cm with ample base foliage and has deep-rosy-purple flowers.
The most effective species is C. *nepetoides*. From an enduring compact rootstock come somewhat twiggy sprays, to 40 cm, of small, light-blue flowers in late Summer to make a very pleasing display. It grows in sun or part shade. None of these minty-odoured plants is fussy and can be divided in Spring.

* CALANDRINIA

Calandrinia umbellata is a pretty, succulent plant with narrow leaves and violet-red flowers on 11 cm stalks. 'Amaranth' is more of a carmine colour. They flower in July and on through September, and are therefore valuable in the garden. They are very good for the rock garden.

CALCEOLARIA

Above: *Calceolaria darwinii* must have a sheltered place to grow in.

CALCEOLARIA

The dwarf alpine species are mostly quite hardy. They do best in well-drained humus-rich soil, but dislike hot sunny positions.

C. *polyrrhiza* spreads below ground and forms grey-green rosettes. Yellow pouches come on 10 cm stems. A larger hybrid, 'John Innes', is more desirable, and both need frequent replanting. It is true that these daintier species are not reliable everywhere, but they are worth some effort to please.

C. *arachnoidea*, with its woolly rosettes, dislikes winter wet. Flowers on 15 cm stems are purple-red.

C. *biflora* has twin yellow pouches, 20 cm, but the choicest of all is C. *darwinii*. In a sheltered place and gritty humus soil, its flowers on 10 cm stems are brownish-yellow, with a white band.

C. *tenella* grows with a creeping habit, has small bright-green leaves, and its 5 cm stems carry pouched yellow flowers. In practice young plants do best and seed is worth collecting where species do not readily divide.

C. *falklandii* and C. *fothergillii* are also worth trying, but C. *integrefolia* is a half-hardy, semi-shrubby plant. It makes shapely, leafy 40 cm bushes with a long season, June-October, of yellow flowers, and is very showy in 'Boughton', a burnt-orange colour.

Left: *Caltha palustris*, the native Marsh Marigold, shows its yellow flowers in Spring.

Caltha

Marsh marigolds occur wild in the temperate regions of the northern and southern hemisphere. There are about 40 species which all like moist to wet soil. Attractive combinations can be made with irises, primulas, *Lysichiton* and *Leucojum*. Some varieties only produce sterile flowers, in which case propagation is only possible by division. In all other cases propagation can take place from seed. Sowing should take place as soon as the shiny seeds are ripe, and they should germinate in Spring. Sow in boxes with moist soil.

CALTHA

The marsh marigolds make a fine show in Spring and early Summer in any soil which does not dry out. They will grow in quite boggy conditions and are best divided after flowering.

C. *leptosepala* is a demure little plant with white flowers on 15-20 cm stems above rounded leaves in May-June.

C. *palustris* is the native Marsh Marigold and a good marginal subject, but is less reliably perennial than the double 'Plena'. This is first rate with large glistening yellow flowers on somewhat weak 20 cm stems, April-May.

C. *palustris* 'Montrosa' has even larger flowers on prostrate branching stems a little later.

C. *palustris* 'Minor' is a single yellow which roots down as it spreads. The tallest and latest to flower is C. *p.* var. *polypetala*, growing to 60 cm where moist. It has large and lush green leaves and branching stems of yellow flowers, May-June.

CAMASSIA

These lily relatives are early-flowering from bulbs and become dormant long before Summer ends. The best known is C. *leichtlinii* with lax narrow foliage and 100 cm spikes carrying starry flowers in early Summer. C. *cusickii* is blue, and 70cm high. The most pleasing of the variations in colour is the blue, but the double 'Plena' is creamy-yellow on strong spikes. Any well-drained soil suits them in a mainly sunny position and replanting should be in early Autumn.

Early flowering *Camassia* species are available in blue and yellow shades and should be grown in well-drained soil.

CAMPANULA

This large and infinitely varied genus contains some excellent subjects, both alpine and for borders and beds. They are not very fussy as to soil and have no objection to some shade even if sun is preferred. Almost all are easy to divide in Spring or early Autumn.

Although blue is the basic colour in campanulas (Bellflowers), there is such wide variations in height and habit that they form an important asset in decorative gardening. Most of them are reliable and trouble free and have few soil fads or fancies, adaptable to sun or partial shade. They can be increased by division in Spring but seldom come true when raised from seed.

Amongst dwarf-growing dual-purpose kinds, C. *carpatica*, in shades of blue as well as white, grows neatly from 15-30 cm, making a show of upfacing bells frome June to August.
C. *muralis* (syn. C. *portenschlagiana*) is lavender-blue, only 10-12 cm high, but has an amazing capacity for flowering and creeps slowly below ground.
C. 'Stella' is really excellent with starry flowers spreading out from a mounded plant, often flowering twice. It can also be effective as an indoor pot plant.
C. *alliariifolia* 'Ivory Bells' is, of course, white, a long-lived variety of a free-flowering species. From June to August, 45 cm sprays carry dangling bells, though they are not so large as the smoky-blue flowers of C. 'Burghaltii' (also 45 cm), which also has a long flowering period.
C. *glomerata* has several forms, but the flowers are clustered.
C. *g.* 'Joan Elliott' is violet-blue, 145 cm, for May and June.
C. *glomerata* 'Nana Alba'is white, 45 cm, June to August, and 'Purple Pixie' July to September.

Below: *Campanula portenschlagiana*, with *Corydalis lutea*.

CAMPANULA

The tallest is C. *glomerata* 'Superba' which carries terminal violet clusters on 75-90 cm stems in June and July.

C. *lactiflora* makes a more fleshy root and bears open heads of lavender-mauve bell-flowers in high-Summer on erect 90-120 cm stems. There is also a white and the slightly pink C. *l.* 'Loddon Anna' which grows 120-150 cm.

C. *latifolia* grows strongly to 120 cm for June and July, the variety 'Brantwood' being violet-purple; and, apart from a white variety, there is the exquisite pale-lilac-blue 'Gloaming'.

C. *persicifolia* is not so long-lived as most, but during June and July makes a good show.

C. *p.* 'Telham Beauty' is the best blue, but a more reliable variety with the same form of saucer-covered 90 cm spikes exists in C. *latiloba* 'Percy Piper', with rich blue flowers. Finally, for those who like double flowers, the 60 cm C. *trachelium* 'Bernice', powder blue, is worth growing for the June-August period, and C. *rapunculoides* is pretty with purple-blue flowers on 60 cm stems, but it is a pernicious weed in growth and spread.

Dwarf campanulas

Dwarf campanulas are of special value, for most of them flower after the spring flush of alpines is over. Some species are very choosy or difficult, others are short-lived and a few are weedy. The list below includes all those worth recommending as having reliability and merit, including good cultivars such as 'Birch Hybrid'. This flowers on-and-off for much of the year, forming neat clumpy plants with upturned flowers of deep lavender-blue to 15 cm.

C. *carpatica* is best seen in its named varieties. All flower in the June-to-August period with mainly upturned cup or saucer-shaped flowers above bushy summer growth. 'Blue Moonlight' is china blue, 15 cm; 'Chewton Joy' has a profusion of smaller, light-blue flowers, only 10 cm tall. 'Hannah' of similar habit is pure white; and 'Isobel' deep blue, 20 cm. C. 'Constellation' and 'Stella' are both hybrids of compact mounded habit with outspreading sprays of lavender-blue flowers for many weeks.

C. *carpatica* var. *turbinata* and its cultivars grow more like dwarfer *carpatica* types in shades of blue and violet. 'Molly Pinsent', 'Stansfieldii' and 'Norman Grove' are hybrids with clumpy growth, not evergreen, making a mounded display in varying shades of lavender-blue in July and August, 10-20 cm tall. All the above are virtually trouble free in any well drained soil, limy or acid.

C. *garganica* is of similar habit, but more tightly mounded, but there are taller variations as well as the choicer, deep-lavender-flowered 'W.H. Paine'. These are good wall plants.

Above: Campanula *lactiflora* 'Prichard's Variety', not mentioned in the main text, is one of several good varieties.

Left: Campanula *persicifolia* makes a great show during June and July.

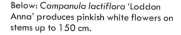

Below: Campanula *lactiflora* 'Loddon Anna' produces pinkish white flowers on stems up to 150 cm.

Creeping campanulas

Campanulas with a creeping habit, dying back in Winter, include the dainty blue C. *cochleariifolia*, the white 'Hallii', and larger, deep blue in 'Oakington'. A new variety, 'Elisabeth Oliver', is a charming double powder-blue. All are 6-8 cm. 'G.F. Wilson' also runs below ground, to carry large violet-blue flowers 8-10 cm; C. *pulla* has dangling purple-blue bells to 6 cm; and C. x *pulloides* resembles a larger edition of it at 12 cm. These types wander somewhat and may need curbing. Not so with C. *portenschlagiana* (syn. C. *muralis*) which has clumpy growth and lavender-blue flowers about 12 cm, useful in walls in sun or shade.

The true harebell C. *rotundifolia* does not take well to cultivation, though there are easier variations in deep-blue and white, in 'Covadonga' and 'Spetchley White'.

One species to avoid for being weedy is C. *poscharskyana*. Campanulas can be divided in Spring and C. *carpatica* germinates well from seed, in mixture. All associate happily with dwarf shrubs and sedums, yellow or pink. There are many more alpine species in existence for those wishing to grow them.

Campanula *poscharskyana* spreads rapidly and therefore should only be planted in areas where it will not be a nuisance.

Campanula

Bell flowers occur wild only in the northern hemisphere, especially in Southeast Europe, the Far East and also in the Himalaya mountains and North America. Practically all species originate from mountain areas, although there are some woodland and steppe species. *Campanula* may be grown in varying conditions. In shady places a combination with, for instance, ferns, *Aruncus* and *Astilbe* is very attractive. In the border especially, the tall species are suitable together with poppies, lilies, *Oenothera* and *Achillea*.

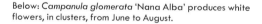

Below: C*ampanula carpatica* 'Chewton Joy' remains compact (10 cm), and forms a wealth of light blue flowers.

Below: *Campanula glomerata* 'Nana Alba' produces white flowers, in clusters, from June to August.

CARDAMINE

CARDAMINE

These are not for dry conditions but are otherwise easy to grow in sun or part shade. They make readily dividable plants, best done every two years.

C. *latifolia* makes lush green mats of rounded leaves and gives a bright display in early Summer of lilac flowers on 40 cm branching heads.

C. *pratensis* is the native cuckoo flower. Though pretty, it is scarcely a garden plant, but there is a much dwarfer double form 'Plena', also lilac-flowered.

It needs frequent replanting.

C. *trifolia* is white-flowered and vigorous, flowering in Spring on 20 cm heads.

Left: *Cardamine pratensis*, the native cuckoo flower, is also available in a double form.

CARDIOCRINUM

These spectacular lilies need well-drained rich soil and some shade. As bulbs they should not be planted deeply; and though they die after flowering, bulbils have to be nursed.

Both they, and seedlings if raised, take a few years to reach flowering size. Success comes with care and perseverance, with strong 200-300 cm stems topped with large white trumpets on C. *giganteum*.

A little less tall is C. *yunnanense*, also white.

Both have handsome heart-shaped leaves and neither needs staking.

The variegated forms of *Carex morrowii* make eye-catching, evergreen ground coverers.

Cardiocrinum giganteum takes several years to reach flowering size, but the tall stems with their white trumpets, make this plant well worth growing.

CARDUNCELLUS

Carduncellus rhaponticoides is quite outstanding with its evergreen rosette of leathery leaves (up to 20 cm across), close to the soil. In early Summer comes a large, rounded, stemless head like a ball of lilac-blue. The plant is easy in well-drained soil and the fleshy roots can be used as cuttings for increase.

CAREX

This is sedge, and as a genus has little to commend it for garden cultivation.

As a species, C. *morrowii* is useful evergreen ground cover but the cultivar 'Evergold' (C. *morrowii* 'Aurea Variegata') is outstandingly valuable. The bladed leaves, of bright golden-yellow with a thin green line, arch over to cover 30 cm or more across as a shapely mound, effective throughout the year, and only 30 cm high. It has many uses amongst dark-green dwarf conifers, or between red or blue flowering plants as an edging, or even as a pot plant.

Best divided in Spring it is not fussy as to soil or position except that it dislikes dense shade.

C. *stricta* 'Aurea' prefers sun, light soil, to make clumps of erect golden blades. It is a compact, fully evergreen plant. A smaller hybrid with a silvery sheen is seen in 'Tinneys'. Both are easy to grow, dividable in Spring.

CARLINA

These are ornamental thistles, but those below are not weedy and have considerable garden value. They are easy to grow in sun, and can be increased by root cuttings or division.

C. acanthifolia is a rarely-seen species having a wide flat rosette of jagged leaves for most of the year. In the centre will come a spectacular stemless thistle head of lilac blue in Summer.

C. acaulis, though of a somewhat similar habit and more vigorous, is not often seen as stemless. The form C. acaulis 'Caulescens' is more likely to be available, and this has arching stems up to 25 cm with smaller flowers.

Flowering time is June-August.

* CASSIA

Cassia hebecarpa is a bushy perennial with leaves reminding one of robinia, the false acacia. Even the flowers show some resemblance, though they are yellow. Flowering time is August-September. It is not quite hardy when young, but older plants cause no trouble in Winter: a beautiful solitary plant for a sunny site.

CATANANCHE

Catananche caerulea is another cut-and-come-again plant and the papery cornflowers on single 60 cm stems have good cutting qualities.

The fleshy rooted plants are amazingly free and long-flowering, June to September, but such profusion takes its toll in exhaustion after 3 or 4 years. 'Cupid's darts' — the folk name of this plant — is best in sun and a well-drained soil, and is very drought resistant. Increase is either from seed or root cuttings in Spring, 8 cm long, placed in a frame.

CAUTLEYA

Cautleya 'Robusta' is an exotic looking subject which grows strongly in a sheltered position and rich moist soil, not too alkaline. The roots are fleshy with a central crown and radiating thongs, active only 5 cm deep, and in cold districts a little covering from November to March is advised in case of severe frost.

In early Summer the reddish sheathed shoots develop to open out rather like compact-growing sweetcorn, but in July the yellow lipped flowers make quite a show against a backcloth of lush greenery.

Depending somewhat on moisture, height varies from 75-120 cm and, where happy, there is an attractive display until well into Autumn.

Planting is best in Spring and care must be taken not to injure the rather brittle roots and crowns.

Carlina acaulis 'Caulescens' forms stemless thistle heads flowering June-August.

Catananche caerulea flowers abundantly over a long period, from June to September, but in so doing the plant exhausts itself and should be exchanged after 3 to 4 years.

Cautleya
The 5 species of this genus all originate from the Himalaya mountains. Besides Cautleya 'Robusta', you may sometimes find C. gracilis also offered. It is a 30-50 cm tall plant with golden yellow flowers from August to September. Cautleya makes a good combination with grasses and ferns. The plants are somewhat similar to Canna.

Cautleya 'Robusta' needs a sheltered position. Produces exotic flowers from July to well into Autumn.

CENTAUREA

Above: *Centaurea* 'John Coutts' produces fine pink-tinted cornflower-like blooms.

Right: *Centaurea montana* flowers in May-June. Varieties are available in all shades between pink and purple.

Below: *Centaurea macrocephala* grows almost 1.8 metres tall, with an abundance of yellow flowers.

Below: *Centaurium scilloides* is an alpine for sunny places.

CENTAUREA

These are best described as perennial cornflowers, though the wild knapweed is in fact a *Centaurea* too. They are easy to grow in any well-drained soil as well as being long-lived, and respond easily to division.

'Steenbergii' has been popular for several years as the best form of C. *dealbata*. It has deep-pink flowers in June and July, on very robust growth with greyish foliage, but the newer variety C. 'John Coutts' has even larger flowers of a more delicate shade of pink.

C. *macrocephala* is a giant with large green leaves and stout 180 cm stems, carrying fluffy yellow flower heads from June to August.

C. *glastifolia* is like a smaller-flowered but more dainty C. *macrocephala*, but is not often seen.

C. *ruthenica* is also tall but of more graceful appearance with dark-green, deeply-cut leaves and carrying lemon-yellow flowers for a long season.

C. 'Pulchra Major' is handsome for its fine silver-grey foliage and erect 90 cm spikes of large tufty pink flowers in June-July.

Dwarf centaureas

Dwarf centaureas have their place, and nothing looks prettier than the 40 cm C. *hypoleuca* with its silver foliage and pink flowers and a much longer season than the May-June flowering C. *montana* varieties in pink, violet and purple.

Other dwarfs, with good silver-grey foliage, are the 45 cm C. *rigidifolia* and the 25 cm C. *simplicicaulis*. The latter does not flower very freely, but makes quite attractive ground cover. Both these have pink flowers in June-July and are tidier growing than the rather vigorous C. *montana* which is rather floppy and makes a good deal of spread for all its short flowering season.

Generally, centaureas are sun-loving plants and, as is often the case with subjects having grey or silver foliage, prefer to be in dry rather than damp, ill-drained soil. Another generalisation applies to centaureas, which is that those that flower early are best divided or planted in Autumn, whereas later- flowering kinds are best in Spring, but pot grown plants can be moved at either season.

CENTAURIUM

Centaurium scilloides is a neat-growing alpine once known as *Erythraea diffusa*. It has 8 cm sprays of clear pink flowers from a green tuft, best in sun. It is not long-lived but may be raised from seed.

CENTRANTHUS

Centranthus ruber. The old name 'valerian' lingers for this ubiquitous plant which will naturalise even in walls by self-seeding. The colours vary from white to reddish-pink, but the most attractive is the deep red which may be listed as C. *atrosanguinea* or C. 'Coccineus'.

They flower for many weeks June-September with leafy stems up to 90 cm.

CEPHALARIA

Cephalaria gigantea (syn. C. *tatarica*). This is a massive-growing, long-lived scabious, with primrose-yellow flowers June-August. A well-established plant will take up a metre-square space, making a leafy bush and needing no supports. Flowers of pin-cushion type come on short stems above, but such a plant needs to be well in the background.

Seed is a method of increase, less tedious than division.

CERASTIUM

This genus includes the well-known but pernicious 'snow-in-Summer'. Although it makes a bright show of white flowers above grey foliage, it is so invasive that many a rock wall or garden has been ruined by it. The roots are very penetrating and almost impossible to curb or eradicate without dismantling. It should never be introduced where other choicer plants are to be grown, but there is one species worth having in C. *columnae* (*Cerastium tomentosum* var. *columnae*) which is an intensely silvery-leaved carpeter with white flowers, and a modest spread above ground.

Above: *Centranthus ruber* – the best variety of this is the deep red 'Coccineus'.

Below: *Cerastium tomentosum* var. *columnae* is a good, bright flowering, modestly ground covering plant.

Cerastium

In nature the enormous abundance of species within one genus is often conspicuous. With *Cerastium* more than 100 species are known, which are mainly annuals. They only occur in the northern hemisphere, often in regions with steppes and poor soil, although there are also typical alpine kinds. Many species spread rapidly and develop richly flowering carpets which are very useful in the garden. It is almost exclusively the grey-foliaged species and forms which are cultivated. Propagation is simple and can be done by division.

CERATOSTIGMA

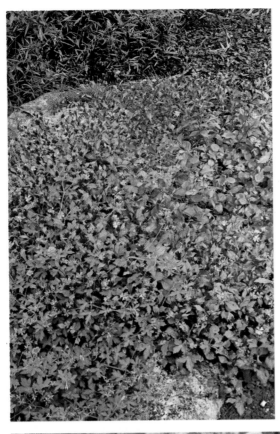

Ceratostigma plumbaginoides, showing its sky-blue flowers together with the autumn colour of the leaves.

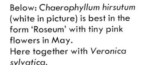

Below: Chaerophyllum hirsutum (white in picture) is best in the form 'Roseum' with tiny pink flowers in May.
Here together with Veronica sylvatica.

CERATOSTIGMA

Ceratostigma plumbaginoides is useful for banks, but not for small sites for its underground progress may be troublesome. It forms a carpet of leathery leaves on 20 cm stems tipped with sky-blue flowers in late Summer, and with leaves colouring in Autumn. It is easy to divide.

* CHAENARRHINUM

This genus has 20 species, all of them native in Europe and W.Asia. They are closely related to the genus Linaria. Some species are not quite hardy, but with some extra care they will do very well.
C. glareosum is native in Spain. It grows in the mountains up to 3000 m. Stems are 30 cm high. Flowers are violet with some yellow, appearing June-July.
C. origanifolium has lilac flowers with stems reaching 25 cm high. The sub-species C. o. crassifolium comes from Spain again. The colour of the flowers is lilac.
C. villosum grows in northern Mediterranian areas. Its violet flowers appear in June-July.

CHAEROPHYLLUM

Chaerophyllum hirsutum. Despite its resemblance to cow parsley, the form 'Roseum' is a very showy plant. The heads of tiny pink flowers come on erect 60 cm stems to bring a welcome early display in May. It is easy to grow in sun or part shade and has no vices.

CHEIRANTHUS

As perennial wallflowers these are showy and some are perfumed. All prefer poor and dry soil to rich and moist, and in these conditions will live longer. Some are separated into the genus Erysimum, but are included here as being practically inseparable.
C. cheiri 'Harpur Crewe' is an old-fashioned double yellow, sweetly scented with flowers above erect bushy growth to 35 cm.
C. mutabilis 'Constant Cheer' is basically violet-mauve, tinged amber, and is seldom out of flower, growing to 25 cm.
C. 'Jacob's Jacket' is dwarfer and more spreading at 20 cm, with heads of multicoloured flowers in Spring and early Summer. 'Moonlight' makes a low spread of greenery to 15 cm, covered in lemon-yellow flowers. 'Orange Flame' is quite descriptive, as is 'Sunbright'. The last three are all low-growing and longer-lived than the first three,

from which autumn cuttings can be taken to renew old plants.

Cheiranthus are good wall plants as one would expect, and look attractive with *Cytisus* and helianthemums.

CHELONE

Chelone barbata is a near relation of penstemon and is pretty enough, but lacks longevity. For 2-3 years, seed-raised plants will throw graceful 60 cm spikes, arching a little and carrying tubular flowers June-August. Colours may vary from scarlet-red to clear-pink. Plants have ample basal leaves but not much spread and they dislike wet and shade.

C. *glabra* makes light-green 30 cm bushes with lilac-pink flowers nestling. It is compact in growth and reasonably long-lived.

C. *lyonii* is a good perennial, bush of form, and has a long succession of pink rounded flowers, 30 cm, June-August.

C. *obliqua* is very different and reliable in every way. The leafy spikes stand stiffly to 60-70 cm, carrying curiously shaped carmine-rose flowers which suggested the folk name 'turtle head'. Roots spread slowly to make bold clumps, easily divided in Spring, since it flowers for several weeks in late Summer and Autumn. The white form 'Alba' is also desirable.

CHIASTOPHYLLUM

This is the updated name for *Cotyledon simplicifolia*.

It is one of the best of all rock garden plants, but it dislikes a very dry position. Otherwise, it will grow in sun or shade; and from rosettes of green, thinly succulent leaves, sends up 15 cm sprays on which dangle small yellow flowers for many weeks. It responds to top dressing with peat or soil as an alternative to replanting more deeply every two to three years.

Easy to divide, it contrasts attractively with *Campanula* and blue *Veronica*.

Chelone obliqua 'Alba' is a reliable white-flowering 'turtle head'.

Above: *Cheiranthus* varieties – pictured is 'Moonlight' – are very reliable wall plants.

Below: *Chiastophyllum oppositifolium* (syn. *Cotyledon simplicifolia*), is a good and attractive rockgarden plant, which will thrive everywhere if the soil is not too dry.

Chionochloa

This is a genus of grasses from Australia and New-Sealand. Recently one species was introduced which proved to behave well in our climate: *Chionochloa conspicua*, Hunangamoho-grass. This species originates from New-Sealand. It builds big mounds with stiff leaves up to 1,2 m tall. The flower spikes reach up to 1,5 m. They stand rather erect. The flower panicles give a yellowish impression. Flowering time: July-August. Propagation by seed or division.

CHRYSANTHEMUM

Chrysanthemum uliginosum grows over 1.8 metres tall with white daisy-like flowers on top of narrow-leaved stems.

Chrysanthemum weyrichii is a small species, suited for the rock garden.

CHRYSANTHEMUM

This large and varied genus needs to be described in sections somewhat arbitrarily to avoid confusion. There is no practical reason, for example, to include the very distinctive *Pyrethrum* as *Chrysanthemum* coccineum.

What most people know as chrysanthemums are the single and double, small or large-flowered, which are to be seen in abundance in the latter part of the year as florists' flowers or pot plants. Over 1,000 varieties of these have been registered.

A few are quite hardy and perennial and provide a welcome display in Autumn. Some make a good spread of leafy bush formation, such as the button-flowered, rosy purple 'Anastasia', 80 cm. 'Bronze Elegance' is barely 60 cm, also button-flowered, along with 'Meikyo', deep pink, 'Mandarin', orange-yellow, 'Peterkin', orange bronze, whilst 'Sunbeam' is bright yellow and earlier to flower at 40 cm and 'Peter Sare' is a neat-growing, single pink.

These perennial types may be divided in Spring, but there are strains offered as seed which give a colourful mixture of mainly singles and which flower the first year if sown under glass in March. They are best treated as annuals but the so-called 'Koreans' are more perennial.

Those following are more identifiable as species.

Worthy species

C. *arcticum*, (syn. C. *yezoensis*) although not truly alpine, will make a late show, being only 25 cm tall. It has white, pink-tongued daisies from vigorous, matted roots in Autumn.

C. *corymbosum* is sometimes listed under 'Pyrethrum' and it has that kind of foliage, finely dissected but greyish. The white daisies on strong 120 cm stems are profuse, coming in early Summer and often again later if cut back. They do best in sun and good drainage but are easy and reliable from division.

C. *hosmariense*, given a warm sunny spot, will flower on and on. The white daisies, 15-20 cm, stand just above a mound of delicate filigree foliage of silvery hue all year round, but it pays to replant more deeply if after 2-3 years it is seen to need rejuvenating.

C. *leucanthemum* is the early-flowering dog daisy as distinct from the marguerite or shasta daisy. Scarcely any improved cultivars are now seen and I still regret having lost one 40 years ago named 'Rentpayer'. Two German varieties tried since have not proved reliably perennial.

C. *maximum* is the shasta daisy and so well-known as to need little description. Indeed 'Esther Read' has been so popular as a florist's flower that its generic name has dropped away. This is, of course, the best-known double, but others now exist. The next most popular is the taller (90 cm) 'Wirral

Supreme', but it is not fully double.

For the border, the single flowered are more effective. 'Elisabeth' and 'Thomas Killin' have prettily-fringed petals. These are 80-100 cm tall but the dazzling white single 'Snowcap' is only 40 cm.

The flowers hide the plant itself in high Summer. *C. nipponicum* is dwarf and not very different from *C. arcticum.* It has white flowers in Autumn, 20 cm.

C. parthenium is mentioned under *Pyrethrum.*

C. x rubellum is a race of obscure origin, of single-flowered cultivars in late Summer and Autumn from vigorous, hardy roots. 'Clara Curtis' is the oldest and still one of the best, single pink, 80 cm. 'Duchess of Edinburgh' is bronzy-crimson. 'Mary Stokes' is pale yellow, of similar height, but several other dwarfer ones exist.

C. uliginosum is the tallest of the white daisies and the last to flower. The narrow-leaved stems run up to 200 cm, brightening the late autumn scene. Roots are inclined to wander a little in good moist soil, but it is reliable and valuable in almost any sunny position.

Chrysanthemum

Although some species are annuals or shrubs, most chrysanthemums are perennials. In total some 200 kinds are known. Besides the well known perennials which are generally offered for the garden, there is also a group of plants for the keen gardener which are particularly suitable for rock gardens. They do need special attention however. Some of these kinds are:

C. *alpinum*, 15 cm, white
C. *argenteum*, 30 cm, white to pink
C. *atratum*, 30 cm, white
C. *cinerariifolium*, 40 cm, white
C. *densum*, 30 cm, yellow
C. *maresii*, 25 cm, white with yellow.

Above: *Chrysanthemum maximum* 'Wirral Supreme' is one of the best known shasta daisies.

Right: One of the large-flowered, double chrysanthemums, which come under *Chrysanthemum* indicum-hybrids.

Below: *Chrysanthemum leucanthemum*, the ox-eye daisy, is an early flowering species.

Below: *Chrysanthemum* x *rubellum* forms are hardy, vigorous and available in single-flowered cultivars at several heights.

CHRYSOGONUM

Chrysogonum virginianum is a small plant seldom found in garden centres, with a long flowering season beginning in May and lasting until October.

CHRYSOGONUM

Chrysogonum virginianum is a demure little plant which begins flowering in May, and, where happy, scarcely stops until October. To be happy, soil should be light, deep and not lacking in fertility, and with a low lime content.

The plant grows neatly with soft green leaves above which the 25 cm flower-sprays nestle, and apart from being fully hardy and long-lived, division of older plants is easy. It is by division every 3 years or so, plus some soil enrichment when replanting, that its longest flowering properties are encouraged. It is, however, a relatively rare plant and seldom offered.

CICHORIUM

Cichorium intybus is the blue-flowered 'chicory', a pretty culinary plant in its own right, but there is a seldom-seen pink form 'Roseum'. They grow from deep fleshy roots, and above the basal foliage come 100 cm stems carrying charming, fluffy, daisy flowers for many weeks, June-September. They need good drainage and sun, and like limy soil. Propagation is by spring division or root cuttings.

Cimicifuga racemosa is one of the tallest growing species of these outstanding garden plants suitable for moist soils.

Cimicifuga

There are about 10 species of this genus which all flower some time between July and October.

The late flowering kinds make a good combination with plants which already have their Autumn colours and evergreen plants, such as bamboos and evergreen *Rhododendron*. Also a combination with autumn-flowering anemones and ferns is very attractive.

The early flowering species give off an unpleasant smell. The plants often seed themselves.

CIMICIFUGA

These are outstanding and distinctive plants for good, deep soil which does not dry out. All have delicate, deeply-divided foliage which is fully complementary to the slender spikes. These branch gracefully to produce pokery tips of creamy or ivory-white flowers in later Summer and Autumn according to species, varying in height from 100 to 200 cm. None ever needs support and where happy the fibrous rooted clumps will become quite massive. Spring division of old plants requires the two-fork technique. They do well in part shade.

C. *cordifolia* has handsome dark foliage and creamy white flower-spikes branching erectly, 120 cm, August-September.
C. *dahurica* has fluffy pokers and a very graceful, overall appearance at 150 cm, a little later than C. *cordifolia*.
C. *racemosa* has imposing spikes 150 cm tall in July-August. The creamy-white pokers come above abundant foliage.
C. *ramosa*, though similar in habit to C. *racemosa*, has fuller spikes and grows strongly to 200 cm, with side spikes making a long season, August-

September. Two purplish-leaved forms are much
sought. One is 'Atropurpurea', but 'Brunette' is
even deeper-leaved, contrasting superbly with the
fluffy white 'bottle-brushes'.

C. *japonica* var. *acerina* (syn. C. *acerina*) is more
slender than others, with deeply divided foliage
and erect flower spikes to 120 cm in late Summer
and early Autumn. The cultivar 'Silverax' is a more
decided white.

C. *simplex* is the latest to flower and makes a fine
display of bold ivory-white 'bottle-brush' spikes,
with ample greenery. The clumpy plants become
large and very effective at 180 cm, especially if
next to a late-flowering blue *Aconitum*. The
cultivars 'White Pearl' and 'Elstead' are more
likely to be listed and they do not differ
appreciably.

CIRSIUM

The best known C. *rivulare* also has the name C*nicus
atropurpureus*. They stand for a handsome thistly
plant with jagged leaves and strong spikes to 120
cm carrying wine-red tufty flowers, June-August.
C. *japonicum* grows more stiffly to 100 cm and this
too has crimson flowers and dark, jagged leaves.

Cirsium rivulare resembles a
tall thistle, with warm-red
flowers during the Summer
months.

CLEMATIS

Clematis integrifolia. The cultivar 'Hendersonii' is
quite the best form of this unusual herbaceous, non-
climbing *Clematis*. Though stems are somewhat lax,
an established plant makes an attractive display
from June to August and can be safely left to itself
for many years. It is perfectly hardy and can be
divided, as can the more robust C. *heracleifolia*
types, of which C. 'Crepuscule' is a very good
variety. The sky-blue flowers on erect 1-1.2 m
bushes have curled-back petals, faintly perfumed,
and keep on for many weeks after mid-Summer.
These are two out of the ordinary subjects which
please their owners and intrigue visitors unfamiliar
with them.

The species C. *recta* does not live up to its name
and the 100-120 cm stems need supporting. The
flowers of creamy white come clustered atop the
stems and have a faint scent. The purplish leaved
'Purpurea' is best for foliage.

Clematis integrifolia
'Hendersonii' is herbaceous and
non-climbing, but once happily
established, makes a splendid
show during Summer.

Above: *Clintonia andrewsii* forms blue berries after pink flowers, which are shown in May-June.

CLINTONIA

This small genus of choice shade-loving plants is rarely seen. They need a humus-rich lime-free soil. C. *andrewsii* has oval base leaves and 50 cm clusters of small pink bell-shaped flowers, May-June, followed by deep blue berries. It is of slow growth, needing careful division.
C. *umbellulata* is more robust, but the clustered flowers are greenish-white and fragrant: not spectacular, but interesting.

CODONOPSIS

This, too, has bell-shaped flowers like some campanulas, but these are very distinctive in having exquisite markings inside the flowers which tend to droop from lax, tenuous stems.
They are unusually distinctive and are best planted where they can hang down a bank or over a rock or wall.
C. *clematidea* has light blue bells on 20-25 cm stems and C. *ovata* is somewhat similar at 15-20 cm, flowering June to August.
The fleshy roots do not respond to division, but plants may be raised from seed sown under glass.

Codonopsis ovata produces campanula-like flowers on 15 cm stems from June to August.

* COMMELINA

Commelina coelestis (syn. C. *tuberosa*) is just one of the about 150 species known, but the only one worth growing. It comes from Mexico. Up to 70 cm in height, it is an impressive plant with heavenly-blue flowers. It is not hardy, so you have to take the tuber out in Autumn and keep it cool during Winter. You can plant again in May. A close relative is *Tradescantia virginica*.
Commelina does very well together with *Montbretia* and *Hemerocallis*.

Codonopsis
Although mainly one species (C. *clematidea*) is offered, there are 30 kinds, which all flower between July and August. Do not put them close to other perennials, because *Codonopsis* is very rampant. They are climbers which, even if they hang over stones, often climb upwards again.
C. *convolvulacea*, up to 3 m high, violet-purple flowers in July; C. *rotundifolia*, with up to 1 m long stems, can flower as early as June with yellow flowers.

Commelina coelestis must be lifted in autumn to over-winter in a dry cool place, since it is not winterhardy.

CONVALLARIA

The lily-of-the-valley, *Convallaria majalis*, is a firm favourite but needs a place by itself. The horizontal roots and shoots run only 2-5 cm below ground and spread quickly where suited in shade or sun, but take a year or more to establish. It is unique for perfume. 'Fortin's Giant' is the finest.

COREOPSIS

The type most often seen is C. *grandiflora,* usually raised from seed, but though flowering is profuse, plants seldom recover from one season's exhaustive performance. Not so with other lesser known kinds.

C. *verticillata* makes ample growth below ground with which to carry on for years and the growth above ground is quite delightful. The neat, narrow-leaved bushes reach 45-60 cm and from June to August are covered with a long succession of bright yellow flowers. 'Moonbeam' has primrose-yellow flowers, whilst the golden flowers of 'Zagreb' come on bushlets only 25 cm tall.

The cultivar 'Grandiflora' is slightly larger and deeper coloured.

C. *auriculata* 'Superba' has a long season of golden flowers with a brown centre, and is reliably perennial.

C. *lanceolata* is extra good in the variety 'Golden Gain' but needs to be cut back before flowering ends to encourage new basal growth for survival. C. *l.* 'Goldfink' is a charming midget with quite large flowers only 15-20 cm above close-tufted plants. These have a small brownish centre-zone. Flowering is profuse from June to early September, but where any lack of basal growth is noticed by that time, a cut-back to ground level should encourage it to begin, and with this renewed basal growth, no winter loss should occur. Spring division of the above *Coreopsis* is advised.

CORONILLA

These belong to the vetch tribe and need sun as well as good drainage.

C. *montana* makes a shapely, twiggy mound 25 cm high, set with bright-yellow pea flowers, June-August.

C. *minima* may be a dwarf form. It is smaller in every way and stems are almost prostrate.

Both are deep-rooting, long-lived plants, for a sunny position.

Convallaria majalis, flowering together with violets, makes a pleasing combination.

Coronilla minima is not frost hardy, so it needs protection throughout Winter.

Coreopsis auriculata 'Superba' can reach 80 cm and will show its golden flowers from June to August.

CORTADERIA

Cortaderia
There are about 15 species which occur in South America and New Zealand of which *C. selloana* is the most widely available.
Rather newly cultivated is *C. dioica*, a low growing kind. *C. richardii* originates from New Zealand. The plant has up to 1 m long leaves and a yellowish white inflorescence, but is not completely hardy.
With all *Cortaderia*, mainly female plants are cultivated because their inflorescence is more attractive.

Left: *Cortaderia selloana* varieties are most effective as specimen plants. They need space and full sun to be happy.

CORTADERIA

This is the well-known pampas grass (*Cortaderia selloana*) of which several variations are now in commerce. These include some which vary only in height, others having variegated or golden leaves. Since all are most effective grown as specimen plants, they are best purchased as pot grown and a selection should be made on site.
Given a place in full sun, perhaps with an evergreen background, it is to be recommended.

CORTUSA

This is very close to *Primula* of the type with soft rounded foliage, for a shady but not boggy place. The best known is *C. matthioli* having purple-magenta flowers above pretty indented leaves in May-June. 15 cm.
The species *C. m. pekinensis* is somewhat similar but flowers are near to red.

CORYDALIS

This is a genus from which only a few make good garden plants because they are either short-lived or have thin tap-roots. This makes the production difficult for sale.

C. cashmeriana is in a class by itself. Though barely 10 cm high, it is fully perennial from tiny claw-like tubers. In Spring the glaucous ferny foliage is a prelude to little sprays of glistening ice-blue flowers in April-June. It is not easy to please but does best in gritty, humus soil in a cool position. It grows best in northern climes where humidity is high.

Below: *Cortusa matthioli* has warm purple-magenta flowers in May-June.

Corydalis
Practically all of the 200 or so species of this genus originate from the temperate zones of the northern hemisphere. Most are annuals. *Corydalis* has a special way of spreading seeds. The seeds have an extension which attracts ants, which then spread them.
Most kinds naturalize easily and often in places in which other plants have difficulties existing. Propagation from seed is simple. Only *C. cashmeriana* must be divided (immediately after flowering).

Corydalis solida makes a bold display in Spring of purple-rose flowers.

C. cheilanthifolia is a short-lived evergreen but seeds itself. Its tap roots produce abundant ferny foliage and the yellow flowers come on 30 cm sprays for many weeks, May-July.

C. ochroleuca is of somewhat similar habit with more glaucous, evergreen foliage, and the creamy-white flowers on 20 cm stems carry on for months.

C. solida makes a bold display in Spring of purple-rose flowers on 15 cm stems from bulbous, spreading roots. It dies back to dormancy soon after flowering.

COSMOS

Cosmos atrosanguineus (syn. *Bidens atrosanguinea*). This has a dahlia-like habit and a tuberous root which needs to be lifted and stored over Winter, or well protected if left outdoors to prevent frost penetration. It is worth the trouble, for on leafy, bushy growth come deepest-crimson single flowers of unusual charm for weeks, from June to October, and smelling of chocolate.

COTYLEDON – see CHIASTOPHYLLUM

CRAMBE

Crambe cordifolia, the seakale, species has clouds of small pure-white flowers on widely branching 100 cm stems in early Summer. It needs space, but leaves a gap with not much foliage for the rest of Summer. It is nevertheless a spectacular plant and long-lived, increased from root cuttings.

CREPIS

From amongst a welter of weedy species are two good garden plants.

The finest is *C. incana* which, with its fluffy pink flowers on 25 cm stems from June to September, is a first-class plant. It has fleshy roots which will produce root cuttings but has no outward spread from the clump of grey dandelion-like foliage.

C. aurea has upright greenery with sprays of very deep orange flowers at 20 cm from June to August. Plants divide readily in Spring.

The flowers of *Cosmos atrosanguineus* have a chocolate scent.

Crambe cordifolia blooms marvellously in early Summer, but leaves a bit of a gap in the border, once flowering is over.

CRINUM

CRINUM

These have large bulbs with good base foliage all Summer and are hardy in all but coldest districts. They can be left alone for years and still flower freely.
C. capense (syn. C. longifolia) has white trumpet flowers on 80-100 cm stems in Summer. Narrow leaves arch over and are pale green.
C. x powellii is a hybrid of real merit with rich green foliage and strong stems carrying large pink lily-like flowers to 100 cm in late Summer. The bulbs are large and produce offsets which expand into clumps if left alone. Both are for sun and well-drained soil. There is a beautiful rare white form 'alba'.

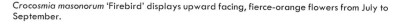

Crinum x powellii carries lily-like flowers on strong stems in late Summer.

Crocosmia masonorum 'Firebird' displays upward facing, fierce-orange flowers from July to September.

CROCOSMIA

For convenience and simplicity the closely allied Curtonus, Antholyza, Montbretia and Tritonia are included here under the one name. The latter two are generally less hardy, but hybrids between them and the first two have proved hardy and very popular.
C. masonorum has proved to be a first-rate plant in its own right, as well as being a fruitful parent. All of them grow from corms which need to be planted 7-10 cm deep and are adaptable to any soil, sun and good drainage. This applies to all crocosmias and all have a steady spread to make congested clumps in a few years.
C. masonorum has abundant rushy foliage and wiry sprays to 90 cm, July-September, carrying brilliant orange flowers. The variety 'Firebird' is even brighter, with larger flowers which face upwards effectively. A rare yellow form exists named 'Rowallane'. 'Lucifer' is quite outstanding, earlier and taller at 100 cm, with foliage not far short of this height. The flowers are intense, flame-red. 'Spitfire' is a little later and less tall at 75 cm, orange-flame. 'Bressingham Blaze' has a more decided orange shade, and 'Jenny Bloom' grows vigorously, with charming deep butter-yellow flowers at 90 cm. 'Bressingham Beacon' is more like a shorter 'Lucifer' at 80 cm. 'Emberglow' is only 60 cm tall, a glowing deep-reddish shade, and the fiery 'Vulcan' is of similar height, flowering August-September. Some of the older species and hybrids are worth growing. These are more often classed as Monbretia but two should be avoided except when their rapid spread does not matter. They are C. x crocosmiiflora and C. x pottsii, both deep orange at about 60 cm. It is better to grow others which, if somewhat tender, can be given winter protection.
'His Majesty' has large orange-red flowers, as does 'Emily Mackenzie' which is late-flowering. 'Jackanapes' is bi-coloured yellow and red.

'Solfatare' is apricot-yellow with bronzy leaves and is rather tender, and 'Star of the East' has extra large light-yellow flowers. Finally, the species C. *rosea* is distinct for being pink, but is somewhat spindly.

CRUCIANELLA – see PHUOPSIS

CYANANTHUS

For humus-rich gritty soil, these *Campanula* relatives have large blue flowers on more or less prostrate summer growth, from deep fleshy roots. They like sun but not dry conditions.
C. *lobatus* is most often offered, flowering terminally.
C. *integer* (syn. C. *microphyllus*) has small-leaved recumbent stems ending in purple flowers.

CYCLAMEN

A place may sometimes be found where some of the hardy cyclamen will flourish and add interest. All they need is some shade and good drainage. Most of them have flowers at only 5-10 cm high, and when in leaf these too are attractive. Corms should not be planted more than 2-3 cm deep and can be left as a permanent bed. They can only be increased by seed sown as soon as ripe.
C. *cilicium* is pink with marbled leaves.
C. *purpurascens* (syn. C. *europaeum*) has crimson, scented flowers and C. *hederifolium* (syn. C. *neapolitanum*) in both pink and white are all late Summer and Autumn flowering.
C. *orbiculatum* (syn. C. *coum*) has several variations for late Winter and Spring flowering, and the larger but less hardy C. *repandum* is bright crimson, also in Spring.
They look attractive when planted with or beneath such dwarf shrubs as daphne, rhododendrons, azaleas and shrubby potentillas.

CYMBALARIA

(syn. *Linaria*). Two species should be mentioned, if only as a warning, for they are fast spreaders below the surface. Both have quite pretty rounded leaves and tiny lilac or mauve flowers of virtually no height in Summer. They are C. *aequitriloba* and C. *hepaticifolia*.

The *Crocosmia* hybrid 'Emily McKenzie' is a late-flowering orange-red beauty.

Right: Hardy *Cyclamen* cannot stand wet positions, and prefer some shade.

Cymbalaria
Be careful with the species from this genus (especially in rock gardens), because they are very rampant and tend to crowd other plants. Some kinds may become weeds in spite of the fact that in severe Winters they may get frozen.
The least aggressive species is not mentioned on the opposite page, as it is not readily available, namely C. *hepaticifolia* with violet purple flowers from May till September.
Another species C. *muralis* is common in many parts of Europe. The plant has a peculiar habit: flowers, which at first were directed towards the sun, bend away from the light after pollination spreading their seeds over a big area.
There are some varieties: 'Alba' with white flowers (the species has violet-purple flowers) and 'Globosa' which for some time shows a somewhat global plant shape.

Below: *Cymbalaria* species look lovely, but spread quickly below the surface.

CYNARA

* CYNARA

This is the well-known Globe artichoke. The best species for the garden is C. *scolymus*. Growing up to 2 m high, they are very impressive plants, flowering August-October. In a solitary position, they are quite spectacular.

CYNOGLOSSUM

Cynoglossum grande would be a very good subject but for its rather floppy habit. It has fairly large leaves and 50 cm stems carrying lots of intense blue flowers June-July.
C. *nervosum* is less tall at 30 cm and has smaller flowers, but is fully garden-worthy and needs no supporting. Both are very easy to grow and divide for increase and are more reliable than the related *Anchusa*.

Cynara scolymus is the ideal globe artichoke for ornamental gardens. They are best displayed as specimen plants.

Below: *Cynoglossum nervosum* is very easy to grow and has pleasing, intense-blue flowers.

CYPRIPEDIUM

This is a section of the orchid family which always appeals, and of which 'Lady's Slipper' is the best known (C. *calceolus*). They are not easy to grow or raise from seed, and plants collected from the wild mostly die. Where suited, in cool peaty soil with some shade, distinctive pouched flowers, topped by four petals above, hold an unfailing appeal.
C. *calceolus*, already mentioned, is the most-often available, with brownish-yellow flowers. It likes a little lime or mortar rubble in with a light peaty mix, and firm planting in Autumn. 30 cm high, its flowering time is May-June.
C. *pubescens* has a light-yellow pouch with brownish petals, above the usual leaf-sheathed stem. It flowers May-June, 50-60 cm.
C. *reginae* is indeed the queen, highly prized and priced if it can be bought at all. The outer petals are white over a pink pouch. 30 cm high, it flowers May-June.

* CYRTOMIUM

This fern likes moist conditions and can stand some shadow. It does very well in rather acid soil, e.g. in combination with *Rhododendron* and other winter-green plants, which it needs for protection in Winter as well.
C. *fortunei* is the best known. It grows up to 60 cm. The species origin is Japan.
C. *macrophyllum* is 50 cm high, with a brighter foliage than C. *fortunei*, and more hardy.

Cypripedium calceolus, the well known 'Lady's Slipper', has brownish-yellow flowers and grows best in slightly limey, moist soil.

Below right: *Cystopteris bulbifera* is a dwarf form for shady sites. It spreads quite easily.

Below: *Cyrtomium fortunei* prefers acid soils and does not mind some shade.

CYSTOPTERIS

Cystopteris bulbifera also spreads, although not invasively, but it is a dwarf form at 25 cm producing little bulbs. It is easy to grow and quite decorative in a shady nook.

Cystopteris
This genus is represented practically everywhere in the world, although the number of kinds are limited to just 18.
Besides C. *bulbifera* you may find:

C. *dickieana* which likes shade. A small species with up to 10 cm long leaves. C. *fragilis* is quite rampant and is found all over the world. It is better to keep this kind away from the garden.

DEINANTHE

Succulent *Delosperma cooperi* displays warm red flowers with a white centre.

Deinanthe caerulea only thrives on well fertilised, light soils.

Delphiniums need a lot of care in order to produce their best.

DACTYLORHIZA – see ORCHIS

DEINANTHE

Deinanthe caerulea is a choice but not difficult plant for good soil, preferring some shade, but disliking lime and heavy soil. It forms a slowly expanding mat which is easily divided. The rounded crinkly leaves and 12 cm stems are tipped with waxy, deep-blue flowers in Summer.
D. bifida grows strongly to 60 cm in cool, rich soil. The leafy stems are topped by clusters of waxy, nodding, white flowers, June-August.

* DELOSPERMA

This succulent 'moon-flower', with three important species, flowers in June-August. They do very well in combination with plants like *Sedum*, *Sempervivum*, *Opuntia*, *Jovobarba* etc. They need sun and well-drained soil.
D. brunnthaleri flowers in bright shades of pink.
D. cooperi the best known and available has red flowers with a white centre.
D. sutherlandii flowers pink with a yellow heart. It is a plant for the specialist, because it needs careful (Winter) protection. Avoid wet conditions!

DELPHINIUM

Delphiniums do not come to perfection without effort. They need deep rich soil, are not immune to pests and diseases, and almost all need staking to avoid the havoc strong winds can cause.
Specialists think nothing of producing spikes up to seven feet tall, but more recently it has been realised that for ordinary and modern gardens, such heights are troublesome to cope with if not somewhat incongruous as well. This applies especially to named varieties which can only be propagated by division or basal cuttings. This makes them expensive to produce and to buy; and since there has always been a demand for the more cheaply produced seed raised plants, a good deal of progress has been made towards achieving reliability, as far as colours are concerned, from seed.
Some of these strains include the blood of shorter-lived types and what are still known as D. 'Pacific Hybrids' contain some very rich colours, including pinks and purples, as well as true blues. They can be sown under glass and by keeping them on the move, they will flower later in the same year, but are not likely to live more than two or three years, as a general rule.

The longer-lived mixtures or strains from seed will mostly survive for five years, and occasionally much longer; but for long life, the vegetatively produced varieties are supreme, provided the soil is well drained and plants are kept healthy and free from slug damage.

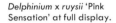

Planting is safest in Spring just as new growth begins; and when dividing old plants, healthy shoots with young fibrous roots should be selected, discarding any woody or damaged growth.
D. 'Lamartine' is one of the belladonna varieties. These have smaller flowers on more branching, slender spikes than the more ususal and mostly taller varieties. They too flower in June and July but need less space and are generally quite reliable and good for cutting. Apart from 'Lamartine', there is the sky-blue 'Blue Bees' and the deep violet-blue D. 'Wendy' and a clear mid-blue D. 'Peace'. D. 'Pink Sensation' could also be included here. It is a charming long-flowering plant but not very robust, growing only 75-90 cm high from a fairly small plant.
This, and the belladonna mentioned above, must be increased by division or basal cuttings in Spring.

Delphinium x ruysii 'Pink Sensation' at full display.

Mixed Delphinium hybrids showing a good range of colours.

Delphinium belladonna-hybrid 'Piccolo'.

The trustworthy Delphinium hybrid 'Blue Fountain' does not need much space.

Delphinium

Most of the almost 400 species of Delphinium are annuals. The dominant flower colour, as with Campanula, is blue.
Besides the garden varieties mentioned and the small D. nudicaule for enthusiasts the following kinds are of interest, and are suitable in a natural garden or for the rockery):
D. brunonianum, up to 40 cm, light blue, July-September; the plant has a special scent.
D. cashmerianum, up to 40 cm, deep violet, June-July, becomes rather broad.
D. grandiflorum, up to 50 cm, bright blue, June-July. A dwarf variety 'Blauer Zwerg' also exists, only 20 cm high.
D. semibarbatum, more than 1.5 m tall, June-July. Very attractive, but rather difficult species, because it does not like wet conditions.

DELPHINIUM

'Galahad' is one of the well known Pacific Giant hybrids that have strong colours. They are rather short-lived.

No list of varieties among the taller delphiniums need be made. They can only be obtained from specialists whose catalogues will give full descriptions for each, but full account should be taken of height. It is too late, often enough, to stake delphiniums when flower buds are showing because they are then already weakened by wind or by their weight. Nowadays there are named varieties that do not attain more than a modest 120 cms or so, and these are easier to cope with. The somewhat short-lived Pacific varieties come fairly true to colour in named varieties as well as a mixture. There is also 'Blue Fountain' coming fairly true, and this is both of modest height, 100-120 cm, and reasonably long-lived.
D. chinense is dwarf and short-lived, but very showy with lots of bright blue flowers on bushy 30 cm growth and easy from seed. *D. formosum* is very pretty with stumpy 30 cm spikes of deep blue and fully perennial.
D. nudicaule is short-lived, small rooted, with slender stems, to 30 cm the main attraction being its colour — a deep orange red. *D.* 'Zalil' is also unique for colour, a pale yellow, dangling from strong 80 cm spikes, not spectacular, but a good garden plant in light soil and a warm position.

Below: *Deschampsia cespitosa* is an easy to grow grass with elegantly bending leaves.

Dentaria digitata is easy to grow and has white flowers April-May.

DENTARIA

These make a cheerful if rather brief display in early Spring. Easy to grow and adaptable to shade and dry soil, they can be used between shrubs. Division is in Autumn.
D. digitata has masses of lilac flowers on 30 cm stems rising from congested fleshy roots.
D. pentaphyllos flowers in April-May, but is white in panicles on 50 cm leafy stems.

DESCHAMPSIA

Deschampsia cespitosa is a very pretty grass 80 cm high which is easy to grow in any but dry soil. It makes compact, hefty clumps of narrow blades arching over, and airy sprays of tiny greenish flowers. The variety 'Bronze Lace' is most attractive in June-August.

DIANTHUS

A large number of the many cultivars are adaptable either as alpines or in frontal groups of taller perennials. A few are tiny, slow growing and choice enough to grow in an alpine house, though hardiness is a strong feature for the majority. Having merited the attention of breeders for over 200 years, there are hundreds still in existence including what are known as 'border pinks' and 'carnations'. Not many of the latter however make good garden plants. As old-fashioned scented and colourful flowers, interest in 'pinks' has revived and some specialists offer a wide range.

Although *Dianthus* of the taller range, i.e., pinks or border carnations, are by nature quite long-lived, some tend to become ragged with age, flowering less freely. They all like sun and good drainage and prefer limy soil. A cut-back and mulch may improve vigour, but cuttings pulled off with a heel are not difficult to root in a sandy mixture after flowering.

Above: *Dianthus deltoides* flowers abundantly from May to well into August. They are easy to grow and require very little care.

Right: Left undisturbed, this *Dianthus deltoides* 'Splendens Alba' will gradually cover quite an area. All varieties are great carpeters.

DIANTHUS

Above: *Dianthus alpinus* blooms on stems of about 6 cm tall with rather large flowers.

Above left: *Dianthus plumarius* is another fine border species, producing flowers in abundance.

Left: *Dianthus* 'Doris' is a nicely scented, pink-flowered, border carnation.

Below: *Dianthus gratianopolitanus* is the new name for the well-known 'cheddar pink'.

Dianthus

The genus *Dianthus* with about 250 species, originates mainly from the eastern Mediterranean, although some kinds have been found elsewhere (in Japan, and North America). Most species like chalky soil. In nature almost without exception they grow in dry, sunny places. Therefore, they are extremely suitable for well drained boxes and troughs.

It is rather simple to propagate *Dianthus* from seed, but because many kinds can easily be hybridized, one can never be sure that seeds will produce the true species.

Dwarf or Alpine Dianthus.

These consist of many species as well as hybrids which for convenience are less than 15 cm high. Some are silvery-leaved, others are green or in-between. Some trail whilst others make mounds, tufts or cushion-like growth. Sun and good drainage is even more essential for all these. The list below gives examples only, since so many exist.

D. alpinus is green leaved, slowly mat forming, with large flowers of rosy red on 6 cm stems in early Summer.

D. x arvernensis forms vigorous silvery mats set with a wealth of smallish pink flowers on 8 cm stems, June-August. There are at least three slight variations on this theme, 'Garland', *D. x lemsii* and 'La Bourbille'.

D. barbatus includes the sweet william, but dwarfer and somewhat rare forms, all green-leaved, exist. They include 'Cassers Pink', 15 cm, 'Spark', 8-10 cm, and the old 'Napoleon III', 20 cm.

D. deltoides is popular and easy from seed, trailing as a green carpet set with small but very bright flowers, May-August. Some have dark-purplish foliage.

D. caesius is the cheddar pink and now renamed, sadly, *D. gratianopolitanus*. It is the parent of many good hybrids including doubles. All make neat, silvery hummocks. Most are pink, but white and near-red are available, all 8-12 cm, in early to mid-Summer.

D. freynii and such as *D. microlepis* var. *musalae*, *D. simulans*, are of the close tufty type, slow growing and needing gritty soil. Flowers are pink, often stemless, and all in the choice bracket. *D. noeanus* (syn. *D. petraeus*) is rare but not difficult. Narrow, congested foliage, grey-green, forms a delicate mound on which white flowers up to 15 cm appear for many weeks.

D. neglectus is now named *D. pavonius* and dislikes lime. It forms low pads and has very large flowers in shades of pink, 15 cm. A few hybrids have come from this which are more reliable. One of the best of all dwarf dianthus is 'Ischriach Dazzler'.

D. squarrosus is easy to grow, with deep-green foliage and much-fringed white flowers, highly fragrant on 20 cm stems.

DICENTRA

DIASCIA

But for their lack of complete hardiness, these would be first-class perennials. They are still worthwhile, however, and cuttings which can be kept safe over Winter are not difficult to root. In good well-drained soil and sun, they will flower for most of the Summer and Autumn.

D. cordata is dwarf and loosely mounded. Above the small deep green leaves come 15 cm sprays of pink flowers, best in the form 'Ruby Field'.

D. elegans is mat forming with sprays of pink flowers.

D. rigescens has strong spikes up to 50 cm, crowded with rich pink flowers making a spectacular display.

D. vigilis grows vigorously during Summer and has rather arching sprays of light pink flowers at 50 cm.

Diascia cordata is not completely hardy, but a nice pink-flowering dwarf.

Dicentra spectabilis is one of the loveliest of all plants for late Spring and early Summer.

DICENTRA

'Bleeding heart', 'Dutchman's breeches' and 'Lady in the bath', are names for D. spectabilis which is one of the loveliest of all plants for late Spring and early Summer. The root is ugly with its fleshy fangs, but the shoots emerging from it enhance their early promise as they unfurl with fresh-looking deeply-incised leaves. Through these arch out branching stems to 60 cm or more, from which dangle the locket-like flowers to which such folksy names have been given, though to see how the last mentioned of these applies, the flower has to be held upside down.

Flowering lasts for several weeks from May onwards and for all its fragile appearance, the plant itself is fully hardy.

Its only needs are for reasonably good well-drained soil, and to be sited where the strongest winds do not harry it. Old plants can be increased by very careful division, for both roots and shoots are brittle.

D. eximia and its varieties make some spread, with less fangy roots, and make a mound of pretty glaucous foliage. The type is a rather dull rose-pink, but in the variety D. formosa 'Adrian Bloom', the individual flowers are much larger and of a ruby-red shade on sprays 40 cm high, from May to July and often longer.

85

DICENTRA

Dicentra

A small genus belonging to the *Papaveraceae*. In total there are some 15 species. Only a few species are cultivated.

The name 'Dutchman's breeches' only refers to the species *D. cucullaria*. This is a native of the U.S.A. and flowers from April till May. The flowers have the well known, tear-like shape and are white with a yellow tip. The plant is about 20 cm high and starts its rest period very soon after flowering.

Top left: *Dicentra eximia* varieties spread modestly. Flower colours are mostly in soft pink tints.

Left: *Dictamnus albus* 'Purpureus' is a red-flowering form of this deep rooting species.

Right: *Dierama pulcherrimum* produces elegant bell-shaped pink flowers from July-August.

Dictamnus albus 'Albiflorus' makes a great show for several weeks in May-June.

D. 'Bountiful' is also large-flowered, but less richly coloured. 'Luxuriant' is very similar to 'Adrian Bloom' but 'Bacchanale' is a deep wine-red and dwarfer than the rest.

D. *eximia* 'Alba' lacks vigour as a white, and 'Pearl Drops' is the one much to be preferred. It has abundant glaucous foliage as a base to the white flowers on 30 cm sprays. These dwarfer dicentras appreciate good light soil and are easy to divide, though roots are fleshy and brittle.

Replanting may be necessary after 2-3 years.

DICTAMNUS

Dictamnus fraxinellae has been changed in name to *D. albus* to make for confusion, and the former *D. fraxinella*, of which a white form exists, is simpler. Deep-rooting plants send up strong spikes of lilac flowers up to 100 cm. In light soil and full sun they make a splendid show for some weeks. The white is uncommon but quite attractive.

All dislike disturbance and division is not recommended. Seedlings take up to 3 years to flower.

DIERAMA

D. *pulcherrimum* is also known as 'fairies wand'. The 130 cm arching sprays dangle pink bell-shaped flowers charmingly above long grassy evergreen leaves in July-August: not a plant for coldest climes.

D. *pumilum* is only half the height, but the congested corms forming the rootstock of dieramas have more vigour. This is easier to place being less tall. The variety 'Hermia' has virtually the same satiny pink flowers.

All like a fairly moist soil and sun, but not boggy clay or chalky marl. Spring division is simple but plants can be left alone for years.

DIGITALIS

None of the foxgloves are long lived perennials but all are freely raised from seed. They are easy to grow in well-drained soil and are not averse to some shade.

D. ferrugiena is unusual for its small rust-coloured flowers along the strong 100 cm stems.

D. grandiflora (syn. D. ambigua) forms a neat leafy clump and has spikes to 60 cm of soft creamy-yellow flowers, June-August.

D. x mertonensis is by far the most showy. It has good base foliage and strong spikes of quite large 'foxgloves' of bright-pink, suffused-orange flowers, June-August up to 100 cm. It seldom survives more than 2 years, and though division is possible, it comes true from seed.

* DIONYSIA

The 40 known species of this genus (which can be thought of as something between *Primula* and *Androsace*) all come from West or Central Asia. The flowers appear from the beginning of March until the end of May on very short stems in yellow, pink or violet colours.

Most species are suitable only for the alpine house, but two of them do very well in the garden, though they need some winter protection.

D. aretioides is rather easy to grow. It stands some shade and wet conditions. The single yellow flower measures about 1.5 cm. 'Gravetye' and 'Paul Furse' are very rich flowering.

D. tapetodes, again with yellow flowers and greyish-green leaves, is available in several types. The ones with grey leaves are the most hardy. Both species are typical alpine plants.

DIPHYLLEIA

Diphylleia cymosa is a rarely-seen plant of considerable merit for fairly moist rich soil and some shade. From clumpy roots emerge large umbrella-type leaves. Above them, up to 80 cm, come stems carrying a head of small white flowers, which are followed by violet berries in Autumn to go with tinted foliage.

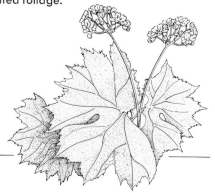

Above: *Digitalis ferrugiena* forms unusual, rust-coloured flowers, during July and August. The plants can be grown in any good soil and will adapt to some shade.

Right: *Dionysia* species for the garden all show yellow flowers. These are typical collector's items for the alpine garden.

DIPLARRHENA

Above: *Disporum* is related to Solomon's seal (*Polygonatum* species), taking a similar form and producing dangling bell-flowers.

Left: *Diplarrhena moraea* is a rather tender, evergreen plant with white flowers showing some touches of purple and yellow.

Below left: *Dodecatheon media*, one of the 'shooting stars' with leathery leaves and hanging flowers.

Diplarrhena

This is a genus related to *Iris* with 3 species, originating from Australia. Besides *D. moraea* which agrees best with our climate, sometimes *D. latifolia* is also available. The latter is taller (more than 50 cm) and has blue-with-yellow flowers. However, it is less hardy and is more suitable for the alpine house.

DIPLARRHENA

Diplarrhena moraea is a choice but tender plant with 15 cm bladed evergreen leaves. Wiry stems carry very pretty white 30 cm three-petalled flowers having a touch of purple and yellow at the centre. It will survive over Winter in most districts but litter cover round the plants is a wise precaution.

DISPORUM

This is a small genus related to Solomon's seal and best grown in some shade on light soil, not bone dry.

D. oreganum is a disputed name and stands for a leafy but not evergreen plant, mounded in form. The ivory-white bells on 30 cm stems develop into orange berries. Roots divide readily in Spring.

D. sessile is also known as 'Oakesiella', but only a variegated form is worthy. Even so, it runs underground to emerge with short, pointed, colourful leaves and 10 cm stems of tiny white flowers. This too is for shade.

DODECATHEON

These aptly named 'shooting stars' have deeply-reflexed petals with prominent yellow centres. There are several species which do not vary greatly, all having long leathery leaves and flowers hanging loosely in a clustered head 20-25 cm high in Spring. They need no special soil, but resent very dry shade. All die back to dormancy from August to March and can be increased both from seed and by division.

Colours vary a little from pink to magenta crimson. The species *D. media* and *D. pulchellum* (syn. *D. pauciflorum*) are most often offered. The 30 cm 'Red Wings' is the brightest.

They are effective amongst ferns, *Anemone nemorosa* and *A. ranunculoides*.

DORONICUM

These undemanding plants make a brave show in Spring. All are yellow, ray-petalled, daisy-type flowers, easy to grow, and divide in Autumn, thriving in sun or part shade.

D. austriacum is rather obscure and apt to be confused with D. caucasicum (syn. D. orientale) which is quite dwarf and flowers in April-May at 15 cm. Flowers are 6 cm across.

D. cordatum (syn. D. columnae) is also dwarf at 20 cm and does well in moist soil. It has good, light-green, bare foliage and erectly-held yellow flowers.

D. 'Miss Mason' is intermediate for height at 45 cm and flowering time and is a first-rate plant with ample foliage and vigour.

D. plantagineum is now seen only in the form 'Excelsum'. More often named 'Harpur Crewe', it is the latest and tallest at about 80 cm with fine yellow flowers, good for cutting.

D. 'Spring Beauty' is, to date, the only double-flowered and is deservedly popular. Flowers come on 40 cm stems and are 6-7 cm across, making a bright display in April-May.

Above: *Doronicum* 'Spring Beauty' is the only double-flowered *Doronicum* available.

Right: *Doronicum caucasicum* is a rather small species that flowers April-May.

Below: *Douglasia laevigata* is a collector's item for alpine lovers. It displays deep-pink flowers in June.

DOUGLASIA

Truly alpine in character, these form tight, grey-green pads or cushions of slow but steady spread, studded with almost stemless flowers. They are worth ensuring a good gritty soil in sun.

D. laevigata is a rarity with deep-pink flowers in early Summer.

D. vitaliana is the best known, with grey-green pads and yellow flowers. Its form *praetutiana* (sometimes listed as a separate species) is tighter growing, with more silvery foliage and freer to flower. Division is after flowering.

DRABA

Above: *Draba imbricata* looks very much like *D. rigida* var. *bryoides* with yellow flowers on neat hummocks.

Dracocephalum species generally produce flowers in shades of blue.

Dryas octopetala is a mat-forming European alpine which produces nice seed-heads after flowering.

DRABA

These are all spring-flowering plants, most of them cushion-forming in small green rosettes. All need sun and good drainage.

D. aizoides has deep-green rosettes and makes a bright show of 8 cm high yellow flowers Of similar habit, *D. dedeana* and *D. x salomonii* have white flowers.

D. bruniifolia and *D. repens* are the easiest to grow, the latter spreading quite quickly, rooting down with short runners. Both are yellow, 5 cm tall. These are all increased by division or seed, suitable for scree or an alpine house.

D. rigida, *D. imbricata* and *D. mollissima* form very neat hummocks of slow growth, set with yellow flowers only 3-4 cm. All flower March to May.

DRACOCEPHALUM

The name means 'dragon head', and the flowers are lipped but not exciting. The most vigorous is *D. sibiricum*, but this plant is now assigned to the genus *Nepeta*. It has violet-blue flowers, on 90 cm stems, above a spreading root system. *D. ruyschianum* is more demure and needs a warm place. The flower spikes are above low greenery, violet blue, and 40 cm in Summer.

D. grandiflorum is more showy, with spode-blue flowers in heads at 30 cm.

DRYAS

These mat-forming plants with leaves deep-green above and silvery beneath, produce quite large flowers of 'strawberry' formation, followed by fluffy seed-heads.

The best-known — common in the European Alps — is *D. octopetala*, but this does not flower so freely as *D. x suendermanii* and *D. vestita*. None has flowers more than 12 cm high. Cuttings are taken in early Autumn or new plants can be grown from seed. Full sun and well-drained, gritty soil is required.

DRYOPTERIS

Dryopteris filix-mas indicates the well known 'male fern'. It is one of the most adaptable and widely grown, with fronds up to 80 cm long where moist, and is more or less evergreen.

D. erythrosora requires some shade and humus-rich soil to give of its best. The young fronds are glossy green, maturing lighter to give charming overall greenery, 50 cm.

D. borreri (syn. *D. affinis*) is one of the best evergreen ferns with 80 cm fronds.

D. pseudo-mas 'Crispa' as crinkly tips, 40 cm.

D. pseudo-mas 'Cristata The King', is very imposing with fronds up to 90 cm: a splendid specimen from a stalwart base.

D. pseudo-mas is also known as *D. affinis*.

Above: *Dryopteris filix-mas*, the 'male fern', thrives wherever the soil is moist.

Dryopteris

Like other succesful ferns, *Dryopteris* occurs all over the world. There are about 150 species. Most of them are not of much interest for our gardens, but the kinds which are cultivated have played an important part in good garden design throughout the centuries. Many perennials with a pastel coloured inflorescence stand out better against a background or carpet of green *Dryopteris*. *Dryopteris* can also give shelter to early flowering bulbs, or form an element of liaison between different groups of plants.

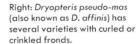

Right: *Dryopteris pseudo-mas* (also known as *D. affinis*) has several varieties with curled or crinkled fronds.

Below: *Echinacea purpurea* 'Robert Bloom' is a strong stemmed variety with rosy flowers.

ECHINACEA

The 'purple cone flower' is quite outstanding for late summer display and easy to grow in any good well-drained soil and sun. Clump-forming plants grow compactly to produce stiff, leafy stems topped with large rayed flowers having a central cone. Only the species *E. purpurea* is seen, the yellow cone flowers being rudbeckias. Improvements have been made, but the once popular 'The King' has given way to the variety 'Robert Bloom' and the slightly variable 'Bressingham Hybrids'. These are strong-stemmed at 100 cm and are not faulted by having low, drooping petals as has 'The King'. The latter has large purplish-pink flowers and a less erect habit at 120 cm, but 'Robert Bloom' is a warmer rosy shade. A white variation exists but is not exciting. Old plants divide readily in Spring and seedlings take two years to flower.

ECHINOPS

Echinops ritro, the 'globe thistle', does not grow much over 100 cm and may be left undisturbed for years. The blue flower heads' over the jagged, bluish-grey leaves, adds a special touch to any garden.

ECHINOPS

The 'globe thistle' is an attractive plant with its grey and jagged foliage, and stems carrying rounded blue flower heads from mid-Summer onwards. Some kinds are rather too coarse-growing for small gardens, but the more compact are not only effective, but can be left alone for years with no attention beyond cutting back one season's growth when faded in readiness for the next to come. Any but damp soil will suffice and they are drought resistant, whilst flowers are of value for cutting.

The best known is *E. ritro,* and at 90-100 cm is imposingly erect, without being too tall, as is inaptly named *E. humilis.* 'Taplow Blue' is a variety with paler blue flowers than *E. ritro.*

E. 'Blue Cloud' is large-flowered, 120-150 cm, and *E.* 'Veitch's Blue' of good colour at a similar height.

The little-known *E. gmelinii* is 75 cm, free flowering and neat growing, the colour being slightly lighter than *E. ritro.*

The larger *Echinops* make massive plants and need ample space, but all will divide with a spade or knife and will come from root cuttings as well as from pieces of root accidentally left in the ground.

Echinops
In nature these thistles grow in sunny, mostly steppe-like regions of eastern Europe, Asia and the eastern Mediterranean.
Only a few species are worth cultivating. Those that are cultivated make a beautiful combination with other sun-loving perennials, such as *Achillea, Inula, Gypsophila,* various grasses and *Allium* species.
If you wish to use *Echinops* for dried flowers, you have to cut them early, preferably before the first flowers open.

EDRAIANTHUS

The species *E. pumilio* forms tight silvery cushions set with violet-blue 5 cm flowers in Spring and is best in scree soil. This is the species most often offered, but there are others a little taller and less attractive with deep green, narrow leaves.
E. caudatus (syn. *E. dalmaticus*) is about the best, 15 cm. All species are best increased by seed.

The silvery-leaved cushions of *Edraianthus pumilio* bear bright violet-blue flowers in June-July.

* ELYMUS

This grass is available in 3 species. *E. arenarius,* strong spreading, is blue-green all over. The leaves roll in when dry. It is very decorative. *E. glaucus* is the most blue tinted species, very good in small gardens, but hardly available.
E. racemosus has green leaves. They are easy to grow and inclined to be invasive.

Elymus arenarius is a fast spreading, blue-green, very decorative, grass.

EOMECON

E. chionantha is a pretty, spring-flowering member of the poppy family and best grown amongst shrubs. It spreads quickly below ground to become a nuisance with other perennials. The nodding, white flowers come above attractive, glaucous, grey leaves, of rounded shape, and the roots are fleshy with orange sap. It is not for sunny, dry situations.

EPILOBIUM

One or two dwarf kinds of willow herb are worth growing where not too dry.
E. glabellum makes a loose mound of greenery, 20 cm high, and has a profusion of ivory-white flowers for much of the Summer.
E. 'Broadwell Hybrid' comes from a cross between this and the short-lived pink species *kai-koense*. It has purplish-bronze foliage and creamy-white flowers at 15 cm for many weeks. These may be increased by seed, cuttings in early Autumn or division in Spring. They look attractive with campanulas and summer-flowering Gentians.
The species *E. macropus* should be avoided for its invasiveness.
Two taller species, though seldom offered, are worth growing.
E. fleischeri has greyish, narrow leaves and upright 30 cm leafy stems carrying small rose-pink flowers, June-August.
E. rosmarinifolium (syn. *dodonaei*) is a rare but charming subject. Willowy stems rise to 100 cm, grey leaved and with a long display of pink flowers.

EPIMEDIUM

The dwarfest of these are of real value in a cool position. They have very pretty foliage, forming a dome over their slowly expanding roots. Leaves are fresh until Winter frost, and in Spring comes the display of starry flowers followed at once by new foliage. None is fussy as to soil, though best where not dry.

E. alpinum makes rosy-purple flowers on wiry 20 cm stems, whilst 'Rubrum' is reddish pink.
E. grandiflorum 'Rose Queen' grows compactly with a profusion of pink flowers only 15 cm tall.
The best white is *E. x youngianum* 'Niveum', with a neat habit and specially good foliage. Division in Autumn is best, the roots being quite congested and tough.
Epimediums have value as edging plants to a path where shady, and associate effectively with any blues such as *Omphalodes* and *Mertensia*.

Epilobium glabellum displays creamy-white flowers during summer.

Epimedium alpinum 'Rubrum' (newly listed as *E. x rubrum*) prefers a rather cool position to show its reddish pink flowers at their best.

EPIMEDIUM

Right: *Epimedium* x *versicolor* is another nice, small species, of which several varieties exist with interesting leaf-colours.

Left: *Epimedium* x *youngianum* 'Niveum' is a very good dwarf for a cool position.

Bottom: *Eremurus stenophyllus* thrives best in a warm position and shows spectacular flowering during Summer.

The hybrid 'Frohnleiten' has deep yellow flowers above 30 cm foliage. This and the *E. perralderianum* type are evergreen. The smaller *E. macranthum* (listed under *E. grandiflorum* now) and *E. youngianum* are not, but they are dwarf enough to contrast with alpines given a cool position. One of the brightest is the deep orange flowered *E. Warleyense*, semi-evergreen.

Eremurus
Besides the tall 'Ruiter hybrids' and the somewhat lower *E.* x *isabellinus* hybrids there are different species, often with varieties, which are readily obtainable.
E. elwesii flowers lilac pink, 'Albus' white.
E. robustus has pink flowerbuds, but flowers white, more than 2.5 m high.

E. stenophyllus, dark yellow, 1 m high, but rare.
E. himalaicus, yellow, 1.2 m high.
Eremurus makes attractive groups with, for instance, *Asphodelus*, *Kniphofia* and *Papaver orientale*.

EREMURUS

These stately plants are somewhat troublesome to grow, but do best in warm climes and need good drainage. The fleshy brittle roots radiate laterally from a central nub and care to plant them flat and shallow with added sand is needed. They also need sun and annual mulching. Staking is often necessary and leaves fade quickly after flowering. That said, the choice is open between such species as the hybrid strains of modest height – 100-150 cm with richly-varying coloured spikes – or the massive 200-300 cm in pink, white and yellow. They are all spectacular in the June-July period.

ERIGERON

These are valuable members of the daisy family which always flower freely during the June-August period. Good drainage is their main requirement and a preference for being planted – or divided when necessary – is early Spring rather than Autumn.

'Foerster's Liebling' (Darling) is a reliable pink with almost double flowers on 50 cm stems.
E. 'Rosa Triumph', a little lighter in colour, is another of 'Foerster's darlings', and though E. 'Prosperity' was one of my raising, it has exactly the same habit of a sturdy, clumpy plant, the 45 cm flower stems carrying semi-double mauve-blue flowers in June and July.
Other good erigerons exist in the upstanding 60 cm E. 'Amity' with lilac-rose single flowers, and the single pink E. 'Charity'.
E. 'Adria' is a fine, near-double mauve-blue at 75 cm, and the old pink 'Quakeress' is still worth growing.
E. 'Schwarzes Meer' grows erectly to 60 cm with deep violet-blue semi-double flowers but
E. 'Dignity' is a dwarfer, single deep blue.
E. 'Gaiety' is single, deep-pink and E. 'Sincerity' a single lavender-blue.
The dwarfest of modern hybrids is E. 'Dimity', which with others ending with 'ity' were names I chose. This has soft foliage and stems radiate to make a low mound only 10 in high, carrying firstly orange-shaded buds which turn to pink as they open. This variety needs to be cut back immediately flowering is over and better just before, in order to promote the renewed basal growth it needs for over-wintering.
E. simplex is a now-rare white species, May-June, 25 cm. Of similar height and flowering time comes E. howellii, very pale lilac, 20 cm. E. salsuginoides is somewhat similar but freer to flower. E. philadelphicus is pink at 60 cm but is apt to be short lived or to wander. The unique deep-orange of E. aurantiacus, 25 cm, is alas short-lived. All these species flower in early Summer, but E. mucronatus (syn. E. karrinskianus) flowers all Summer with masses of small pale-pink daisies on 25 cm mounds, sometimes seeding itself.
The dwarf E. leiomerus has lavender blue flowers on 12 cm stems. This section comprises types which are two-way subjects, but there are several true alpine species in existence, if not often listed in catalogues.

Above: Erigeron 'Darkest of All' is a good model for a wide range of hybrids, that come in a variety of colours.

'Schwarzes Meer' is an Erigeron hybrid with violet-blue, semi-double flowers.

ERINUS

Erinus alpinus 'Dr. Hähnle' is a good plant for poor soil with rosy-pink flowers.

ERINUS

The one species available is *E. alpinus* which varies in colour but not in habit. They grow in a compact, non-spreading, tufted formation; and if not very long lived, they are easily reproduced from seed. The type has lilac-mauve flowers on 5-7 cm spikes and *E. alpinus* 'Albus' is its albino. The most popular are the pink 'Mrs. Boyle' and the deeper rosy-pink 'Dr. Hahnle'.

They are best in poor soil and will grow happily in crevices and chinks.

Eriogonum umbellatum needs a sunny position in well-drained soil.

Below: *Eriophyllum lanatum* is best grown over a bank or wall.

ERIOGONUM

Eriogonum umbellatum makes a mat of leathery leaves from which rise 15 cm stems of creamy-yellow flower heads, June — August.

Several more species exist, some choice, and all for sun and well-drained soil, not too limy.

ERIOPHYLLUM

Eriophyllum lanatum is good where it can hang over a retaining wall or on a bank. It has silvery, indented leaves, and above comes a long succession of yellow daisies. It has a rapid but not dangerous spread and is easily curbed with shears, keeping it as a dense mound, if required, at about 25 cm: not choice, but useful.

ERODIUM

These also much prefer stony soil and full sun, and in these conditions are long-lived. All have open, saucer-shaped flowers and more-or-less evergreen foliage.

E. chamaedryoides (syn. *E. reichardii*) makes glossy green tufts, studded with white, pink-veined flowers for most of the Summer, as does the pink-flowered *E. chamaedryoides* 'Roseum'. Both are only 4-5 cm high.

E. corsicum is a little larger with greyish leaves and deeper pink-to-red flowers, but is best in an alpine house.

E. guttatum, E. macradenum (syn. *E. petraeum*) and *E.supracanum* (syn. *E. rupestre*) are much alike, all about 12 cm, with ferny-grey foliage, light pink flowers, prettily veined purple. Growth is a little woody but not so much as in the beautiful *E. chrysanthum*, which will mound up to 20 cm to carry lemon-yellow flowers.

All these are very long-flowering and deep-rooting plants which can be divided with care.

E. manescavii and *E. carvifolium* are much alike and larger than the rest at 30 cm. They form a clumpy mound of finely-cut foliage set with rosy-pink flowers for many weeks.

ERYNGIUM

The name 'sea holly' applies only to *E. maritimum*, and though pretty, it is a plant that does not take to inland gardens. Other species will grow strongly from fangy roots in well-drained soils to give a charming display of bluish flower bracts, often with stems blue as well.

E. alpinum has green, rounded leaves, and flowers of rich blue, larger and deeper than any, on 70 cm stems, July-September.

E. bourgatii is one of the prettiest and has silvery, deeply-cut and somewhat prickly foliage. It has erect shortly branched stems to about 60 cm carrying quite large silvery-blue flowers above a spiky base.

E. amethystinum is green-leaved, but the flowers are deep-blue, whilst *E. x tripartitum* carries a sheaf of smaller blue flowers on 90 cm stems.

E. planum is strong growing but less blue, but *E. variifolium* has very pretty marbled foliage, close to the ground, and erect branching stems to 75 cm of blue flowers.

E. giganteum is silvery all over, and though very effective, it dies after flowering; and seedlings for replacement must be a matter of forethought. There are a few entirely green species, with fearsome looking evergreen foliage in large rosettes.

E. bromelliifolium, E. serra and *E. proteiflorum* are three of them which may appeal to some, and, like most species, are not difficult and are long-lived.

Erodium manescavii is one of the tallest species at 30 cm. The rosy-pink flowers are shown between June and September.

Eryngium alpinum flowers in a warm-blue shade from July to September.

ERYTHRONIUM

EUPATORIUM

These are good for rear positions but do not like to be starved or bone dry. Otherwise they are easy to grow but need adequate space. All are herbaceous.

E. ageratoides (syn. *E. rugosum*) makes a massive leafy bush up to 120 cm, tipped with abundant heads of fluffy white flowers, July-September.

E. purpureum is a good garden plant for all its 250 cm height. Stems are strong and leafy and the large heads of rosy-purple are effective for several weeks of later Summer.

E. p. 'Atropurpureum' has purplish foliage and deeper coloured flower heads, but the white 'album' is less distinguished. Old clumps need two forks as levers for division best done in Spring.

Eupatorium purpureum 'Atropurpureum' has purplish foliage and strongly coloured, impressive flower heads.

ERYSIMUM – see CHEIRANTHUS

ERYTHRONIUM

The common 'dog's tooth violet' is *E. dens-canis* which has purple-rose flowers in Spring on 15 cm stems. It has marbled leaves, but more desirable are some lesser-known species. All are Spring flowering bulbs with a long dormant period from July to early March.

E. californicum also has handsome marbled leaves and large creamy flowers, 15 cm tall, with reflexed petals.

E. x 'Pagoda' is yellow and *E. x* 'White Beauty' is also lovely. They need a cool but open soil, and if planted 10 cm apart will make a brave show as they increase naturally where suited. If interplanted in Spring with dwarf *Mimulus*, the blank spaces they leave in Summer will be effectively filled.

E. tuolumnense is soft yellow, carried on 35cm stems.

Above: *Erythronium* 'Pagoda' is a 'dog's tooth violet' with yellow flowers, and thought to be a variety of *E. tuolumnense*.

Eupatorium
The species of this genus (more than 600) occur only in the northern hemisphere. They are plants which grow at the water-side and therefore need rather moist soil. Plants which prefer similar circumstances are for instance *Ligularia*, *Hemerocallis*, *Iris pseudacorus*, *Trollius* and *Filipendula*. With these plants many attractive combinations can be made, especially if you also use grasses and ferns.

EUPHORBIA

Some members of this large genus have a distinctive beauty, but very few are sufficiently dwarf and compact to be treated as alpines. The range of garden worthy kinds includes some for shade and ground cover, but it is amongst the taller ones — 50 cm and more — that some first-class subjects are available to garden lovers. And they are deservedly popular.

Beginning with the dwarfest, *E. cyparissias* is a pretty romper, best away from slower-growing alpines. It has narrow silvery leaves and heads of sulphur yellow in early Summer, 20 cm high. *E. myrsinites* is a beauty and dwarf enough amongst alpines because its silver-blue leafy stems splay out close to the ground. The quite large heads of sulphur yellow come in early Summer. Though not likely to live more than 3-4 years, seedlings, best moved when young, usually appear to maintain a group.
E. amygdaloides makes a good ground cover in sun or shade with a fairly rapid evergreen spread of deep-green, and has 30 cm stalks of greeny-yellow flowers in Spring. There is a purplish-leaved form as well as one with variegated leaves.
E. robbiae (syn. *E. amygdaloides* var. *robbiae*) is on similar lines but taller at 50 cm.
E. polychroma sends up its bright sulphur-yellow flower heads before the leaves in April. As the leaves follow to form a bushy 50 cm plant, the flowers fade imperceptibly and it remains green till November. A purplish-leaved form has also emerged.
E. wallichii also grows bushily as does the somewhat similar *E. x martinii*. They have thicker stems, longer leaves and larger greeny-yellow heads at about 60 cm, May-July.
E. seguieriana is narrow-leaved, greyish, with an abundance of stems and flower-heads up to 50 cm, lasting a long time. I have not found this, however, reliably perennial.
E. griffithii 'Fireglow' is outstanding for colour. New spring growth soon reveals deep fiery-orange heads in May and bush out and up to 90 cm, to remain green till Autumn. Roots spread steadily, but apart from curbing now and then, this can be left alone for years.
E. characias is always a favourite, but needs light soil and full sun, unlike those above which are very adaptable. Thick stems to 100 cm have long bluish-green leaves and very handsome yellowish heads in Spring which slowly unfurl.
E. wulfenii (syn. *E. characias* ssp. *wulfenii*) is much the same and the variety 'Marjery Fish' is magnificent.
E. palustris makes large green bushes of Summer growth, topped by yellow-green heads. At 120 cm this is a reliable perennial with no vices.
E. longifolia is also long-flowering and a splendid long-lived subject for rear positions at 150 cm, flowering for weeks June-August.

Above: *Euphorbia myrsinites* forms large flower heads of a bright yellow colour in early Summer. The silver-blue stems stay close to the ground.

Euphorbia griffithii 'Fireglow' produces fiery-orange flower heads in May. This impressive plant can reach 90 cm in height.

EUPHORBIA

Euphorbia characias is a tall plant – up to 100 cm – for light soil and full sun, with thick stems and bluish-green, rather long leaves. The flowers appear in Spring.

E. sikkimensis is the tallest of the sulphur yellow species at 180 cm, of graceful willowy form, but the early shoots are bright crimson.

Some euphorbias will divide, but most of them will come from seed, though slow. Cuttings of others need to be under glass to root.

EURYOPS

Euryops evansii makes a neat silvery bushlet, giving a long succession of golden daisies on short stems. Best treated as an alpine, it requires sun and well-drained soil where it remains well clothed over Winter at about 25 cm.

Right: *Euryops evansii* is a really showy alpine with golden-yellow, daisy-like flowers above silvery leaves.

FERULA – see FOENICULUM

FESTUCA

Some of the fescue grasses are well worth growing. They are clump-forming and evergreen, and easy to grow without losing compactness.
F. glauca makes an excellent edging of needle-leaved tufts of blue. The flowers are unobtrusive, but newer, bluer forms are coming along.
F. capillaris is not reliably perennial, but the newly introduced *F. tenuissima* is more so, and has almost silky green foliage above which come buff-yellow plumes on waving slender stems, at 60 cm.

Festuca glauca looks good set amongst rocks and stones, but is equally as good for edging.

FILIPENDULA

Although most of these are moisture loving, they are easy to grow in sun or part shade, formerly known as herbaceous spireas. Now names are confused and I prefer to stick to common usage as always.

It would be misleading to apply the common name 'meadowsweet' to all the filipendulas, since it applies only to the wild *F. ulmaria*, of which only one form is of real garden value. This is the golden-leaved *F. ulmaria* 'Aurea' which, given fairly moist soil with some shade, makes a most attractive mound from its foliage alone, from April to October. The flowers are nondescript and the 60 cm stems are best cut back once they reach full height to promote renewed foliage.

F. palmata 'Rubra' (syn. 'Purpurea') needs similar conditions of moisture, and the leafy bushes are topped with glowing rosy crimson heads 90 cm high in June-July. This is a choice plant, but *F.* 'Elegantissima' with glistening pink is more robust and less in need of shade. It grows to 120 cm and there is a similar but much dwarfer pink species in *F.* 'Elegans'.

F. digitata (syn. *palmata*) 'Nana' makes hummocky growth, with deep-green fingered leaves and has deep red flowers on 30 cm stems from June to August. All these are responsive to moisture and plenty of humus, but have a rather brief period in flower if this is denied. All are easy and safe to divide in Autumn or Spring.

The one *filipendula* suitable for ordinary soil, even if dry, is *F. hexapetala* (syn. *F. vulgaris*), but the type is much inferior to *F. hexapetala* 'Plena', which carries heads of dazzling white flowers in June-July. The 60 cm stems rise from deep-green carrotty foliage, and the roots are somewhat woody.

F. hexapetala 'Grandiflora' grows 75-90 cm and the heads of creamy white are slightly scented, as well as being attractive to bees. The two last named are long-lived and trouble-free, but mulching as for astilbes is advised for the remainder.

Above: *Filipendula hexapetala* 'Plena' carries heads of dazzling white flowers in June-July.

Right: *Filipendula vulgaris* (now called *F. hexapetala*) does well in any soil, but is not as good as the variety pictured above.

Filipendula

The only 10 species of this genus grow in the temperate zones of the northern hemisphere. In fact, they are water-side plants and therefore *Filipendula* makes a good combination with *Tradescantia, Lythrum* and other plants which like moist soil.

Also when the plant is not flowering the palmate leaves of *Filipendula* are very attractive.

Some species, such as *F. ulmaria* are very suitable for naturalizing in larger gardens along the side of ponds.

FOENICULUM

Foeniculum vulgare is the culinary fennel, but the purple-leaved form is decidedly ornamental with its delicate foliage. The flowers, as yellowish heads, come on strong stems in Summer up to 200 cm. It comes true from seed and makes stout, deep-rooting, long-lived clumps in any soil, best in sun.

The ornamental value of the culinary fennel (*Foeniculum vulgare*) is clear once the delicate flower heads appear. Many herbs and even vegetables are suitable additions to the ornamental garden.

FRAGARIA

Frankenia thymifolia shows its pink flowers from June until well into September if the weather is good.

Francoa ramosa with *Hebe* and golden bamboo in a Somerset garden.

FRAGARIA

This includes the strawberry, and now there is one which is worth growing for its bright pink flowers, occasionally fruiting. It is named 'Pink Panda' and grows just like a strawberry with runners, but the leaves are smaller and shorter.
Flowering is spread over many weeks of Summer but it needs curbing if amongst other perennials.

FRANKENIA

Known as the 'sea-heath', *F. thymifolia* makes a close carpet of deep green only 3 cm high, with a profusion of open pink flowers from June to September. It is best in dry or sandy soil and losses occur in cold wet districts in Winter.
Propagation is from summer cuttings, or division in Spring.

FRANCOA

This slightly-tender plant is hardy in most districts. It is evergreen, reminding one of a large-leaved *Heuchera*. Given a sheltered spot in sun or part shade, it sends up long wiry stems carrying a short spike of light-pink flowers. As a pot plant, the stems can be trained to arch over, hence the name 'bridal wreath'.
The species *F. appendiculata*, *F. ramosa* and *F. sonchifolia* are much alike.

Fritillaria michailovskyi is especially suited for the rock garden. The bell-shaped bi-coloured flowers have a striking effect.

FRITILLARIA

Fritillaria imperialis is 'Crown Imperial'. It forms a cluster of bulbs if left alone; and in Spring come stout stems up to 100 cm or more, carrying handsome lily trumpets at the top. It is available in both a bronzy shade and in pure yellow. They fade away as quickly as they develop and, if bulbs are disturbed, emit an unforgettable odour. *F. meleagris* is a native from N.W. and Central Europe and is very good for naturalising. The very pretty purple-spotted bells appear in April and May. Lots of varieties are as suitable as the species. 'Aphrodite' (white), 'Pomona' (white violet-spotted), 'Poseidon' (purple-red) and 'Saturnus' (bright violet-red) are some of them. 'Contorta' shows a remarkable tube form.
F. michailovskyi, and *F. involucrata* are some of the othe lesser-known species worth growing. They do especially well in the rock garden.

Fritillaria
All fritillarias are bulbous plants which flower in Spring. There are some 100 species most of which grow in the countries around the Mediterranean. Especially the small flowering kinds are rare, real enthusiasts' plants which are often grown in rock gardens. Not only *F. imperialis*, but also many other species have bulbs which have un unpleasant smell. Some species for the keen gardener are:
F. armena, 20 cm, violet-brown with yellow flowers.
F. pontica, 45 cm, greenish flowers.
F. persica, a tall species: up to 90 cm, violet flowers.

The fiery-orange flowers of this *Fritillaria imperialis* variety may be red or yellow in other varieties.

Fritillaria meleagris. The purple-spotted form is the native species, but many varieties are available.

FUCHSIA

Fuchsia 'Tom Thumb' is a true dwarf with carmine-purple flowers and very suitable for the rockgarden.

Gaillardia 'Goblin' is one of the smallest hybrids of this genus, with beautiful two-tone flowers.

FUCHSIA

Although generally classed as shrubs or indoor plants, some are suitable for rock gardens etc. and can be grown outdoors. If good pot-grown plants are obtained in Spring and inserted deeply, they will survive Winter frosts, especially if on the south side of conifers etc. In very cold districts, a covering of litter will give additional protection.

They flower from new growth, and old stems should be cut back in Spring. All flower from July onwards.
F. pumila makes neat little bushes 15 cm tall with red and violet flowers.
F. 'Tom Thumb' is a little taller and more robust with carmine-purple flowers at 20-25 cm.
Cuttings are taken in Summer.

Taller hardy kinds may be used as herbaceous perennials because they need to be cut hard back in Spring. They flower on the new growth and continue from about July till late Autumn, needing no attention for years.
When ordering plants, make sure they are hardy varieties and plant them deeply. The species *F. magellanica* should be avoided in rainy western areas where it has already run wild. Such varieties as 'Mrs. Popple', 'Chequerboard', 'Mme Cornelissen' and 'Empress of Prussia' are quite reliable at about 50-100 cm, and the golden-leaved form of *F. magellanica* is worth having. This has small red flowers at 80 cm, but the others are much larger and very effective in giving a late but long-lasting display.

GAILLARDIA

Gaillardia grandiflora. The 'blanket flowers' are nothing if not showy, but are apt to flop in rich soil. They need full sun and good drainage to be reliably perennial; and to encourage new basal growth, should be cut hard back just as flowering — June through August — ends. Most of them have soft petalled flowers 8 cm across, and are excellent for cutting. They produce lots of new young plants from their roots if old growth is spaded off in early Spring, but seed is likely to yield a mixture of colours.
'Ipswich Beauty' is half-and-half yellow and bronzy- red, 'Wirral Flame' much more reddish-bronze, 'Mandarin' the best for flame-orange brilliance; and finally, 'Croftway Yellow' is all yellow. These all attain about 80 cm but 'Goblin' is quite dwarf with bicolor flowers at 30 cm. Spring division is safest. None breeds true from seed.

* GALAX

Galax urceolata is a very choice ever-green perennial with repetitive, shiny, leathery leaves. The plant reaches up to 30 cm with flower stems up to 40 cm: it is a beautiful plant. The leaves are used for flower arrangements. *Galax* needs moist soil, and rather acid conditions. So a combination with e.g. *Rhododendron* does very well. Flowering time is June – July.

The evergreen *Galax urceolata* is very popular with flower-arrangers. It grows best in an acid soil.

GALEGA

Galega officinalis is 'goat's rue'. Its forms are showy with pea-shaped flowers on leafy bushes up to 150 cm from stout, tough-rooted clumps. They are not fussy except for sun and good drainage and flower for several weeks, June-August. Apart from a white, there are named varieties with pinkish, lilac and rosy-mauve shades. It is not too difficult to divide and may be raised from seed. *G. orientalis* has spikes of rich-blue flowers on deep-green leafy stems in early Summer up to 130 cm. Its roots may run in some soils, but I have never found it a nuisance, nor is it at all common.

Galega officinalis, the goat's rue, forms leafy bushes up to 150 cm, decorated with pea-shaped flowers in June-August.

GALEOBDOLON – see LAMIUM

GALIUM – see ASPERULA

Galtonia candicans, the Summer hyacinth, grows up to 120cm with pure white flowers on top of stout stems.

GALTONIA

The bulbous, *G. candicans*, 'Summer hyacinth' is pure white, 100-130 cm, smooth near the top. It is trouble free, given sun and good light soil. Bulbs should be planted 8 cm deep and can be interplanted to good effect between such as June-flowering iris. The pure white flowers July-September make excellent contrast.
G. princeps is less tall and more adaptable. It gives plenty of green-bladed leaves and greenish-white tubular flowers on 80 cm stalks in late Summer. It has no objection to dryish soil.
G. viridiflora is not often seen; and though the greenish flowers may appeal to arrangers, it is rather inconspicuous in the garden, having flowers on 80 cm stems.

Galtonia
Besides a combination with Iris, *G. caudicans* is also very suitable between plants whose foliage dies down early, such as *Dicentra* and *Papaver*. A composition with grasses, *Monarda, Rudbeckia* and, for instance, *Anchusa* can be very attractive. The genus *Galtonia* only comprises 3 kinds which are mentioned opposite. All three are natives of southern Africa, where in fact they flower in Winter and early Spring.

GAURA

Above: *Gaura lindheimeri* produces white flowers touched with pink, all through the Summer and Autumn.

Top left: *Genista sagittalis* displays best over a bank or wall. It forms dense ground-covering evergreen mats.

The shrubby *Genista tinctoria* 'Royal Gold' grows to a 50 cm high evergreen bush, covered with golden flowers during the early summer months.

Gentiana acaulis is an easy-to-grow, evergreen alpine which flowers profusely.

* GAURA

Gaura lindheimeri is rather bushy with pinkish white flowers during Summer and Autumn. The plant reaches up to 120 cm, is very hardy, and good for dry, sandy soils.

GENISTA

All are shrubby, but some are quite prostrate and make a splendid display in early Summer.
G. delphinensis (nowadays thought to be *G. sagittalis* as well) has large yellow flowers on tightly congested mats. It does best in scree soil and grows to 10 cm.
G. pilosa spreads as twiggy evergreen mats with masses of yellow flowers, also 10 cm.
Best over a wall or bank, *G. sagittalis* does not flower so freely, making prostrate mats of flat stems to give evergreen and complete ground cover. The above are to be considered alpines, but *G. pilosa* 'Lemon Spreader' is more suitable as a frontal border subject. It has light-yellow flowers, above dense greenery to about 25 cm.
G. tinctoria is for similar usage but the best to grow are the double-flowered 'Plena', forming low evergreen bushes to 30 cm in Summer, yellow flowered. The cultivar 'Royal Gold' is twice as tall and makes a fine display.

A light clip after flowering keeps them shapely and, given sun, they are not particular as to soil, other than where wet and sticky.

GENTIANA

This is a name almost synonymous with alpines, and no collection is complete without some of them. They are best divided into three groups, according to flowering time. Those that flower in Spring like lime in the soil, though it is not essential. They also need a sunny position, as do the summer-flowering species, which will grow well in either limy or acid soil. With one exception, however, the autumn gentians will not grow in limy soil and need a cool position away from strong sun in peaty or leafy soil. All need good drainage.

G. acaulis is easy to grow, but flowers erratically in the Spring, and no sure way of enticing it to flower profusely and regularly has been found. It makes clumpy growth, at ground level, of evergreen rosettes.
The rich-blue, trumpet flowers appear in Spring, 10 cm. Clumps will divide but need to be planted very firmly.

G. *verna* is much smaller, with more open Spring flowers of intense blue. It needs scree soil and appreciates the addition of cow manure. It is best increased by seed sown under glass after being frozen.

The summer gentians are easy in any reasonable soil. The species G. *septemfida* is most often offered, flowering from June to August with loosely-held blue trumpets to about 20 cm. There are other species akin to this – mostly good garden plants, but not easy to divide and best raised from seed.

Autumn gentians, the lime haters, grow with white thong-like roots, and have narrow grassy foliage-like stems terminating in blue trumpets from August to October, at about 10 cm. Shades vary from electric-blue in the one lime-tolerant species G. *farreri*, to the deeper-blue variations and hybrids of the best known G. *sino-ornata*. The roots will fall apart for multiplication, and it is good practice to replant in Spring every two or three years. It is bad practice to plant where the soil can dry out or bake, and for a group they can be set only 10 cm apart. These late gentians are ideal for peat-bed cultivation.

There are taller gentians for use as border perennials, but some are difficult to obtain or establish. Given good light soil, not too dry , and some shade, G. *asclepiadea* is superb for late Summer. Its habit of narrow leaves on slender arching stems gave rise to the name, 'willow gentian'. Rich-blue trumpets, but slightly variable sometimes, hang from stems up to 90 cm where suited. There is also a white form.

Though division of old plants is possible, they resent disturbance and young seed-raised plants thrive best.
G. *lutea* is of noble appearance but is not easy to establish in my experience. Again, young seedlings are best, and in sun and good soil the stiff leafy spikes will attain 100-130 cm. The outstanding feature is that it is yellow-flowered.

Other blue gentians for frontal positions could include the lovely G. *makinoi* – if it can be located. It is rare and unfortunately difficult to please, but the rich-blue flowers from the leaf axils of its 40 cm spikes are entrancing.
Two less exciting but interesting species are G. *andrewsii* and G.*waltonii*. They have small blue trumpets as a terminal cluster on 25-30 cm stems in Summer. Neither is difficult.

Above: *Gentiana septemfida* is one of the most generally available species of this alpine genus. Easy-to-grow and flowering freely from June to August.

Right: *Gentiana sino-ornata* has given rise to a number of hybrids, mostly in rather deep-blue shades.

Below: *Gentiana lutea* is the only yellow-flowered species within this genus.

GERANIUM

Geranium cinereum 'Ballerina' is one of the best varieties of this species with beautiful lilac-pink flowers.

Below: Geranium dalmaticum is a good, pink-flowering species, but needs frequent replanting.

GERANIUM

What is surprising about hardy geraniums is not merely their wide variety, but that their value as good garden plants has taken a long time to be appreciated. It could be the upsurge of interest in perennials generally, coupled with the notion that they were largely indoor or Summer bedding plants. But almost all geraniums are fully hardy and the indoor type are not geraniums at all, but pelargoniums.

None of those recommended below is excessively tall and the list begins with those most suitable as alpines. Some of these are quite adaptable in front of taller perennials.

Alpines and others

G. cinereum and its forms and hybrids vary from 10-15 cm in height. They form neat clumpy plants and the species itself has ash-grey, deeply-indented basal leaves giving cup-shaped pink

Geranium
Of this genus about 300 wild species are known. A typical habit of almost all species is that they explode their seeds in some way or other! Cranesbills occur in very different regions of the temperate climatological zones, from low meadows up to high in the mountains. Therefore suitable species may be found for any kind of garden. Many species can stand shade, and so can be used under trees and shrubs. Most of them are easy plants which need little care. In some cases not only is the inflorescence attractive, but so also is the Autumn colour.

flowers. 'Ballerina' is a hybrid of highest merit, the lilac-pink flowers being prettily veined crimson. 'Apple Blossom' is pure light pink and 'Laurence Flatman' has quite large flowers, heavily blotched and veined. The subspecies subcaulescens is vigorous with green leaves and vivid magenta flowers and G.c.s. 'Splendens', though less robust, is close to salmon-pink. All these flower May-August but 'Ballerina' often goes on and on. They all need sun and very well-drained soil. Spring division provides increase.

G. dalmaticum has vigour and is adaptable, though the pink flowers last only a few weeks in early Summer on 10 cm stems. Both this and the white form 'Album' respond to frequent replanting as they tend to grow out of the ground.

G. farreri is slow to expand and needs very well-drained soil. I find it does best in sandy, peaty soil. The large pink flowers on 12 cm stems have black centres nestling above the grey-green leaves.

G. sessiliflorum 'Nigricans' has coppery-brown leaves on compact mounds. The small white flowers, only 6 cm high, are not significant and self-seeding makes good occasional casualties.

Dual purpose geraniums

Those below in the 15-30 cm height range are mostly dual purpose, increased by Spring division.

G. 'Anne Folkard' is a hybrid with a long display of vivid magenta-purple flowers. It makes a wide Summer spread of gold-tinted greenery from a compact root, June-September. 20 cm.

G. x cantabrigiense with light pink flowers, June-August, is 15 cm.

G. himalayense is now correct for G. grandiflorum, low growing with a quite brisk below ground spread into matted clumps. An early display of blue cup-shaped flowers on 30 cm stems is even more effective in the double form 'Plenum'.

G. 'Johnson's Blue' is deservedly popular with masses of blue flowers on 30 cm stems in early Summer, from compact clumpy growth.

G. macrorrhizum too has a good spread and is dense enough for ground cover. The leaves are scented and flowers come on little clusters at 30 cm just above the foliage in early Summer. The species is light pink but much deeper in 'Bevans', more of a lilac in 'Ingwersens' and white in 'Album'. 'Variegatum' is one with pretty foliage, but is apt to be straggly.

G. malviflorum gives a fine show in Spring of blue flowers at 30-35 cm, and then dies away till Autumn to give Winter leafage. Roots are somewhat invasive.

G. procurrens romps with such abandon that although only 10 cm high in flower, it is out of place amongst alpines. It roots down as it runs and has rosy-purple flowers and is best for ground cover between shrubs.

G. pylzowianum spreads quickly below ground, for Summer foliage cover with pink cups. 12 cm.

G. *renardii* has only a short flowering season, May-June, but the pale lilac flowers are followed by a dome of soft rounded leaves, an attraction in themselves, 30 cm.

G. x 'Russell Prichard' makes a bright display of large magenta-pink flowers on semi-prostrate stems above grey foliage. It needs a warm spot, being slightly tender, and resentful of winter wet.

G. *sanguineum* and its forms make sturdy clumps, with a show of 25 cm magenta-red flowers on the type, but clear pink in 'Holden Variety' or 'Splendens'. G.s. *lancastriense* (syn. G. *sanguineum* var. *prostratum*) is more prostrate at 15 cm, and this too has clear-pink flowers from June-August. 'Shepherd's Warning' has deep rose-pink flowers for a long time, 15 cm, above strong green tufts.

G. *wallichianum* is available only in 'Buxton's Blue' and is a delightful plant. From a very compact root, deep-green mounds up to 30 cm are studded with light – blue, paler-centred flowers for weeks on end after June, till well into Autumn. I find it does best in sun with light soil, but it is adaptable for part shade.

Taller growing geraniums

Those over 30 cm are all easy to grow in any well-drained soil and some are good for shady places.

G. *armenum* (syn. G. *psilostemon*) makes a hefty bush of greenery up to 120 cm in good soil, and is a trifle lax. The flowers from June-September are a fierce magenta, but less so with the hint of pink in 'Bressingham Flair'.

G. 'Claridge Druce' will grow in sun or even dry shade, with purplish flowers on 70 cm stems above ample grey-green foliage. It has vigour and adaptability and is virtually unequalled.

G. *clarkei* 'Kashmir Purple' and 'Kashmir White' are new names for clumpy plants with good base foliage and a long season in flower at about 30 cm.

G. *endressii* is a strong grower, with ample greenery, clump-forming in sun or shade. 'Wargrave Pink' at 50 cm in June-August and 'A.T. Johnson' are much alike.

G. *grevilleanum* along with G. *albanum* and G. *lambertii* make a good summer spread of trailing habit. The pink-to-lilac flowers nestle above the dense greenery, about 40 cm, June-August.

G. *libani* gives an early display of blue cups on 60 cm stems, forming compact roots, but lies dormant and leafless till Winter.

G. x *magnificum* – still sometimes listed as G. *ibericum* – makes a fine show of large blue flowers, 60 cm, above a mass of foliage in June-July. Cut hard back after flowering for neatness.

G. *phaeum* has variations, the stately purple form having the name 'Mourning Widow'. Flowers are small on 70 cm stems, May-June, but it will also grow well in dry shady places. The white 'Album' is very effective.

G. *pratense* is the 'cranesbill' and this also has

Geranium macrorrhizum is available in many fine varieties, flowering in pink, lilac and white shades.

The cranesbill, *Geranium pratense* exists in both double and single form.

GERANIUM

Geranium sylvaticum 'Mayflower' shows bright flowers in May-June.

variations. The best single-flowered is 'Mrs Kendall Clarke', with large light-blue flowers on 60 cm stems, June-July. A white and pink exist as it does in the three double but smaller-flowered forms in light and deep-blue and white, less vigorous than the singles, all having a somewhat woody root.
G. sylvaticum flowers in May-June on 75 cm stems, and the variety 'Mayflower' makes a very pleasing display of light blue.
So does the white 'Alba' and the pink 'Wanneri'. All are easy to grow in sun or shade.
G. wlassovianum makes a steady spread of deep velvety greenery and a long season of violet cups, June-September at 50 cm.
It is easy and adaptable.

Left: Geum hybrids, like this double ruby-red 'Rubin', flower abundantly, often in striking colours.

Below: Geum 'Borisii' is early flowering (May-June), but may flower for a second time later in the year.

GEUM

Almost all in cultivation are hybrids. They are easy to grow and prefer sun, and most divide readily.
G. x 'Borisii' is deservedly popular. On evergreen hummocks come deep-orange flowers on 30 cm stems, May-June, and often a lesser show later on. A new variety, 'Nordeck', 20 cm, flowered for most of the 1987-88 Winter in my garden.
G. chiloense gave the well-known 'Mrs Bradshaw', red, and 'Lady Stratheden', yellow. They are both fully double-flowered on 60 cm stems, June-August, but need to be raised from seed, having about a 3-4 year life span and not being easy to divide.
Hybrids of *chiloense* and *coccineum* are 'Fire Opal', rich red double, and 'Dolly North', double orange, and are increased by division, but with me they lack the vigour they had 50 years ago.
G. 'Copper Tone' makes neat mounds, having single deep-yellow flowers above at 25 cm.
G. 'Georgenberg' is of similar habit, the coppery-yellow flowers dangling on 25 cm stems, June-August. 'Lionel Cox' is another of this type.
G. reptans is dwarf enough to class as alpine. It has woody surface-rooting stems, bright-green leaves set with yellow flowers, May-July. The best of the dwarfs is 'Baby Tangerine' with bright-orange flowers 10 cm high, rather like a tiny *G. x 'Borisii'*.
G. rivale likes moisture but is adaptable, making leafy clumps, and having strawberry-pink flowers at 50 cm, June-August.
G. rossii is quite distinct for its carroty leaves and 20 cm sprays of bright-yellow flowers, May-June.

GILLENIA

Gillenia trifoliata has slender willowy stems carrying masses of tiny white flowers to give a charming airiness. The branching 100 cm stems need no supports and it is adaptable to almost any soil, sun or part shade.
It is also long-lived with tough roots, but will divide best in early Spring.

GLAUCIDIUM

Glaucidium palmatum is, for those who can acquire and grow it, a real treasure. In humus-rich soil and some shade, 50 cm light-lavender poppy-like flowers come above broad indented leaves, May-June. It is hardy but not for exposed positions.

GLOBULARIA

These are true alpines and of value for small sites, with low tufts of dark evergreen leaves. Flowers come as little blue fluffy balls in early Summer.
G. incanescens is a choice species best in scree conditions, and flowers are bright powder blue only 7 cm high.
G. cordifolia and *G. meridionalis* (syn. *G. bellidifolia*) are a little larger, of easy growth at 10 cm, whilst *G. trichosantha* and *G. elongata* are both 15-20 cm and more robust in growth. Old plants are best divided in early Autumn or Spring.

GLYCERIA

Glyceria aquatica 'Variegata' is a rushy grass for the waterside, though it will grow in any moist soil with a modest spread. The blades are up to 50 cm and flowers insignificant.

Gillenia trifoliata invariably produces tiny white flowers, wherever it is planted.

Right: *Glaucidium palmatum* forms poppy-like flowers in May-June.

Left: *Globularia elongata* is rather robust for this alpine genus, with a height of 20 cm.

Below right: *Glyceria aquatica* 'Variegata' displays best beside water.

Glaucium

Not dealt with elsewhere in this book, but perhaps worth a brief mention, this genus belongs to the *Papaveraceae*, with mainly annual and biennial species.
There is one species that, although not long-lived, may be classified as a perennial: *G. flavum*. This is a plant which occurs in various coastal areas of Europe. It has attractive, bluish-green foliage. The height is 30-60 cm and it flowers with yellow poppy-like flowers between June and August.

GONIOLIMON

Goniolimon tataricum is the so-called 'statice', flowering from July-August.

Below: Gunnera manicata is an impressive perennial with giant leaves, well worth growing in larger gardens, but unfortunately not hardy in cold districts.

GONIOLIMON

These close relatives of Limonium, with leathery leaves in flat rosettes, are merely grown for their spectacular flowers.

G. speciosum flowers in Summer, purple-red on 30 cm stems.

G. tataricum flowers as high, but ruby-red. This is the so-called 'statice'. The plants do not stand to wet conditions during the flowering period (July-August).

Increase is by root-division.

GRATIOLA

Gratiola officinalis is not spectacular but is interesting with upright leafy stems and near-white, small flower-spikes to 70 cm in Summer. Plants have clumpy, fleshy roots, easy to divide and not difficult to grow in sun.

Gratiola officinalis, although perhaps not the most showy of plants, does well in sunny places.

GUNNERA

This is a genus of great contrasts, grown for foliage rather than flowers.

Leaf size varies from 5 cm, to over 100 cm in the case of G. manicata. This is a waterside subject and the huge, jagged-edged leaves are large enough on 150 cm stems to serve as an umbrella. The stocky plant becomes massive and will take up a 2-metre space when established. It is not hardy in cold districts, nor is it evergreen. Flowering is a stumpy black cone.

G. magellanica and G. hamiltonii are spreaders in dampish places, forming unaggressive mats of small leaves, crinkly and shiny.

GYPSOPHILA

This includes both border and alpine kinds. All require good drainage and sun. The charming folk name of 'baby's breath' applies to the single-flowered G. paniculata. From a sturdy top or fangy root, this makes a considerable summer spread of somewhat tangled twiggy branches forming a cloud of tiny white flowers.

G. 'Bristol Fairy' has larger, double flowers, and both will reach 90 cm high and as much in diameter when at their best. 'Flamingo' is similar but pale pink and less reliable. Both this and 'Bristol Fairy' are best propagated by grafting onto the single G. paniculata, which is raised from seed.
G. 'Compacta Plena' is like a smaller edition of the double 'Bristol Fairy' and covers the same period in flower from June to late August. This is also the period for two pink varieties, but it must be said that in both the 45 cm G. 'Pink Star' and the prostrate 'Rosy Veil', the colour is but faint. They are, however, good perennials capable of covering a fair amount of space and having a long period in flower.
Those suitable as alpines include the tufty G. cerastioides with white, pink-veined flowers in Summer, only 5 cm high.
G. repens 'Dubia' have bluish-green-leaved trailing stems and a bright display of small clear-pink flowers. 'Dorothy Teacher' is extra good, but 'Rosa Schönheit' is the deepest pink cultivar I know.
All these make excellent wall plants and can be increased from cuttings.
All gypsophilas like sunny well-drained conditions; and as the generic name states, they revel in chalky soil.

HABERLEA

Haberlea rhodopensis is a plant for north-facing crevices, like its better known relative Ramonda. The deep-green, puckered leafy rosettes are long-lived and give little sprays of lavender-blue flowers 12 cm in early Summer.
Under the name H. ferdinandi-coburgi is a species with flowers a little larger, flecked gold.

HACQUETIA

The one species H. epipactis is best in some shade and is included not only because it grows well in dampish or heavy soil, and is long-lived, but because it flowers in earliest Spring.
The flowers are in sulphur yellow heads, 15 cm tall, and when these are over, there comes a low canopy of green leaves from its tough clumpy roots.
Division is best in Autumn and it is quite adaptable also for peat beds.

Gypsophila repens 'Rosa Schönheit' ('Pink Beauty') shows the most impressive pink flowers within the genus Gypsophila.

Haberlea
This is a small, very special genus. Special, because the plants have been found as fossils from the Tertiary Age. If they are left alone, and they like their position in a sheltered place without direct sun, they are very long-lived and can form large groups. This enthusiasts' plant needs and loves lime.

Centre: Haberlea rhodopensis has lavender-blue flowers in early Summer and does best in north-facing crevices.

Hacquetia epipactis produces yellow flowerheads in very early Spring. It will withstand some shade and dampish or heavy soil.

HAKONECHLOA

Hakonechloa macra 'Aureola' in the author's garden at Bressingham.

HAKONECHLOA

Hakonechloa macra 'Aureola', although not evergreen, is one of the brightest of all dwarf grasses. The blades arch over in abundance to give complete ground cover, of a decided golden hue from April to November. Barely 30 cm high, the blades come from tough but dividable roots, and grow well in any reasonable soil and sun. A green type is also of value.

* HAPLOPAPPUS

These *Aster*-related beautiful flowering plants are very showy in the rock garden. They need a sunny spot. All flower from June till some time in August. They can be increased by seed, cuttings and division, but are not hardy in cold regions.
H. acaulis is up to 10 cm high.
H. croceus (with bigger flowers: 7 cm instead of 3 cm diameter) grows taller: 50 cm. Other species sometimes offered are *H. coronopifolius* and *H. lyallii*. All are worth growing. The general flower colour is yellow.

Haplopappus croceus is, with a height of 50 cm, one of the tallest species within this genus.

Below: *Hebe* 'James Stirling' is a shrub, but may be used as an alpine plant. It grows up to 20 cm.

HEBE

Although these are shrubs, some of the dwarfest kinds are very suitable as alpine plants. Some make shapely evergreen bushes of conifer form. These are virtually leafless and are grown for their evergreen form of dense colourful branches. Some are golden like the 20 cm 'James Stirling', but there are others of gold or green hue. The true *H. cupressoides* 'Nana' makes a deep green bush, 30 cm high. Other dwarf hebes grown for flowering exist in a quite wide variety, mostly to be seen at garden centres in pots. Lilac, blue and violet flowers on short spikes are the rule, and they are good value if dwarf varieties are chosen.
They can be clipped for neatness after flowering, and cuttings are easily rooted, but some are rather less than hardy.

HELENIUM

These are indispensible for sheer display, but are liable to suffer from neglect. After 3-4 years they become starved and produce more stems than can be fed. The result is shrivelling stem leaves even before they flower. It can be easily remedied by lifting and dividing in early Spring, using only the most vigorous outer shoots and replanting in enriched soil. The old tall varieties should be avoided as they mostly require supporting, especially if in one-sided borders.

Heleniums provide some very rich colouring, and amongst the best varieties H. 'Gold Fox' is outstanding, with its streaky orange and flame-brown shading. It grows to about 90 cm, as do e.g. the very attractive and sturdily upright H. 'Coppelia'. In the same height range and in the same June-August period, H. 'Moerheim Beauty' is a favourite, with bronzy-red flowers; H. 'Mahogany' is a similar colour but later flowering, and H. 'Golden Youth' a warm deep yellow. There is a good selection at this intermediate height. For August-September flowering, H. 'Baudirektor Linne' can be recommended as a tawny orange-red.

H. 'Bruno' is close to being mahogany red, and H. 'Butterpat' a rich yellow. These attain 120 cm which is plenty tall enough for any Helenium; for where hemmed-in conditions prevail, the taller they grow the more likely they are to need support, since the flowers are carried on terminal heads, tending to make them top heavy if stems are weakened by lack of air and light.

The dwarfest heleniums are the earliest to flower — and often the longest flowering. H. 'Crimson Beauty' is more brown than red, but the flowers open on bushy leafy plants barely 60 cm high. H. 'Wyndley' has larger flowers in which orange-yellow is streaked with reddish-brown, also with a bushy habit little more than 60 cm. H. hoopesii is distinct for its leathery leaves and sprays of golden-yellow flowers.

HELIANTHEMUM

The so-called 'rock roses' are somewhat shrubby, but best included here as they are very popular and to be considered as indispensable alpines. Most of those offered are cultivars in a wide variety of names and colours, from white to pink, yellow, red, orange, brown and many intermediate and bicolour shades. There are also some double-flowered, and many have silvery foliage. Some are of prostrate growth, others are more mounded up to 25 cm in height, but all respond to clipping back after their early summer flowering has ended. This promotes tidiness, some being of quite vigorous growth, and may result in a second flowering in late Summer. None is difficult to grow and will flourish in quite dry or poor soil — their only dislike being of wet conditions. All will come easily from cuttings under a frame, best taken after flowering or in early Autumn. Only two distinctive species need be mentioned. H. lunulatum makes erect little greyish bushes

Helenium 'Moerheim Beauty' is an appealing variety with bronzy-red flowers.

Right: Helenium autumnale 'Pumilum magnificum' is not a hybrid, but a somewhat uncommon variety of the species autumnale. Hybrids are generally preferred.

Below right: Because of their rich range of shades, Helianthemums are very popular. Pictured is the hybrid 'Ben Ledi'.

Helianthemum
The 80 species, or so, originate from the Mediterranean and central Asia.
They can stand drought very well and, especially the English hybrids, are hardy (which cannot be said of many species). Because very often the stems grow too long, it is advisable to cut them back immediately after flowering (August). It is important to do this at the right time, because the new growth has then time to mature before the Winter. In this way frost damage is avoided.

Helianthus

Important to us as perennials, sunflowers originate from North America. They are strong plants which need little care and produce excellent cut flowers. The flowers are especially popular with bees. The attractive yellow flowers are sterile along the edge of the disc, and only the centre can form seed. *Helianthus* likes a little lime in the soil and appreciates some old stable manure every year. In order to maintain a rich flowering, replanting (every two years) is recommended.

about 20 cm covered for a long period in small, pure yellow flowers.

H. serpyllifolium is also yellow, but its green growth is completely prostrate and it flowers in May and June. Helianthemums are so varied in form and colour that they benefit from association with blue-flowered plants to give the complete colour spectrum.

HELIANTHUS

The name literally translated from the Greek means 'sun flower', but the perennial kinds have little resemblance to the rather grotesque annual species. There are some perennial kinds which are very weedy, spreading quickly below ground, and sending up stems 150-180 cm high with single yellow flowers on top. These are simply not worth growing and are a menace amongst better subjects. It is far better to fork them out and insert instead the compact-rooted kinds, which include double-flowered varieties and have a much neater, though still robust, bushy habit, coming under the species *multiflorus*.

The 150 cm *H*. 'Loddon Gold' is a fine double variety with flowers, up to 10 cm across, covering the plant on short stems.

H. 'Triomphe de Gand' and 'Morning Star' are semi-double, of similar height and with little variation in colour. None needs supporting.

Helianthus decapetalus 'Capenoch Star' is a good example of a single variety of these 'sunflowers'. Often double and semi-double varieties are preferred.

They are far better subjects than the rampant single kinds.

These better *Helianthus*, which are at their best in July and August, are easy to grow in any ordinary soil, but do respond to reasonably good treatment such as an occasional mulch.

Division is best in Spring, but some thinning out should take place rather than allowing overcrowding to spoil them.

H. salicifolius (syn. *H. orgyalis*) is much later to flower and taller, with willowy stems up to 230 cm. They carry narrow drooping leaves and are topped by single yellow flowers. The roots have a modest spread.

Helianthus salicifolius flowers in Autumn on willowy stems up to 23 cm.

HELICHRYSUM

Helichrysum milfordiae needs a warm spot and if happy, will provide you with many crimson-backed white flowers during Summer.

Helichrysum bellidioides has grey-green leaves, covered with white flowers in Summer.

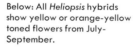

Below: All *Heliopsis* hybrids show yellow or orange-yellow toned flowers from July-September.

HELICHRYSUM

This much-varied genus includes species forming low mounds to shrubby ones of 60 cm or more. Many have silvery foliage and some are tender, but all prefer full sun and well-drained soil.

H. bellidioides makes prostrate mats set with crispy white flowers 5 cm above grey-green leaves in Summer.
H. coralloides is a choice shrublet with scaly, leafless branches. It is an interesting curiosity with occasional yellow flowers, and grows to 25 cm.
H. milfordiae makes a silvery pad set with white, crimson-backed flowers in a warm spot, 5 cm, also summer flowering.
H. orientalis is vigorous and mat-forming with narrow grey leaves and clusters of golden, fluffy heads. It is a showy little plant, 20 cm.
H. virgineum also needs a warm spot — or an alpine house in cold regions. It has silvery base leaves and 20 cm stems carrying small pink bracts which open out to crispy white flowers.
H. 'Sulphur Light' is a hybrid with a long season of clustered sulphur-gold flowers on 30 cm stems.
H. splendidum, though strictly a silvery evergreen shrub up to 60 cm, is not out of place with perennials, with deep yellow flowers. It is a little tender. Not so *H. angustifolium* (syn. *H. italicum*), with narrow grey foliage smelling of curry. The 50 cm stems carry yellow clustered flowers. Both can be sheared in Spring to promote neatness.

HELICTOTRICHON – see Avena

HELIOPSIS

This, too, indicates 'sunflower', but for sheer display over a long period, July-September, they are scarcely equalled. They grow from compact dividable clumps and only the tallest, if in rich or damp soil, are likely to need supporting. All those in cultivation are hybrids of *H. scabra* (syn. *H. helianthoides* var. *scabra*). All are in yellow shades and some, such as 'Golden Plume', are almost double, rich orange-yellow at 100 cm. 'Incomparabilis' is similar but flowers are a little smaller at 8 cm diameter. Both have overlapping petals. 'Ballerina' is semi-double and 'Patula' and 'Gigantea' (130 cm) are single-flowered. The less vigorous 'Gold Greenheart' is semi-double, light yellow with a hint of green. The largest orange-yellow single is 'Desert King', but one wonders how or why the celebrated Karl Foerster raised and named so many. Although *Heliopsis* add to the dominance of yellow in late Summer, I rate them highly as excellent perennials.

HELLEBORUS

These evoke the annual thrill of another Spring with their promise and magic. But there are still garden lovers who do not realise what a range exists, though some are still rarely seen. The 'Christmas rose', *H. niger*, is still outstanding for earliness, though it does not live up to its name outdoors except here and there or when under cloches. Not that it matters greatly, for it is still the depths of Winter when the first white, golden-centred flowers appear amid the deep-green leaves. It likes a cool root run, neither soggy nor starved; and though its preference is for some shade, competition with tree roots should be avoided. A light mulch is helpful, applied in Spring, and young plants are easier to establish than old. Indeed, divisions of old plants often languish rather than grow. Increase can be made by seed, but this is a slow process.

It is usually cheaper to buy young nursery-grown plants and, having chosen a semi-shady place, prepare it well; then, after a year or two in which to become firmly established, it should flower year after year from January to late March.

H. orientalis are much more adaptable and reliable than *H. niger*.

Flowering from February to April, they carry the name 'Lenten rose'. They come in a colour range from white through shades of pink to plum purple, at a time when old leaves, which have been evergreen for 10-11 months, are fading. As soon as the flowers begin to fade comes a new crop of leaves, giving a canopy over the roots which helps keep the soil cool in Summer.

H. orientalis can withstand considerable summer dryness but what they most prefer is high or dappled shade, or the northerly aspect of a wall. They are not fussy about soil, but respond to a light mulch after flowering.

Great improvements to the colour range have been made by Mrs. Helen Ballard. Some are close to yellow, whilst others have charming speckles within the flowers. Occasionally, named varieties are offered, but these are much more expensive. Old plants can be divided in Autumn, though this may spoil flowering for one season. When planting, roots should go well down, leaving the crown buds only just below ground level.

Stems vary in height from 30 to 50 cm, but the very early *H. atrorubens* and *H. abschasicus*) are rather shorter. Both have deep maroon flowers.

H. colchicus is pink-flowered in clusters, and apart from flowering sometimes in Autumn as well as early Spring, has evergreen leaves.

H. corsicus is also evergreen, but the leaves come from stems which may loll over somewhat and lengthen till a large terminal head of pale apple-green flowers opens in April. This and its hybrid *H. x sternii* make quite large plants and from seed take 3 years to flower fully.

H. nigercors is a cross between *H. niger* and *H.*

Helleborus

The 20 species, or so, which grow wild in central and southern Europe, and the western part of Asia, are difficult to distinguish from each other. They hybridize very easily, so that many hybrids are produced. Some are sensitive to fungus diseases and, if different ones are put together, they can easily infect each other. Try to avoid this in your plant scheme.

The Christmas rose makes a fine combination with grasses, ferns, small shrubs and other early flowering plants.

Helleborus niger, the 'Christmas rose', is one of the earliest flowering perennials.

Left: *Helleborus corsicus* is a fairly large evergreen with green flowers in April.

corsicus, whilst *H. kochii* is a free-flowering white, akin to *H. orientalis*.

H. viridis is a rare beauty with apple-green flowers on 40 cm stems for a long time, February-April. The tender *H. lividus,* with its fine foliage and pinkish-green scented flowers, is hardy only in the warmest districts. Division retards them for a season; and though most of them can be raised from seed-sowing in Autumn, none of the *orientalis* type is likely to breed true.

Below: *Helleborus orientalis* hybrids are quite adaptable to shade and are available in a nice range of colours.

HEMEROCALLIS

HEMEROCALLIS

It is not an unalloyed blessing when hybridists go all out to widen the range of a good subject. Fifty years ago there were no more than a score or so 'day lily' cultivars, but now there are many hundreds, due largely, as with hostas, to American enthusiasts. Trials are held to shorten the list in the hope of suggesting the best for colour, constitution, etc., but inevitably, each of several trials comes up with widely-differing short lists of what each considers the best.

It is scarcely possible in this context for me to mention a good representative of each colour variation, taking height, flowering season and other aspects into account. Those wishing to invest, or to widen the range they have already, are advised to study colour catalogues or to see a collection in flower in order to choose. It is not surprising that 'day lilies' have become so popular — especially in America. They are bone-hardy, have abundant complementary rushy foliage, and remain in flower for several weeks. They are not fussy as to soil and will take some shade. They vary in flowering season from May to August and in height from 100 cm down to 40 cm. The latter are the newest trend with breeders, heralded by the little golden yellow 'Stella d'Oro'.

Hemerocallis, for all their ease of culture and adaptability, do respond to good rich soil by

Hemerocallis varieties are available in a wide range of shades, with varying flowering times from May to August, and heights from 100 cm down to 40 cm.

flowering longer and are less affected by drought. In time they make large clumps and where two or more of a kind have been planted as a group, they are apt to become starved through congestion. Large clumps are hard to dig up though not difficult to divide, if need be, with two forks. I have found, however, that little or no damage is caused in taking the easier course of reducing clumps with a sharp spade thrust through plants in situ, either for thinning out or as a means of division, but the spade must go down vertically. With the welter of named cultivars, one is apt to overlook the species — some of which have been their parents.
H. dumortieri, H. minor an *H. middendorffii* are early-flowering and fairly dwarf in shades of yellow.
H. fulva is tall and vigorous with bronzy-red flowers on 120 stems, whilst *H. multiflora* is very late, of similar height, having small but scented warm-orange flowers.

HEPATICA

These demure but delightful plants flower in early Spring. They have fibrous roots and are slow to expand into clumps mounded by dark green, rounded and lobed leaves. The first to flower of the two main species — often in February — is *H. triloba*, now correctly *H. nobilis*.
The bright blue is most often seen and its kinship with the *Anemone* is obvious. It is only 10 cm high, as with the white and pink forms. Doubles of all three exist, but they are rare and expensive.
H. angulosa, now *H. transsylvanica*, is somewhat more robust, with rounded leaves and larger

Hepatica transsylvanica has fine blue flowers in March-April.

flowers of a lighter blue, 15 cm, March-May. 'Loddon Blue' is good, but x 'Ballardii' is superb, a rarity to be treasured. Hepaticas like an open soil and prefer part shade. They also like lime, but they do not like being disturbed once established. Though not difficult to divide, fresh plantings from division are likely to sulk for a year or two.

* HERACLEUM

The enormous showy plants of this genus can become real weeds in the garden. The two species *H. mantegazzianum* and *H. stevenii* are biennials. But *H. lanatum* is a real perennial, which still reaches up to 2.5 m. Flowers are white, June-July.

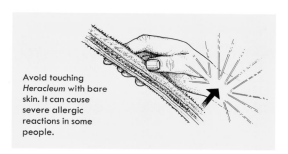

Avoid touching *Heracleum* with bare skin. It can cause severe allergic reactions in some people.

Above: *Heracleum mantegazzianum* is a biennial, but very much like the perennial *H. lanatum*. All Heracleums are very impressive plants, but they can become weedy in the garden.

Hesperis matronalis, the 'dame's rocket', generally has lilac-blue flowers, but white forms are available. The scented flowers appear in early Summer.

HESPERIS

H. matronalis has the folk name 'dame's rocket' and is worthy of inclusion despite its short life. Young plants have good basal leaves and stems branch up to 120 cm to carry a host of small stock-like flowers, mostly lilac-blue but sometimes white. They are scented and last for several weeks in early Summer, will cut well and will grow in poor soil.

Although only two good flowerings can be expected, they come readily from seed, often self-sown to ensure continuity. There are very rare doubles, much less tall, in white and lilac, but these have baffled most plantsmen, including myself, to find a reliable method of propagation, since they do not set seed.

HEUCHERA

Above: *Heuchera cylindrica* 'Greenfinch' has greenish-white flowers on 75 cm spikes.

Below left: *Heuchera x brizoides* 'Scintillation' with its red-tipped, pink bells received numerous awards from the R.H.S.

The spikes of *Heuchera* are very good as long lasting cut flowers.

HEUCHERA

These are of special interest to me because my father grew them as market cut-flowers long before I became a nurseryman. He was also initially responsible for raising crosses, which in time led to several R.H.S. awards and have enriched many a garden, including the now widely-known mixture 'Bressingham Hybrids'. Wherever a garden has well-drained soil, *heucheras* will flourish and add a unique charm to the early Summer scene. They have attractive evergreen foliage which, with overlapping and often marbled leaves of rounded ivy shape, is pleasing even when not in flower. In May, the slender stems rise to unfurl with a spike of small bell-shaped flowers in a pleasing range of colours, from white to pink, salmon, red and crimson, varying in height from 30 to 75 cm and lasting in flower till well into July.

The plants have one fault despite their being fully hardy and long-lived: it is that the crowns above ground gradually extend so that after a few years they become woody and less likely to produce abundant flowers. The remedy is to dig up the plant and pull off some of the crowns which have fibrous roots attached, and after preparing the soil again, plant them back more deeply till only the leafy upper part is above ground, and then firm well. This, and any new plantings can be done best in late Summer or early Autumn, but otherwise they are safe enough to move in Winter or Spring.

Named varieties

The variety H. 'Scintillation' has received the highest possible awards from the R.H.S. and the red-tipped pink bells add much to its brilliance. H. 'Coral Cloud' has smaller flowers on longer stems at 75 cm, with H. 'Firebird' a telling red of 60 cm.

H. 'Freedom' is light pink and dwarf, only 45 cm high; but both H. 'Greenfinch', a greenish white, and H. 'Hyperion', coral pink, are very strong growing with 75 cm spikes.

H. 'Pearl Drops' has small, gracefully carried flowers.

H. 'Pretty Polly' is a large-flowered clear pink barely 30 cm high.

The brightest deep red with large bells is H. 'Red Spangles', with H. 'Shere Variety' more of a scarlet red, both 60 cm.

H. 'Splendour' is outstanding for its glowing salmon-scarlet flowers and H. 'Sunset' has coral red lips to deep-pink bells.

So much for the named varieties, which can only be increased by division. The best strain of mixed colours from seed is undoubtedly H. 'Bressingham Hybrids' in which the full range of colour is seen. H. 'Palace Purple' has become popular for its foliage alone. It is close to being beetroot red, larger and shinier than any others. Although its greenish-white flowers are small, the 80 cm sprays are dainty, coming well after other *Heucheras* in July. Growth is vigorous as it is in another late species *H. villosa*. This grows to 60 cm, with myriads of tiny white flowers.

Some coppery leaved variations of *H. americana* (to which 'Palace Purple' belongs) are on the way. Another worthwhile small-flowered pink *Heuchera* flowering at 70 cm, June-July, is *H. x brizoides* 'Gracillima'.

x HEUCHERELLA

This stands for the cross between *Heuchera* and *Tiarella*, and it has produced the pretty carpeted *H. tiarelloides*, with golden-green foliage 15 cm high, and 25-30 cm spikes of light pink in May and June. This is an easy and useful plant, but the cross also yielded *H.* 'Bridget Bloom', a much choicer subject for good light soil and a little shade. The foliage is domed and very compact; and, where happy, it sends up a long succession of flower sprays giving an overall effect of light pink, from individual flowers which contain both white and pink. Quite often this will flower from May to July and again in September or October. It is a plant worth fussing over a little, adding some leafy or peaty soil where heavy and dividing when need be in August-September.

There is a story behind the plant. Back in 1950 my helper, Percy Piper, needed no encouragement to make crosses. Only tips from me as to what might yield a break were needed. One such was to grow a *Heuchera* and *Tiarella wherryi* side by side and hope bees would do the rest. But no seedlings appeared after 2 years and only one on the third. It was the one, having qualities of both parents. Five years later, by frequent division, it was sent out bearing my eldest daughter's name. As a bigeneric hybrid or mule it does not itself set seed and carries the composite generic parental name.

HIERACIUM

Some of the 'hawkweeds' are weedy, but not those below, and although not choice they are very showy.

H. aurantiacum makes a low pad of greenery and has burnt-orange dandelion-type flowers in June-July, on 25 cm stems. Both this and the silver felty-leaved *H. villosum* are easy in any sunny place. The latter has sizeable bright-yellow flowers, 20 cm, for several weeks, and has a compact rootstock. *H. waldsteinii* has larger, downy, silvered leaves which are effective for months on broad rosettes. The 30 cm stems carry small yellow flowers, but its highest value lies in foliage.

x *Heucherella tiarelloides*, a cross between *Heuchera* and *Tiarella*, is a nice golden-green leaved carpeter, with lovely pinkish flowers in May.

Hieracium aurantiacum produces dandelion-type flowers on 25 cm stems in June-July.

HIPPOCREPIS

Holcus mollis 'Variegatus' (also called 'Albo-variegatus') is very good for edging but spreads quickly.

Horminum pyrenaicum is available in both a deep-blue and a pink flowering form. Since they grow only 20 cm high, they can be used anywhere in sunny or partially shaded sites.

Horminum
The only species of this genus, *H. pyrenaicum*, originates from chalky areas of the Pyrenees. However, on soils with a low lime-content it grows just as well. The species seeds itself quite easily. Because the inflorescence is very modest, it is advisable to plant groups, and in combination with other small alpines. The plant flowers in May-July.

HIPPOCREPIS

Hippocrepis comosa is of the 'vetch' tribe and the wild species is too weedy to consider.
There is a garden-worthy form named 'E.R. Jaines' which, though still vigorous with its deep-rooting matted growth, makes a good show of yellow pea flowers May-July. It is prostrate and needs only a sunny place.

HOLCUS

Holcus mollis 'Variegatus' is barely admissible as a grass for edging. It spreads quite quickly but is easily curbed. The blades are about 15 cm, not evergreen.

HORMINUM

Horminum pyrenaicum has rosettes of darkly evergreen leaves and sprays of small, deep-blue flowers on 20 cm stems which are not unattractive. This, and the pink form 'Roseum', are useful and trouble-free as alpines or frontal groups and will divide readily. They grow in sun or part shade.

HOSTA

There is a special value in having plants which have beauty in both flowers and foliage. In this respect, the hostas, or 'plantain lilies', are well-nigh supreme; and it is small wonder that in recent years, when foliage effect has become more fully appreciated, they have come in for unprecedented popularity.
The remarks made about the multiplicity of *hemerocalis* varieties apply equally to *hostas*, and again it is the Americans who are mainly responsible. The number we have tried and still are trying out at Bressingham before deciding on the best, runs into hundreds. It would be confusing to readers even to recommend some of the newer varieties because it takes years sometimes to be sure which are the best. For example, *H. ventricosa* 'Variegata', which I grew for several years before introducing it in 1962, was voted by the American Hosta Society the premier award for quality in 1987 – in competition with hundreds of newer ones.
But for the partiality of some kinds for shade, with soil not lacking in moisture, hostas have all the qualities one looks for: colour hardiness and longevity, with freedom from trouble as well as beauty and charm. Like several other subjects, the

better the treatment given to hostas – as far as food and drink are concerned – the better the results will be; but many will give good value even if this aspect is somewhat neglected.

They have roots that go a long way down in search of moisture and nutriment, and most of them can stand competition without themselves being aggressive. Some have a wide leaf spread, and often I have planted a group of several plants 45-60 cm apart, only to have to thin them out after 3-4 years' growth. As with large clumps of *Hemerocallis*, it is possible to divide them with a sharp spade, but the back-to-back method with forks will force it asunder with less damage to the fleshy crowns from which growth comes. All die back completely in Winter, and leaves unfurl and enlarge in perfect formation ready for the flower spikes which appear from June onwards.
Those with variegated leaves are best in shade and placed away from strong winds as well as strong sun.

Worthy species and varieties
H. 'Thomas Hogg' is one of the best, and it has lavender-mauve flowers on 75 cm stems, not very different from the wavy edged *H. crispula*, which is rather scarce.
H. sieboldiana 'Elegans' has huge leaves of glaucous blue-green, and a spread of about 90 cm where well established, with 90 cm spikes of pale lilac white.
H. glauca is similar but smaller and *H. glauca* 'Coerulea' has rounded, ribbed leaves that come closest to blue of any.
H. fortunei itself is glaucous-green leaved and has mauve-lilac flowers in June-July. Its form *H. fortunei* 'Picta' comes with vernal leaves showing a bright-yellowish flush, from April to June, when on flowering the leaves turn green.
There is a golden variegated-edged form *H. fortunei* 'Aureo marginata' and also a golden foliage form *H. fortunei* 'Aurea', although the leaves turn a light green as Spring turns to Summer.
H. ventricosa flowers very freely, lavender coloured on 90 cm spikes above handsome foliage, and *H. ventricosa* 'Variegata' has similar flowers but rich- green leaves that are so decked with yellow variegation as to make it one of the finest of all variegated hostas.
H. rectifolia 'Tallboy' is green-leaved with a profusion of upstanding purple flower spikes to 120 cm to make an imposing sight in July and August.
The sturdy 'Royal Standard' is late-flowering, green-leaved, white and fragrant. 'Gold Standard' has green edges to its pale gold leaves but is dwarfer at 60 cm. 'Frances Williams' has great appeal with huge mottled foliage and 'Bressingham Blue' is bluish-leaved and white-flowered. 'Krossa Regal' is another favourite in

Hosta sieboldiana varieties can be recognised by their rounded, huge, blue-green crinkled leaves. 'Elegans' is one of the best.

Hosta undulata has brought forth several varieties which are very much alike, for example 'Medio-variegata' and the pictured variety *univittata*.

HOSTA

Hosta ventricosa is one of the most freely flowering species, on 90 cm lavender coloured spikes.

Hosta fortunei 'Aureo-marginata' is a golden-variegated, lilac-flowering variety.

Right: Houttuynia cordata 'Variegata' is a very popular variety with multi-coloured leaves.

Houstonia serpyllifolia (pictured) is very much like H. caerulea, but faster mat-forming.

Hutchinsia alpina is a white-flowering evergreen for a cool position.

sturdy varieties, but there is much to be said for H. clausa 'Normalis', for though green-leaved and only 40 cm, its purple flowers continue for many weeks.

H. undulata 'Medio-variegata' is wavy edged, much smaller in leaf and only 45 cm in flower, but the foliage remains bright throughout the Summer.

H. lancifolia is neat-growing, and its green spear-shaped leaves overlap in perfect mounded formation, with deep-mauve flowers coming on 60 cm stems in August and September.

H. plantaginea is late-flowering, but some find it shy in this respect, having been planted in a shady place along with other hostas. This is a mistake, for although it grows best in shade and moisture, it needs sun and warmth to induce the charming scented white flowers to appear on their 75 cm spikes.

H. plantaginea var. grandiflora is the best one to go for. Another white is the midget H. minor 'Alba' which barely reaches 30 cm high and has green leaves. It flowers in July-August; but another dwarf, the choice H. tardiflora, has mauve-purple flowers in Autumn.

HOUSTONIA

Houstonia caerulea is a dainty little mat-forming plant with a profusion of blue flowers May-June on 8 cm stems. It prefers a little shade and soil not too dry.

HOUTTUYNIA

Houttuynia cordata romps away with creeping roots in moist soil and above the deep-green base leaves come 20 cm sprays of small white flowers. Both this and its double form are best as marginal plants; it is less vigorous where drier.

In recent years a form with multi-coloured leaves has become popular and is neither fussy as to soil, nor too invasive, making brightly coloured mounds from June onwards. All are slow to emerge after Winter and all have odorous leaves if pressed.

HUTCHINSIA

These demure evergreen, cushion-forming plants prefer a cool position. The leaves are dark shiny-green, deeply divided, and the white flowers come as dainty sprays on 8 cm stems.

H. alpina is most often seen, but H. auerswaldii is even more compact at 5 cm. Both flower in May and June and can be divided in early Autumn.

HYLOMECON

Hylomecon japonicum (syn. *H. vernalis*) is a charming, unusual spring-flowering plant for any cool soil or position. The flowers are as open golden poppies 3-6 cm across in April and May, amid pleasantly green foliage, height 12 cm. The fleshy roots are apt to become congested with age but are easily divided and replanted after flowering or in Autumn.

Above: *Hylomecon japonicum* produces bright golden flowers in April-May. A plant for a cool position.

Left: *Hypericum olympicum* 'Grandiflorum' is a hardy alpine, good for use in crevices, with golden yellow flowers from June to August.

Right: *Hypsella reniformis* is a handsome creeper with pinkish-white flowers during Summer.

Hutchinsia

This genus of alpines has only one species, according to the latest scientific nomenclature, *H. alpina* with the subspecies *alpina*, *auerswaldii* and *brevicaulis*. The first two subspecies like lime, the latter does not. Put them in a position in the rock garden where they get protection from the hot midday sun.
Hutchinsia makes a nice combination with, for instance, *Primula*, *Draba* and *Androsace*.

HYPERICUM

This genus includes well-known shrubs and some good alpine plants, but some lack hardiness. The hardiest are those which are excellent for wall tops or in crevices. They include *H. olympicum* — often listed as *H. polyphyllum* (or *H. fragile*). The flowers are bright yellow with prominent stamens, and in *H. olympicum* 'Grandiflorum' they are 2 cm across in golden yellow. All this type have glaucous foliage and woody growth, and the lemon-yellow *H.* 'Citrinum' and *H.* 'Sulphureum' should not be omitted. All flower from June to August, mounding up to 25 cm.

H. coris is of much neater habit, forming little erect bushes of dark green to about 15 cm, producing starry golden flowers for many weeks from June onwards.

Others, less hardy and best in scree in warm districts or in an alpine house where cold, are the creeping *H. reptans* and *H. trichocaulon*, both deep yellow, 5 cm, whilst *H. cerastoides* (syn. *H. rhodoppeum*) is quite hardy with clumpy, upright, glaucous-leaved stems and light-yellow flowers, with the exception of *H. coris*, which will divide. Hypericums are best from summer cuttings under glass, or from seed.

HYPSELLA

Hypsella reniformis (syn. *H. longiflora*) is an easy-to-grow creeping plant making close green growth at ground level and bearing little pinkish-white flowers for several weeks in Summer.
A good paving plant, it also does well in shady crevices.

HYSSOPUS

Above: *Iberis commutatum* is an easy to grow evergreen, best placed hanging over wall tops.

Left: *Incarvillea delavayi* is a real eye-catcher, amongst other perennials, when it flowers in June.

Iberis

There are some 40 species of this genus, including annuals, semi-shrubs and shrubs. Practically all of them originate from the Mediterranean. Plenty of sun is vital, because plants which grow in some shade do not mature completely, and can get frost damage in Winter.
Do not put *Iberis* plants too closely together, because they will extend moderately within a few years.

HYSSOPUS

These are bush-forming, mainly evergreen plants, needing sun and good drainage. Flowers are small, but as plants they are apt to become leggy, needing the shears occasionally.
H. officinalis is the herbal hyssop, to be found in blue, pink and white, but is grown more grown for interest than display. 50 cm high, it flowers June-August.
H. O. ssp. *aristatus* grows neatly as little evergreen bushes with short narrow leaves of deep green. The thin spikes carry violet-blue flowers, 30 cm, June-August.

IBERIS

The hardiest of these are all white-flowered but are outstandingly showy. The general habit is that of low, dense, shrubby, evergreen growth, which is covered in Spring with rounded heads of pure white.
I. sempervirens and *I. commutatum* are evergreen and excellent for a wall top, capable of long life and hanging over with little or no attention needed.
I. 'Snowflake' is more upright though still evergreen and mound forming to 25 cm, with fine white heads from May to July. Both this and *I.* 'Little Gem' are more compact but the latter is more bushy at 15 cm. Division is possible but summer cuttings produce better plants.
I. saxatilis is best in scree or as a trough plant. It is slow-growing and quite prostrate and covers itself in white flowers only 3 cm high.
Increase is only effected by cuttings.

INCARVILLEA

At first sight, the exotic-looking rosy-red trumpets of these seem out of place amongst hardy perennials. They have some resemblance to gloxinias; and since they appear rather suddenly from bare earth before making leaf, they are all the more startling. The roots are in fact fleshy fangs, and though no sign of shoots may be visible at the beginning of May, by the end of the month they are showing bud if not actually in flower.
I. delavayi is the taller of the species available and gradually run up with dark green, deeply-cut leaves, flowering all through June, till they reach 60 cm or so.
I. mairei (syn. *I. grandiflora*), which has the larger trumpets of deep pinkish-red, begins flowering

only just above ground in late May, and when fully grown is no more than 30 cm high. It has a similar fleshy root; and though these plants are both fully hardy, they need well-drained soil to be long lived, and care with cultivating tools during their winter dormancy. Roots are difficult to divide and they can be increased only by seed.

The salmon coloured 'Bee's Pink' is less reliable, and in my experience seedlings revert to *I. mairei*.

INULA

This includes *Buphthalmum* for practical purposes. With the common name of 'fleabane', inulas may have little herbal value nowadays, but there are a few that merit a place for the show of yellow, finely-rayed flowers they produce. All are easy to grow in ordinary soil and all respond to division in Autumn or Spring.

I. orientalis has large flowers 7-10 cm across, delicately rayed for all its lack of height. It grows to 50 cm but lacks a long flowering period, covering 3-4 weeks only in June-July.

I. ensifolia 'Compacta', by comparison, flowers on and on, from late June to September, with 2.5 cm (1 inch) yellow flowers on bushy growth only 25 cm high.

At more than twice the height, up to 60 cm, *I.* 'Golden Beauty' has a similar long period in flower and a bushy habit. The variety 'Dora' is an improvement in vigour and flower size.

I. hookeri is rather floppy and has soft green leaves. On this dense mass of greenery 60-75 cm high comes a long succession of rayed yellow daisies from June onwards. Plants spread quite quickly and may need curbing after 2 years.

I. royleana, in contrast, is not very robust, but has large yellow flowers up to 12 cm across. It needs a warm place, light soil and full sun as do all inulas except the massive *I. magnifica*. This will tolerate some shade and also moisture, but demands space. Even though the roots are compact, it has huge dock-like leaves and strong, branching stems to 200 cm and a long season of large yellow flowers June-September.

IRIS

This genus offers a wealth of variety, but generally the bulbous kinds are difficult to place in with perennials or alpines. This is because they leave a gap after flowering, yet such dwarf bulbous species as *I. reticulata* and *I. danfordiae* remain popular because they are so bright in early Spring.

Above: *Inula ensifolia* will flower from the end of June until September with pretty, yellow, finely-rayed flowers.

Right: *Inula magnifica* will withstand some shade, but needs space as its branching stems with huge, spreading leaves, grow to over 200 cm tall.

Iris laevigata varieties are well worth growing. They like moist places and do very well beside water.

Above: *Iris kaempferi* varieties are rather fussy in their needs, but available in all kinds of shades.

Left: *Iris sibirica* varieties prefer moist soil to flourish.

Iris

Besides the 200 or so true *Iris* species there are many thousands of varieties, and the assortment is expanded continuously all over the world. They are plants which many enthusiasts like because of the shape of the flowers, which remind one of orchids, and because of the enormous variety of available colours. *Iris* is very often used at the water-side, where it can make a beautiful show. However, there are only a few species which like 'wet feet' (*I. pseudacorus* and *I. laevigata* for instance). Most Irises prefer rather dry conditions.

Non-bulbous alpines

There are several non-bulbous kinds suitable as alpines.

I. chamaeiris is also listed as *I. pumila* and as a group they are like miniature bearded or June-flowering iris. They flower in April and May at heights ranging from 15 to 30 cm and are available in several named varieties. Colours range from white to pink, cream, yellow, as well as blue and violet. Whilst their period in flower is rather brief, they can provide colour where their inclusion is not in conflict with purist views of alpine plants.

I. clarkei is a true species with neat erect foliage and bright blue flowers, flecked and spotted in June at 25 cm.

I. cristata needs cool moist conditions to produce its dainty blue flowers at 15 cm, but the form *I. cristata* var. *lacustris* is only half the size.

I. graminea tends to hide its reddish-purple flowers amid grassy foliage. These are scented, height 15 cm.

I. innominata comes in variable colour, apricot-yellow in the type, but in amongst these appear lilac, purple and lavender. This species dislikes lime, as does the somewhat similar *I. tenax* with lavender-blue flowers. Both reach 20 cm in height, flowering May and June.

Seed-raised plants are better than from divisions. Otherwise, all the above can be divided and replanted after flowering, and they associate effectively with primulas, campanulas and mimulus.

A bewildering range

What was said of the bewildering range of *Hemerocallis* varieties applies equally if not more so to iris, especially the *I. germanica* or 'June flowering'. Every conceivable combination of colours, of which blue, white, purple, yellow or brown-red are basic, exists somewhere or other as a named variety. The upstanding portion of the flower, known as the 'standard' and the drooping tongue-like petal known as 'falls', are often of differing colours, and it can only be a matter of choice from seeing them in flower, or as colour illustrations, that one can make a choice on which appeals most to individual taste. A list of recommendations by word only would be quite inadequate to say the least, because some with several colours merging on the same flowers are virtually beyond accurate description within the limits of space such a book as this imposes.

The June-flowering iris needs sun and good drainage but has no liking for rich soil or manure, other than a lime or phosphatic-based fertiliser. Planting is best in July-September; and when dividing for replanting, the centre parts of an old clump should be discarded. The rhizome itself should not be buried, only barely below the surface, while the fibrous root at the base of each fan should be well down and well spread.

I. sibirica grows rushily to 90-120 cm from a plant that becomes quite large in the moist soil it prefers. They flower under various names in blue, white and deep-purple shades, and though flowers are small, they make quite a show in June-July in the right place.

I. kaempferi have large, wide-open flowers up to 12 cm across. These dislike excessive winter wet, excessive summer dryness, and alkalinity of soil, but where they grow well, they are a real joy. Heights are about 60-75 cm, and colours range from snow-white through many shades of blue and purple. These, and the sibiricas, are best divided in Spring.

Variegated-leaved

Some variegated-leaved iris are worth mentioning. *I. pallida* 'Variegata' has blue flowers in June, and a year-round leafage of glaucous grey-green, strongly marked primrose-yellow. These prefer sun, as does the old-fashioned *I. florentina*, but *I. foetidissima* will also grow in deep dry shade. They have rich green leaves, year round, and rather nondescript flowers, but seed capsules reveal bright-orange seeds in Autumn. Its variegated form seldom flowers, but gives one of the brightest displays of foliage of any in Winter as well as Summer, in sun or shade.

Others worth growing

Others worth growing are *I. kerneriana*, soft yellow, 40 cm; *I. laevigata* 'Rose Queen', a 45 cm moisture lover; *I. chrysographes* 'Black Knight', deepest violet, 60 cm and *I. orientalis* 130 cm, which is like a giant *I. pseudo-acorus*, the native waterside species. Nor should we omit the winter flowering *I. stylosa* (syn. *I. unguicularis*). The little hybrid 'Blue Jimmy' makes a show of blue on 30 cm stems and is vigorous and free.

For lovers of iris there are many more species to be found, but most of the June-flowering cultivars may be the epitome of perfection for many gardeners despite their rather brief spell of glory.

JASIONE

Easy and distinctive plants in the somewhat similar species of *J. jankae* and *J. perennis*, they form evergreen rosetted tufts which bear rounded, fluffy blue heads from June to August on 15-20 cm stems.

Any ordinary soil suits these and they can be divided or reared from seed. They are of equal value for a frontal border position or amongst alpines.

Above: The small *Iris chamaeiris* (syn. *I. pumila*) cultivars are at home amongst alpine plants. Shades are pink, yellow, blue, violet, white.

Left: *Iris germanica* 'Wabash' is a beautiful example of this extensive group of hybrids.

Below: *Jasione* species form evergreen rosettes and bear blue flowerheads during Summer.

Below: *Iris pallida* 'Variegata' has variegated leaves year-round, and flowers in June.

JEFFERSONIA

Jeffersonia dubia (also called *Plagiorhegma dubium*) flowers in April/May.

Left: *Kirengeshoma palmata* forms long, arching flower stems with waxy yellow flowers in August/September.

Facing page: *Kniphofia uvaria*. This species flowers from July until October.

Kniphofia
Red hot pokers can best be combined with other plants which like sun and rather poor soil, such as, for instance, *Verbena*, *Yucca*, *Limonium*, *Nepeta*, *Penstemon*, *Pennisetum*, *Potentilla* and *Gypsophila*.

JEFFERSONIA

This is a genus of only two species related to *Epimedium*, for some shade and humus-rich gritty soil. *J. diphylla* has lobed greyish leaves on wiry stems, 20 cm. In Spring come single white flowers. The more attractive is *J. dubia*, also with lobed but glaucous leaves, but the cup-shaped flowers are pure light-blue, 20 cm.

KIRENGESHOMA

These uniquely beautiful plants are for good deep soil, not limy, and are partial to some shade if not dry. The arching stems carry broad leaves to produce 90 cm sprays of yellow, waxy flowers in the species *K. palmata*. These tend to dangle open-ended and tubular, but in one variation they are held more erectly. Where suited, the plant becomes quite large, but can be divided with two forks.

The species *K. koreana* has more upright stems, and primrose-yellow flowers are held candelabra fashion at 100 cm, but are not so leafy as *K. palmata*. Both flower June-September, but keep greenery until late Autumn.

KNIPHOFIA

No collection of perennials is completely satisfying if 'red hot pokers' are omitted, but not all pokers are red. Nor are all of them tall and stately above lots of rushy foliage. Some grow to only 30 cm or so, with grassy leaves and a profusion of small spikes. They range in colour from near-white through every shade of yellow to orange, on to fiery red. A few are close to 200 cm tall and the flowering period, taking the whole range, begins in late May and ends in October. But the one thing they have in common, though some are only 45 cm high and others a massive 180 cm, is the need for good drainage. Their roots penetrate to a great depth to find all they need even in poor soil: and indeed, I have known plants to be killed by kindness by applying manure or compost in the hope of feeding them well.

They also prefer to be left alone for several years at a stretch; and if planting or dividing, one must be careful to avoid roots becoming dry through exposure, and to make a good deep hole so they do not lie bent or bunched after insertion.

Spring is much the best time for moving kniphofias, but it is safe enough for any that have flowered to plant in August or September. For large old plants, the back-to-back method, using two forks is best, trying as best one can to avoid damage

KNIPHOFIA

Kniphofia 'Little Maid'

Lamium maculatum 'Beacon Silver'.

to the fleshy parts between leaf and root. In some very cold districts or where soil becomes sticky in Winter, a collar of litter around plants after tying up the leaves is good practice. The effect of the former is to keep the soil and roots from freezing and the latter a precaution against slush and damp entering the crowns which might freeze or set up a rotting process.

Having an overall stately appearance, the taller-growing kinds especially are best in some isolation, using a very much dwarfer subject if need be in front so as not to detract.

Not many true species are in circulation, but hybrids abound, and seed-raised mixtures are also offered. In this context it is advisable to list some of the best, whether species or cultivars, on a seasonal basis, beginning with the earliest to flower.

In late May, the first stumpy spikes of the hardy and robust K. 'Atlanta' appear. This is yellow, red-tipped, but K. preacox 'Primaline' is more red overall. Both grow to about 120 cm. The old 'Gold Else' is June-flowering at 70 cm, followed by the dainty lemon-yellow 'Candlelight' 80 cm. 'Fiery Fred' and 'Firefly' are much alike at 90 cm. 'Ada' is orange yellow, 110 cm, but 'Percy's Pride' is canary yellow at 130 cm, whilst 'Green Ice' is ivory, tinged green, 150 cm. These flower at the peak period, July-August, and by no means cover all in cultivation. They are followed by both the tall fiery reds such as 'Samuel's Sensation' and 'Mount Etna' ('The Rocket') and some most attractive dwarfs. The ivory-primrose 'Little Maid' at 40 cm

Lamium galeobdolon (syn. Lamiastrum galeobdolon) is a rapid spreader that will suppress other plants easily.

is outstanding, as is 'Bressingham Comet' at 50 cm, for its red-gold spikes, and 'Bressingham Beacon' of similar height, fiery red. These and the late but tender K. galpinii, deep orange, 35 cm, have grassy foliage.

In contrast, the autumn-flowering K. caulescens has broad glaucous leaves and stumpy spikes of red-tipped yellow. This is hardier than the latest to flower K. rooperi, sometimes listed as 'C.M. Prichard', having 180 cm orange spikes in October.

K. glauca is a clump-forming evergreen grass of greyish-blue hue. It flowers freely, buff-grey on 50 cm stems.

LAMIASTRUM – see LAMIUM

LAMIUM

The 'dead nettle' tribe includes some good ground-cover plants for mainly shady places. These come under L. maculatum and (Lamiastrum) galeobdolon, but the latter is such a spreader that it will take over.

L. maculatum has a silvery blotch to the leaves and pink flowers in Spring. There is also a white, but the best and least rampant form is 'Beacon Silver'. 'Beedhams White' has golden foliage, also slower growing than straight L. maculatum.

L. garganicum is of clumpy growth with pure pink flowers rising above its dense foliage to 15 cm, May-July. L. orvala is quite distinct with deep roots and upright compact growth and spikes of ruby pink, 35 cm, May-June. This too has a white form 'Alba'. All have dead nettle type leaves.

Right: *Lathyrus vernus* flowers in May-June. It is a non-climbing species.

Left: *Lasiogrostis splendens* is a tall grass with pleasing plumes of flowers.

LASIOGROSTIS

Lasiogrostis splendens (syn *Stipa splendens*) and its forms are fairly tall grasses of clump-forming habit. The brownish plumes of flowers reach 130 cm or so in Summer above fairly narrow blades on slender stems, giving pleasing autumn colour.

LATHYRUS

The everlasting (perennial) sweet pea is *L. latifolius*. Being a climber with annually renewed growth, it needs to be specially catered for, but will come from seed. Only white is seen, the best being 'White Pearl', but another perennial climber is *L. grandiflorus* and this has magenta-pink flowers. *L. vernus* makes a good show in Spring, the flowers covering a deep-green-leaved mound up to 35 cm. Roots form a tough and tangled clump and both pink and purple-blue are seen in such cultivars as 'Spring Charm' and 'Spring Delight'. *L. aureus* has a similar densely-mounded habit to *L. vernus,* with deep-orange flowers in clusters, 40 cm, May-June. These non-climbing species are increased from seed or by division.

Lavandula angustifolia varieties, the ever popular lavender, may differ in colour and size, but all are scented.

Lavandula

Lavandula angustifolia with its many varieties is, in fact, the only species of the more than 25 of this genus which is used in gardens. The species is a native of the Mediterranean. If you want to grow lavender in the border, a combination with grasses, such as *Festuca*, and with, for instance, *Echinops*, *Santolina*, *Verbascum* and *Eryngium* is very attractive.

LAVANDULA

Little need be said about these low shrubby grey-leaved plants, well-known as they are and well-loved for edging a path for their scent. A group in which perennials near the edge of a bed is not out of place, but a dwarf variety, such a L. 'Munstead Dwarf', should be chosen and given an annual shearing to keep it neat and leafy.

LAVATERA

Lavatera olbia. Although decidedly shrubby, this tree mallow can fit in with herbaceous perennials because it is best cut back in Spring. Left to itself it will grow to 200 cm, with non-stop flowering from May to September. After 3-4 years, loss of

LAVATERA

vigour must be expected, but it can be renewed
by late summer pull-off cuttings. Full sun and light,
or even poor, soil is preferred to rich and moist
conditions.
L. olbia is bright pink but there is an attractive pale
pink in *L.* 'Barnsley'.
L. cachemiriana is also worthy with clear-pink
flowers on more slender stems, but with a shorter
flowering period in Summer.

LEONTOPODIUM

Leontopodium alpinum is 'edelweiss', having a
charm of its own with silvery leaves and 12 cm
stems carrying curious flowers, whitish and
flannely. It needs sun and good drainage, but
though not specially long- lived, will come readily
from seed.
A more perennial species, but smaller flowered, is
L. crassense at 10 cm, whilst *L. aloysiodorum* is taller
at 25 cm and has lemon-scented foliage as well
as being reliably perennial. All flower in early
Summer.

LEUCANTHEMUM – see
Chrysanthemum species

* LEUCOJUM

The 'Summer snowflake' (*L. aestivum*) is a bulbous
plant, with white flowers in May-June on 40 cm

Top right: *Leontopodium
alpinum*, 'edelweiss', is the
alpine plant for most people.

Top left: *Lavatera olbia*
varieties are all pink-flowered.

Leucojum aestivum is the
bulbous, white-flowering
'Summer Snowflake'.

stems. *L. vernum* is a little taller and flowers in
March-April. Other *Leucojum* species (like *L.
autumnale* and *L. roseum*) are not hardy enough for
our climate. *Leucojum* loves moist soil and stands
some shade. It is good in combination with e.g.
Primula Elatior hybrids and other primulas.

Lewisia cotyledon varieties all make flat rosettes. They prefer to be planted on fairly steep slopes.

LEWISIA

These are some of the most spectacular alpines, but need special treatment for success. For one thing they do not like to be planted on the flat and should be in crevices of rock or peat blocks or on a fairly acute slope. They also need a humus-rich, gritty soil, but they are generally hardy even if they also dislike winter wet or slush. This applies to those with evergreen rosettes, which makes them good alpine house subjects. They have mostly fleshy roots and are increased by seed.

L. *columbiana* is fairly tall, flowering at 25 cm in Spring with loose panicles of pale-pink flowers, deeper in the form 'Rosea'.

L. *cotyledon* is almost a group of variations under different names, but L. *cotyledon* hybrids are very showy in shades of salmon-pink, yellow and white. Loosely clustered 20 cm heads of flowers from broad-leaved evergreen rosettes are a sight to behold in May, June and sometimes later.

L. *rediviva* is deciduous from a short thick root. Large flowers of pink or white come on 12 cm stems in Spring. At least a dozen more species and cultivars are available.

LIATRIS

'Gay feather' is a good name for this showy plant. Though easy to grow in any well-drained soil, it has a fleshy root with no deep penetration and responds to being divided or replanted every 3-4 years because of its tendency to grow out of the ground.

Above: *Liatris spicata* is unusual amongst spike-forming perennials, in the way that it flowers from the top downwards.

Liatris scariosa 'Alba' is a white-flowering variety of this tall species (up to 150 cm) with rather ponderous flowering spikes.

Liatris
These prairie plants from North America, of which 16 species exist, are attractive to bees. The beautiful flowers are also excellent for cutting. *Liatris* combines nicely with, for instance, *Coreopsis, Panicum, Solidago* and *Echinacea.* Beware of voles, they love the rhizomes of *Liatris.*

Deep-green narrow leaves furnish both the plant and the stems which rise up to 90 cm and, by late June, the fluffy little flowers close to the stem open first at the top. This is the opposite to most spike-forming plants, but as flowering proceeds downwards, fading does not seriously detract from what is a quite striking appearance. Cutting back when faded often induces further spikes to flower into August and September, but division is best in Spring.

Though several species exist, L. *callilepis* has been found to be the most reliable of these.

L. *spicata* and L. *pychnostachya* are on similar lines.

L. 'Floristan White' is a more recent introduction growing to 60 cm, and like the others, has compact tuberous roots.

Libertia formosa is the most hardy Libertia species. It forms white flower clusters above dark green leaves.

LIBERTIA

Most of these evergreen rushy-leaved plants are on the borderline of hardiness, but in most localities make a pleasing display in early Summer. They are clump forming, and easy to divide.

L. formosa has dark green narrow blades up to 60 cm. The open white flowers cluster on stems 20 cm above, with yellow stamens. It is the hardiest of those in cultivation.

L. ixioides is somewhat similar, but only 60 cm in flower.

L. peregrinans is also white flowered with somewhat golden foliage, but this needs a warm spot and all are best in light soil and sun.

Ligularia clivorum forms a clump with large-leaved stems. The orange flowers during Summer are very attractive. All Ligularias like moist soil.

LIGULARIA

These handsome plants have been known before as Senecio (q.v.) and one cannot be sure which plants correctly remain under the old name.

In general they like moist soil but are not averse to some shade. Hot sun causes the lush foliage to droop, but turgidity returns quickly without having to water them.

L. clivorum (syn. L. dentata) makes a hefty clump with large rounded leaves and erect branching stems carrying orange flowers in Summer.

The cultivar 'Desdemona' is especially handsome, having purplish foliage and rich orange flowers to 150 cm or more where moist. The green-leaved 'Gregnog Gold' is more compact at 120 cm, but x 'Hessei' is quite massive. All flower July-August.

L. hodgsonii is on similar lines but shorter at 80 cm and the orange flowers open in June.

L. macrophylla is stately at 180 cm with large dock-like leaves, flowering in August.

L. przewalskii is distinct from the above, having slender blackish stems, deeply jagged leaves and 200 cm spikes of small yellow flowers. 'The Rocket' is an attractive variation of similar height – a very imposing plant, compact but sturdy.

L. stenocephala has rounded leaves and strong stems to 180 cm carrying yellow flowers, but is outshone by 'Sungold'. This is splendid with ample greenery up to the 180 cm stems, carrying a wealth of golden-yellow flowers from June to August.

None of the above needs supporting and, though plants will become large, they respond to division with forks.

Below: Ligularia stenocephala 'The Rocket' is another fine variety of this species.

LILIUM

The Lilies are virtually in a class by themselves and, largely because of their special requirements, are not readily adaptable to grow in with a collection of perennials. Some are reasonably so, and the majority prefer sun or only partial shade. Some like dampish soil, but all need good drainage, humus-rich soil, not deficient in phosphates and potash. I have to admit that my own experience with Lilies is limited but of the 20 or more kinds I have grown, some have been rather troublesome, needing frequent replanting with added sand.

The most reliable species have been *L. martagon*, *L. tigrinum*, *L. henryi*, *L. croceum*, *L. regale*, *L. pyrenaicum*, *L. pardalinum*, *L. testaceum* and a few hybrids. The old madonna lily, *L. candidum*, has the fault of withering leaves at flowering time. There is an enticing variety of both species and hybrids for lily lovers and I can but advise some further advance study for those wishing to go in for them.

Above: *Lilium* midcentury-hybrids have upward-facing trumpets and are available in a variety of colours.

Left: The Oriental hybrid lily 'Stargazer' is rather short (50 cm) and is very good for foreground planting.

Right: *Lilium candidum* is the old, but splendidly flowering 'Madonna lily'.

Limonium latifolium 'Blue Cloud' displays myriads of tiny blue flowers in Summer.

Linaria
This genus, with about 100 species from the subtropical areas of the northern hemisphere, is clearly related to *Antirrhinum*. Most species are annuals and biennials, others must be cultivated annually because they are not winter-hardy at all.
Enthusiasts who like special kinds such as *L. triornithiflora* (a perennial from Spain and Portugal, and one of the most beautiful species: 130 cm with large purple flowers) grow them as annuals.

Linaria dalmatica flowers from June to September with yellow snapdragon-like flowers.

Below: *Lindelofia spectabilis* will show its gentian-blue flowers both in sun and part shade.

LIMONIUM

The 'sea lavenders', so-called, are used much for cutting and drying as everlastings, but they also have garden worthiness given sun and good drainage.
L. incanum (syn. *L. dumosum*) sends up wide heads of small, crispy, pink flowers covering the greyish rosette forming plants in later Summer, only 40 cm high.
L. latifolium is taller at 80 cm above large green leaves with wiry branching stems and myriads of tiny deep-blue flowers, best in 'Violetta' or 'Blue Cloud'. They can be increased by root cuttings or seed. Seed is also best for the alpine species. These are not exciting, but are of some appeal having rosetted tufts in the case of *L. cosyrense* and *L. bellidifolium*, with 15 cm sprays of deep violet-blue flowers in Summer.

See also their close relatives, listed under *Goniolimon*

LINARIA

Easy to grow, but rather short-lived, they come readily from seed — often self sown.
L. alpina, though pretty, is short lived but comes easily from seed. Others including *L. aequitriloba* and *L. origanifolia* are tiny, but in the moist soil they prefer, are liable to spread below ground far and wide.
L. dalmatica has glaucous foliage on branching stems up to 100 cm, carrying small yellow snapdragon-type flowers from June to September.
L. purpurea and its pink form 'Canon Went' have more upright growth with wiry 80 cm stems and narrow blue-green leaves. Flowers are small but abundant over a long period. All are longer-lived in poor stony soil, and are best in sun.
See also Cymbalaria. The tiny *L. aequitriloba* is weedy, and the pretty *L. alpina*, with purple flowers is very short lived.

LINDELOFIA

L. spectabilis (syn. *L. longiflora*) has small gentian-blue flowers on 35 cm branching stems. It is somewhat like a smaller edition of *Cynoglossum nervosum* and flowers for several weeks from June onwards and is an easy-to-grow plant in sun or part shade.

LINUM

The perennial flax are brightly coloured, some being blue and others yellow with one or two white-flowered. All are essentially sun lovers for very well-drained soil.

L. arboreum is of low shrubby growth 20 cm high with a display of bright yellow flowers.

L. 'Gemmells Hybrid' is more compact and freer to flower, but both are liable to be damaged by severe frosts.

L. flavum is fully hardy, green-leaved and non shrubby. It is yellow-floweredbut heights may vary from 35-40 cm when raised from seed. These yellows flower from May to August along with others akin to them such as *L. campanulatum.*

White is the colour of the pretty *L. salsoloides,* now correctly under *L. suffruticosum.* This grows to 25 cm but *L. nanum* or *L. prostratum* hug the soil, with wide open flowers.

L. monogynum has a fine show of white flowers on 30 cm stems but is not fully hardy.

Most of the blue flax are fully hardy but none in my experience is long-lived and this applies especially to *L. perenne.*

L. narbonense is a much finer one and taller at 60 cm with azure-blue flowers June-September.

The blue kinds which include *L. austriacum* need to be raised from seed. All have narrow leaves and upright or bushy growth and flower June-September.

Linum narbonense is a hardy perennial, producing beautiful blue flowers.

LIRIOPE

Liriope muscari is a dwarf plant of outstanding merit. It has evergreen grassy foliage forming substantial clumpy growth and in late Summer throws up 30 cm spikes clustered with bright, lilac-purple, bead-like flowers. In any reasonably good soil in sun or part shade, the flowers will still be colourful in late October. It is drought-resistant and has tangled but not fangy roots which makes division with forks not difficult, though plants can be safely left alone for many years. It fits in well as a frontal group, makes an excellent edging, and can be used amongst deciduous shrubs as ground cover.

As a rather unlikely member of the lily family, it is of greater value and more adaptable for temperate climes than other kinds. One of these, *L. spicata,* is a spreader, only 15 cm high with less conspicuous flowers, though good as evergreen ground cover.

L. 'Majestic' is very shy to flower except where hot summers prevail. In such climates the variegated forms flourish effectively but are likely to languish in northern European winters.

All are evergreen where happy.

Liriope muscari flowers from late Summer until well into October.

Lithophragma

Lithophragma parviflora is a new name for *Tellima parviflora,* a real enthusiasts' plant for moist soil with a *Tiarella*-like inflorescence on up to 35 cm high stems. The flowers, white or pink, appear in May-June. The plant loves shade so that it combines perfectly with shrubs. The kidney shaped foliage grows from a rhizome which can easily be divided for propagation.

LITHOSPERMUM

'Heavenly Blue' is one of the best intense-blue flowering varieties of Lithospermum (now called Lithodora diffusa 'Heavenly Blue').

Lobelia cardinalis is beautiful, but not hardy in our climate. Hybrids are more reliable.

LITHOSPERMUM

This generic name has now been discarded in favour of Lithodora, whilst others have been placed under Moltkia.

The much-loved L. 'Heavenly Blue' and 'Grace Ward' are lime haters but the display of intense blue flowers on dark green prostrate growth is somewhat irresistible to all gardeners, flowering as they do for weeks from May onwards. Very few other species exist reliably, but L. oleifolium is grey-leaved with light-blue flowers in Summer, 15 cm, and has roots inclined to wander where suited. See also Moltkia.

LOBELIA

The perennial kinds are totally distinct from blues used for summer bedding. They are much taller; and, indeed, one old variety, the red 'Queen Victoria', is itself used for bedding. There are several more modern hybrids which, though hardy, are not easy to keep over Winter where there is unreliable snow cover.

L. cardinalis itself is hardy where native in N. America, but not in Britain. It is green-leaved and has spikes of brilliant-scarlet flowers.

L. fulgens exists now mainly as hybrids with some fulgens blood. Many have colourful purplish leaves and grow well in mainly sunny positions, not too exposed, dry and starved.

Hybrids have been bred using L. siphilitica as well as L. cardinalis and L. fulgens. Of these, 'Bee's Flame', with beetroot-red leaves and blood-red flowers, has stood the test of time.

'Dark Crusader' is also a strong-growing, deep-purple red, but I have not succeeded in keeping 'Will Scarlet' and 'Cherry Ripe'.

An older hybrid L. x vedrariensis is distinct and reliable, with spikes to 120 cm and purple-violet flowers.

These lobelias contrast well with the yellow ligularias for both colour and the need for similar moistish soil. I find the best means of over-wintering them is to cover with a few inches of litter from November till danger of frozen wet soil is over. By late April or May, new rosettes will fall apart for replanting. They can also be raised from seed, as the old 'Queen Victoria' is, as a more-or-less annual bedder.

L. siphilitica is green-leaved, blue-flowered, at 60 cm, and though hardy is rather short-lived — about 3 years.

L. tupa is very distinct and rarely seen. Its tap roots produce long green leaves and spikes up to 160 cm of browny-red flowers, given good moist soil.

LUETKEA

Luetkea pectinata. This creeper is evergreen, of somewhat mossy rosetted form. The creamy-white flowers on 10 cm stems come in Summer and it gives interesting ground cover in part shade and low pH soil.

LUNARIA

Lunaria rediviva. It is not widely known that this is a fully perennial 'honesty'. It makes a fine show in Spring with masses of lilac-white flowers on stout 100 cm stems in any soil, sun or part shade. It has deep fleshy roots and is long-lived. In my garden its only fault is that it self-seeds rather lavishly.

LUPINUS

Virtually all lupins nowadays originate from the Russell strain. They are so easy from seed that many people prefer this cheaper method, whether they sow their own or buy seeding plants. One should bear in mind, however, that from seed there are reversionary tendencies; and to obtain the best spikes and colours seed must be carefully selected.

Mixed colours, are of course, inevitable from seed; and named varieties to colour are more expensive because they can only be increased from basal cuttings in early Spring. One is no longer able to procure named varieties produced from cuttings, due mainly to virus disease, but hybridists have come out with variations from seed which are fairly true to colour. These are fast-growing and flower the first year if sown in Spring, but are unlikely to survive more than 3 years.

Lupins are not so happy on limy soils as in acid or neutral.

They dislike humus-rich soils too, and should not receive compost or manure, and if they cannot be regarded as long-lived perennials, they are at least adaptable for open as well as shady conditions and town gardens.

LUZULA

These are evergreen grasses with a compact habit, able to flourish in quite shady places. They are especially useful as ground cover under or near trees.

L. nivea makes tufts of broad arching blades, 15 cm long, of deep shiny green, with wiry 30 cm stems carrying heads of near-white flowers in Summer.

L. sylvatica (syn. L. maxima) has narrower leaves and taller 40 cm clustered heads of brownish flowers.

Lupinus Russell-hybrids are available in a wide range of colours.

Luzula sylvatica is a hardy, evergreen grass, with brownish flowerheads.

LYCHNIS

Above: *Lychnis coronaria* is a silvery-leaved evergreen, not very long-lived, but nicely flowering.

Left: *Lychnis chalcedonica* can be over 100 cm tall, flowering bright scarlet-red in June-July.

Lysichiton camtschatcensis (here, together with *Primula rosea*) has scented white flowers.

Lycoris

A special bulbous plant for enthusiasts is *Lycoris squamigera*. If the Summer is sufficiently warm, this plant from Japan grows excellently in our climate. Within a few years large colonies may be formed which early in the year show their daffodil-like foliage. This however dies down towards the end of June, whereas in August the Nerine-like flowers appear. A thick Winter coverage is essential.

LYCHNIS

These very showy, summer-flowering plants include a few dual-purpose kinds. The tallest is *L. chalcedonica* which has clustered upfacing heads of bright scarlet-red above leafy 100 cm stems. Its double form 'Plena' is equally bright and strong in the good soil they prefer, and a sunny position. *L. coronaria* has soft silvery leaves, is tufty of form, and evergreen; but though freely seeding, it is not a long-lived species. The type is vivid cerise and, apart from a pure white, one form 'Oculata' has a pink centre. The most reliably perennial is the bright-pink 'Abbotswood' which may be increased by division.

L. flos-jovis is of tufty habit with grey felty leaves. From June to August, erect 35 cm stems carry clear-pink flowers, best in 'Hort's Variety'.

L. x haageana is green-leaved with heads of mostly bright orange-red flowers of similar height, but quickly flowers itself to death.

Another and better hybrid is *L. x arkwrightii*, and though this too is short-lived, its heads of vermilion-scarlet flowers above purplish foliage is startling.

L. viscaria is included here but it has now been given generic status. This makes a pad of green bladed foliage and in early Summer has 30 cm stems of white or cerise-pink flowers. Much the best form is *L. viscaria* 'Splendens plena', having flowers of bright carmine-rose, much like double dianthus.

The dwarfest are not reliably long lived as alpines. *L. alpina* in purple, pink and white, 10 cm, has a brief life. It is now assigned to *Viscaria*, but *L. lagascae* comes strictly under *Petrocoptis*. It is pretty enough with a long season of clear-pink flowers 10 cm high, but is short-lived. Both these dwarfs can only be increased from seed.

LYSICHITON

The two species are bog plants belonging to the Arum family. They are slow to establish; but, with their deep roots able to take up water, they develop huge glossy leaves.

The best known is *L. americanus* which makes a startling display in Spring of bright-yellow spathes up to 130 cm and taking up more than a metre space.

L. camtschatcensis is less robust and shorter at 100 cm, also in Spring, but with perfumed white flowers.

Both like to be left alone when suited, and increase from seed is a slow process.

LYSIMACHIA

The yellow 'loosestrifes' are useful, long-flowering perennials, easy to grow except where very dry, and in moist rich soil two species are somewhat invasive.

One of these is *L. ciliata* which needs forking around annually to check its spread. It is, however, a pretty but seldom-seen plant with its profusion of small yellow flowers on upright 120 cm leafy stems, June-September.

L. clethroides has white flowers on obtuse terminal spikes 100 cm high in late Summer. It has a steady below-ground spread but no real faults, given reasonable soil in sun or part shade.

L. ephemerum grows compactly with tufty, broad basal leaves and fine spikes to 110 cm of pure-white flowers. This is best in sun and increased by seed rather than division.

L. punctata is a moisture lover but will grow well enough in ordinary soil in sun or part shade. Where moist, it will spread in a widening mat, not difficult to curb or divide. The open yellow flowers, on 100 cm stems, are in whorls and shine brightly for several weeks from June onwards.

Very few species are worth considering as alpines. *L. henryi* or *L. pseudo-henryi* have trailing stems, upturning to a head of yellow flowers.

L. japonica 'Minutissima' makes a close green carpet studded with starry yellow flowers, given a moist shady position.

Summer flowering, and needing frequent replanting, *L. nummularia* is the old 'creeping Jenny' for shady places not too dry. Yellow flowers in prostrate greenery, the golden leaved 'Aurea' is ever popular — but more for hanging baskets than as an alpine, hardy though it is.

Above: *Lysimachia clethroides* has tall white spikes in late Summer.

Right: *Lysimachia punctata* is mat-forming where moist.

Below: *Lythrum salicaria* 'Firecandle'.

LYTHRUM

These are the 'purple loosestrifes', and are amongst the most adaptable of plants for all their association in nature with waterside situations. Any reasonable soil suits them, and their spikes of pink to rosy magenta continue for many weeks in later Summer. The roots are tough and woody and will not divide until plants become quite old. In any case, they can be left to take care of themselves for years, and form erect, twiggy bushes.

Varieties of *L. salicaria* are quite leafy, with profuse but small spikes of intense rose-red in the variety *L.* 'Firecandle'.

L. 'The Beacon' is a little less deep in colour, and both form bushes 90 cm tall, flowering from June to late August.

L. 'Robert' grows only 60 cm with spikes of bright pink.

L. virgatum has less foliage and more slender spikes and flowers a little later, of which *L.* 'Rose Queen' is a favourite pink variety, 45-60 cm high.

MACLEAYA

MACLEAYA (syn. BOCCONIA)

Both species have beautiful foliage all the way up their tall spikes — too attractive to be hidden, even if they need to be in rear or central positions. Their spikes run to 200 cm or so needing no support.
M. cordata itself is rarely seen, but the slightly different 'Flamingo' should be available. The little tubular ivory-white flowers have a hint of pink and come as short branches above.
Roots are somewhat fleshy and will sprout new shoots from eyes to spread modestly.
M. microcarpa has a similar habit but spreads more widely. The spikes, also 200 cm or more, end in tiny brownish flowers, most effective in 'Coral Plume'. Both do best in light soil, in sun or partial shade, flowering July-September.

MALVA

These 'mallows' are easy to grow even in poor soil, given a sunny place, but they tend to flower themselves to death, the remedy for which is often self-sown seedlings.
M. alcea grows strongly to 120 cm, the spikes giving a long display of saucer-shaped, clear-pink flowers. The form 'Fastigiata' is more shapely.
M. moschata is the 'musk mallow', of mounded leafy growth to 60-70 cm. Quite large open flowers continue for many weeks in pink or white.

MARGYRICARPUS

Margyricarpus setosus (syn. M. pinnatus) is a dwarf spreading evergreen inclined to shrubbiness. It has needle-like greenery and inconspicuous flowers, which produce the attraction of pearl-white berries given full sun and good drainage. Height is 10 cm, and increase is from seed.

Above: The pearl-white berries of Margyricarpus setosus.

Left: Macleaya microcarpa spreads profusely and may become a nuisance, but is too beautiful to be ignored.

Right: Malva moschata will flower from July to September.

146

MARRUBIUM

The few species in cultivation are mainly for evergreen foliage effect, but only for mild sunny climes. The species M. candidissimum has soft silvery foliage mounding to 15 cm.
M. velutinum is somewhat similar with a hint of gold in the hairy green leaves.

MATRICARIA – see under Pyrethrum

MATTEUCCIA

Matteuccia struthiopteris is an ugly name for the very elegant 'Prince-of-Wales feather fern'. In almost any shady place, not bone dry, its majestic plumes attain up to 100 cm. The large central crowns will send out ranging shoots below ground to make a broad colony, and care is needed to prevent them from emerging in other plantings. It is not evergreen but remains a firm favourite.

* MATTHIOLA

Matthiola fruticulosa is one of the few perennials within this genus of merely annuals and biennials. It grows 10-15 cm high, spreading beneath the soil surface. The flowers are a dull purple but with M. fruticulosa ssp. vallesiaca they are nearer red. Flowering time: April-May; increase by seed or division.

MAZUS

These are mat-forming alpines with a fair spread below the surface.
M. pumilio has stemless blue and white flowers in early Summer — like a tiny Mimulus.
M. reptans (syn. M. rugosus) has purple-blue flowers 5 cm above toothed green leaves, May-June, and is liable to spread quite quickly.
Both are easy in ordinary well-drained soil and sun.

MECONOPSIS

This genus includes some species of surpassing beauty which are not easy to grow in some gardens. Most of them prefer some shade but not from low overhanging trees. Nor are they happy in windy situations. They all prefer a light or well-drained humus-rich soil, neither wet nor dry.
M. betonicifolia (syn. M. baileyi) is the best known

Marrubium velutinum does well in a sheltered sunny position. Its main features are the colourful hairy, evergreen leaves.

Centre: Matteuccia struthiopteris, the 'Prince-of-Wales' feather fern.

Matteuccia
This genus comprises only 3 species: M. orientalis, M. pensylvanica and M. struthiopteris. The latter two are very similar, but the native M. struthiopteris is light green, whereas M. pensylvanica (up to 2 m tall) is dark green. M. orientalis is also dark green, but stays flatter and develops a flat funnel of leaves. The foliage can reach a length of 1 m. All three have beautiful Autumn colours.

Mazus reptans is a rapid spreader, with purple-blue flowers in May-June.

Meconopsis betonicifolia is not a vigorous perennial, and is generally raised from seed.

MECONOPSIS

Meconopsis cambrica is available in yellow single and orange double flowering forms. They are known for their self-seeding qualities.

Melissa officinalis, 'lemon balm', has little ornamental value apart from scented leaves. The golden-leaved form is better.

Melittis melissophyllum is crowded with pinkish-white flowers in May-June.

of the blue poppies with its yellow-centred, ethereal-blue, open flowers in June-July on 100 cm stems with hairy leaves. Plants are usually seed-raised for they lack full perennial vigour.

M. cambrica is the easiest to grow with yellow poppies on 40 cm stems. It has the fault of seeding around and is best kept where this does not matter. A double orange exists which, unlike most doubles, sets some seed, but not so as to be a nuisance.

M. chelidonifolia is reliably perennial, having a dividable base. The slender leafy stems rise to about 100 cm, carrying light-yellow cups, June-August; a distinctive plant.

M. grandis is a reasonably good perennial which has yielded some variations, but none truly blue even if blue predominates in the wide-open flowers on 100-130 cm stems. Variations include a white and a purplish-blue, and one of the best of the named cultivars is 'Branklyn'.

M. quintuplinervia is quite dwarf at 45 cm and the tufty plants will spread given the right conditions. The blue poppy flowers nod on slender stems in May-June and sometimes later also.

M. x sheldonii is a hybrid of which named cultivars exist. Blue is generally more pronounced and flowers are large on 120-140 cm stems. They are more perennial than M. betonicifolia, and as with others of its class, they flourish best in northern and western regions. Division in Spring is best as seeding is unreliable.

M. villosa is perennial but not reliably so in all districts. It has attractive lobed leaves and nodding clear-yellow flowers on 60 cm stems. It comes easily from seed. Several other species exist but most of them are monocarpic and one, M. regia, is superb for 2-3 years for its wonderful foliage. When it flowers, it dies.

MELANDRIUM – see SILENE

MELISSA

Melissa officinalis is the aromatic 'lemon balm' which is somewhat weedy and lacking in colour. The golden-leaved form 'All Gold' is colourful, making 80 cm bushy growth, but loses colour with flowering. The tiny flowers are not worth keeping; and if cut hard back, base leaves remain golden.

MELITTIS

Melittis melissophyllum is a first-rate plant for a shady spot — even in with shrubs. The deeply penetrating rootstock is compact and long-lived, sending up 50 cm stems crowded with pinkish-white flowers in May-June, the whole plant leafy and too attractive to be overlooked. A pure white form exists.

MENTHA

The taller 'mints' are untidy spreaders and M. *requienii*, the only species to be recommended, is of filmy habit, for crevices and paving. Minute bluish flowers sit on tiny leaves, smelling strongly of mint. It likes dampish soil and usually survives winter frosts.

MERTENSIA

Blue predominates in these and most of them have small bell-shaped flowers. They are not difficult in well-drained soil and may be increased from seed or division.

M. *asiatica* has come to the fore in recent years for its unusual blue-grey foliage. The pure-blue flowers come on prostrate or drooping leafy stems for several weeks, May-August, dying back to a fangy root in Winter.

M. *ciliata* has glaucous foliage and pinkish buds which open to deep-blue flowers June-August, 50 cm. Roots are fleshy and brittle.

M. *coventryana* has dark-green leaves and is mat-forming with shallow roots. Its violet-blue flowers come on 8 cm stems in Spring, as do the sky-blue flowers of M. *echioides* and M. *primuloides*. These two are very similar, mat-forming but not evergreen, both about 10 cm in Spring.

M. *paniculata* is like M. *ciliata* but taller at 70 cm.

M. *virginica* is entrancing. From fleshy brittle roots purplish shoots run up to 50 cm to dangle on arching glaucous-leaved sprays of richest blue bell-shaped flowers. This is a plant to treasure in a sheltered shady place.

MEUM

Meum athamanticum makes a dense mass of filigree aromatic foliage, topped by broad heads of tiny white flowers 60 cm high. It is a deep-rooting, long-lived plant, ideal for a frontal position, and deserves to be more widely grown.

MICROMERIA

These are very dwarf and somewhat shrubby plants, all having aromatic foliage and are best grown in light soil and full sun.

M. *corsica* makes tight silvery hummocks 5 cm high, set with tiny bright-pink flowers for many weeks.

M. *illyrica* has dark-green foliage and blue flowers in later Summer, 15 cm.

M. *piperella* is also highly aromatic. Its stiff 8 cm bushlets are a little thorny and grey, with flowers reddish-purple.

Plants can be divided in Spring.

Mentha
This genus with 25 species is particularly well-known for its culinary and medicinal use. Kinds such as mint belong in the herb garden, where they must be kept under control. The species M. *requienii*, which is described, is the only suitable decorative ground covering plant which can be combined well with small bulbs.

Mentha rotundifolia 'Variegata' is of ornamental value as is M. *requienii*, but less advisable because of its spreading tendencies.

Mertensia primuloides is a mat-forming dwarf (10 cm), with sky-blue flowers in Spring.

Micromeria is closely related to *Thymus* and *Satureja*. All have aromatic foliage.

MILIUM

MILIUM

Milium effusum 'Aureum' is persistently called 'Bowles golden grass'. The 10 cm blades are golden and it has the usual nondescript flowers. It is short-lived and seedlings do not keep to their own plot.

Milium effusum 'Aureum' with its golden leaves, is best displayed in shaded positions.

Mimulus primuloides forms rapidly spreading coppery-green mats, covered in bright-yellow flowers in Summer. It is the smallest species available.

MIMULUS

Some of these are outstanding for brilliance and intricate specklings within their lipped bugle-shaped flowers.

They offer alpines as well as border kinds and in general are easy to grow in any good soil which does not dry out. They prefer sun, and as mat-forming plants, respond to fairly frequent replanting. All are shallow-rooted.

The smallest is M. *primuloides* having bright yellow flowers on close coppery-green mats 5 cm, continuing for many weeks in Summer. It makes quite a rapid spread during Summer in gritty, peaty soil, and has usually survived in past severe winters.

Next in height is the pinkish-flowered 'Andean Nymph' at 8 cm.

Under M. *cupreus* come several hybrids, some of which are short-lived, but come true from seed. 'Whitecroft Scarlet', 'Bees Flame' and 'Wisley Red' are in this group, but M. x *burnettii*, orange, is fully perennial at 15 cm.

M. *guttatus* cultivars are mostly 25-35 cm tall and have the largest flowers.

'A.T. Johnson' is yellow, crimson blotched, but 'Mandarin' is flame-orange and speckled yellow within, whilst 'Harlequin' is tricoloured, primrose, red and yellow.

M. *glutinosus* is somewhat shrubby with orange-yellow flowers on sticky foliage, but falls short of being hardy.

M. *cardinalis*, and M. *lewisii* (syn. M. x *bartonianus*) are hardy, though like the rest are best replanted every Spring. Branching, greyish-leaved stems rise to 80 cm and orange-red flowers are displayed from June to September, but M. *lewisii* is pink. Both prefer goodish soil but are surprisingly adaptable. M. *ringens* likes it moist and is used as a marginal subject. It has narrow-leaved stems to 90 cm and rather small purple-mauve flowers.

Mimulus x burnettii is a trustworthy orange-flowering perennial.

MISCANTHUS

The genus provides some fine, mostly tall grasses, with blades all the way up the strong stems, annually produced. They form tough but compact roots which are not invasive, but merely expand year by year. Any reasonable soil suits them, preferring sun, and divisions are best made in Spring.

M. *japonicus* 'Giganteus', wrongly listed as M. *sacchariflorus*, is the tallest species with erect stems to 300 cm, very leafy, to rustle in a breeze, and massive enough to make a screen. As with all species, growth dies back in late Autumn and is renewed in Spring.

M. *sinensis* has several variations. Most of them grow erectly and well furnished to about 180-200 cm. The blades have a whitish midriff in the green type but one, 'Zebrinus', has lateral bars of buff-yellow. 'Variegata' is a splendid colourful plant but in M. *sinensis* 'Variegatus Strictus' the blades are upward pointing along the stems. M. *sinensis* 'Silver Feather' ('Silberfeder') is best for flowering, which the others often fail to do in northern climes. The plumes run up to 230 cm and are a rare sight even in Autumn when leaves are fading.

M. *sinensis* 'Gracillimus' has narrower, very graceful foliage, and this has a slightly purple-leaved form in 'Purpureus'.

Miscanthus sinensis 'Zebrinus'.

Above: *Miscanthus japonicus* 'Giganteus' is the tallest species with rustling leaves on 300 cm stems. A number of these planted together make a fine screen.

MITELLA

The two species below are evergreen and make good ground cover with deep-green foliage, shiny and crinkly. They are best suited for shady places, not too dry, and are long-lived.

M. *breweri* is the best known. It hugs the ground and has greenish flowers on 10 cm stems.

M. *diphylla* has lobed green leaves and greenish-white flowers on 15 cm stems. Both flower in May-June.

Mitella diphylla

Miscanthus

The dozen or so species all originate from the area between the Himalaya and Japan. There are still kinds which have not been tested in our climate. All available species and varieties can form a fantastic centre of well composed groups of perennials, but they are also worth growing as a solitary plant, such as near a pond, or on the lawn.

MOLINIA

M. *caerulea* another grass of real value, at least in the 'Variegata' form. It makes a mounded non-invasive clump and, though herbaceous, it makes a pleasing display, not only of the narrow, colourful blades, but of the airy sprays of flowers which take weeks to fade. They rise to 60 cm, and clumps will divide best in Spring. It grows best in light soil, not too limy or dry.

Molinia caerulea 'Variegata' is a valuable, colourful, non-invasive grass with nice flower sprays during July-September.

MOLTKIA

MOLTKIA

These are still somewhat confused with *Lithospermum* and *Lithodora*. All are sun lovers from well-drained soil.

M. doerfleri is somewhat tall to be in with alpines at 40 cm, but it is a pretty plant of bushy habit and has short sprays of violet-purple in Summer.

M. graminifolia is sub-shrubby but hardy and long-lived. It has a long succession of sky-blue flowers in clusters above narrow deep-green leaves.

M. petraea is a choice twiggy bushlet of grey-green leaves and has soft-blue flowers 15 cm.

M. x intermedia is taller at 20 cm, also blue, but *M. speciosa* is a rarity worth seeking for silvery narrow leaves and intensely blue flowers.

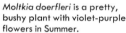

Moltkia doerfleri is a pretty, bushy plant with violet-purple flowers in Summer.

MONARDA

The curiously shaped flowers of the 'bergamot' have a certain appeal, and the leaves are decidedly aromatic even if this does not appeal to everyone. They come in some very bright colours, on erectly branching stems up to 120 cm in moist or rich soil, but less than this where dry.

The plants make a fairly rapid spread of matted-rooting pads and these may need curbing. This is easy enough since they almost fall apart; and with their tendency to wander, one simple method is to dig in the centre parts with a little compost and to plant again some of the vigorous outer pieces in Spring.

The hybrid varieties are the most worthy. They are mostly cross-breeds between *M. didyma* and *M. fistulosa*.

M. 'Adam' is cerise-red, and *M. 'Cambridge Scarlet'* is still popular along with *M. 'Croftway Pink'*.

M. 'Prairie Glow' is bright salmon-red, and *M. 'Prairie Night'* is violet-purple, all growing to a similar height. Monardas are, however, capable of growing quite tall in the second year after planting, in rich or moist soil.

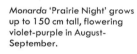

Monarda 'Prairie Night' grows up to 150 cm tall, flowering violet-purple in August-September.

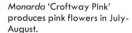

Monarda 'Croftway Pink' produces pink flowers in July-August.

MORAEA

Moraea spathacea (syn. *M. spathulata*) is related to *Iris* but has a fibrous root. It grows with a few long leaves and has bright-yellow Iris-like flowers May-June at 50 cm or so, and demands only sun and well-drained soil. It is easy to divide after flowering.

MORINA

Morina longifolia always attracts attention for it is both curious and beautiful.

Rosettes of base leaves are bright green and a little prickly. Stiffly erect stems carry a long succession, few at a time, of lipped tubular flowers. They are whitish in the bud but turn clear pink and then to near red. Plants are long-lived in sun and well-drained soil, flowering at 90 cm for most of the Summer.

MORISIA

Morisia monanthos (syn. *M. hypogaea*) is decidedly an alpine of virtually no height. Its tight rosetted hummocks of toothed green rosettes are studded in Spring with quite large rich-yellow flowers. It must have sharp drainage being native to sea shores, but is hardy and can be increased from root cuttings as it seldom sets seed and does not readily divide.

MYOSOTIS

This is the 'forget-me-not' genus but does not provide us with many good perennials.

M. alpestris has yielded one or two showy hybrids, all blue, such as 'Ruth Fischer' and 'Mermaid' at 15 cm.

M. rupicola is probably a mountain form of it but is a short-lived little beauty at 10 cm, best in gritty soil.

Morina

All 17 *Morina* species have thistle-like foliage. The only reliable species in our climate, *M. longifolia* can stay in the same place for many years: preferably in the rock garden between stones, and amongst other plants which like dry conditions. The plants must be protected against strong sun, and undue moisture in Winter.

Morina longifolia flowers are unusual. The bud is white, they then turn pink and are almost red by the end of their flowering period.

Right: *Myosotis alpestris* varieties all have blue flowers. Flowering periods are between May and August.

Left: *Morisia monanthos* forms flat rosettes covered with yellow flowers during the Summer.

MYRRHIS

Myrrhis odorata, so-called 'sweet cecily', is a massive grower, displaying creamy-white flowers in early Summer.

Nepeta x faassenii (syn. N. mussinii) flowers from June to September. The scent of these plants is attractive to cats.

The pink, lily-like trumpets of Nerine bowdenii.

MYRRHIS

Myrrhis odorata carries the evocative folk name of 'sweet cecily' and for all its being somewhat massive in growth, it has definite attraction. One of these is the lacy foliage, strongly scented of caraway. At about 100 cm in early Summer, it becomes capped with broad heads of tiny creamy-white flowers. Roots are fleshy and long-lived and its only fault is self seeding.

NEPETA

Most of these have greyish foliage but are not evergreen, with a somewhat astringent odour. Though catmint is one of the commonest of dwarf hardy plants, it remains one of the most widely used. The correct name is reckoned now to be N. x faassenii; but, as it is too well-known as N. mussinii, this is never likely to be accepted. The constant demand for this plant is due to its habit of dying out in Winter through wetness. In dry places it will survive on poor soils to give successive displays, but it does improve for being divided into quite small pieces every 2-3 years.
N. mussinii grows about 30 cm and flowers from June to September, but the taller N. 'Six Hills', with stems about 60 cm, is less neat and tidy. An uncommon variety with much larger flowers exists in N. grandiflora 'Blue Beauty'. This has erect spikes of lavender-blue flowers, 45-50 cm high, from June to August, but the roots are rather rampant below ground and replanting every 2-3 years is advised. This applies also to the much taller, 90 cm N. macrantha which is a somewhat robust spreader. This is also known under two other synonyms, N. sibirica and Dracocephalum supericum. All three nepetas are best planted or divided in Spring, and division of N. mussinii in Autumn may well prove a fatal mistake.
N. govaniana is quite distinct. It not only grows to 100cm in a bushy habit, but carries a long succession of small, light-yellow flowers June-September.

NERINE

This is a bulbous genus for Autumn flowering, but only N. bowdenii and its forms are reasonably hardy.
This has strap-shaped green foliage during Summer, and stems up to 50 cm carry radiating, pink, lily-like trumpets in October-November. The finest form is 'Fenwick's Variety'. Bulbs should not be planted deeply and do best at the foot of a wall, in sun or part shade. Even so, litter

protection is advisable in cold regions.
N. flexuosa and its white form are worth seeking.
Not so tall and a little more tender, its flowers
have delicately crinkled petals.

NIEREMBERGIA

Nierembergia caerulea (syn. *N. hippomanica*) is
short of being hardy everywhere. The 30 cm stems
are leafy and carry deep-blue flowers August-
October. It has no special soil requirements, but *N.
rivularis* (syn. *N. repens*) prefers moist soil in which
it will spread below surface with small deep-green
leaves and large white cups only 5 cm high during
late Summer. This too may suffer if soil becomes
deeply frozen.

> **Nierembergia**
> This is a genus of
> herbaceous plants and
> semi-shrubs. Most of the 35
> species are annuals,
> however. They grow wild in
> Central and South America.
> There is a strong similarity
> with *Petunia*, but the foliage
> is not hairy. Even with a
> thick Winter coverage they
> might freeze and die in
> Winter, therefore it is
> advisable always to take
> up some plants in Autumn,
> and put them in pots in a
> frost free place until the
> Spring.

Nierembergia rivularis spreads
below the surface but is not
hardy everywhere.

OAKESIELLA – see DISPORUM

OENOTHERA

This is another genus in which alpines and taller
perennials are seen as well as such biennials as the
'evening primrose' (*O. biennis* or *O. odorata*).
Yellow predominates and flowers vary in size from
less than 1 cm across to 10 cm. They will grow in
almost any well-drained soil and those below are
fully hardy, much preferring sun.
O. acaulis may still be listed as *O. taraxacifolia*,
which means 'dandelion-leaved'. These are as
rosettes from a tap-root, and clusters of a few
white pink-tinged or yellow flowers come on 10 cm
stems in Summer. It is rather short-lived but mostly
self seeds.
O. glabra is a very worthy plant of compact tufty
growth, having reddish-green leaves and erect
stems to 50 cm.
O. linearis is a good perennial with a dividable
clumpy habit. The 25 cm stems carry multitudes of
small yellow flowers for many weeks, June-August.
O. mexicana (syn. *O. speciosa*) is not very
desirable. It has small pink flowers for a long time,
but seeds itself too freely, 20 cm.
O. missouriensis is for a dryish, sunny slope or bank.
The tap-roots are long lived even in poor soil, and
make a low seasonal spread of greenery set with
large lemon-yellow flowers for weeks on end,
June-September.

Oenothera missouriensis flowers
from June to September
preferring rather dry, sunny
positions.

> **Oenothera**
> This genus originating from
> North America, with about
> 200 species, in some cases
> shows a special habit in that
> they flower during the night,
> and are therefore
> dependent for pollination on
> night-time insects.
> Many species are so-called
> 'pioneer' plants: they
> appear readily in places
> where the soil has been
> worked or on fallow land.
> Most species are not winter-
> hardy in our climate.

OENOTHERA

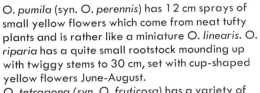
Oenothera tetragona 'Fireworks' has colourful spring foliage, followed by yellow flowers.

O. *pumila* (syn. O. *perennis*) has 12 cm sprays of small yellow flowers which come from neat tufty plants and is rather like a miniature O. *linearis*. O. *riparia* has a quite small rootstock mounding up with twiggy stems to 30 cm, set with cup-shaped yellow flowers June-August.

O. *tetragona* (syn. O. *fruticosa*) has a variety of improvements on the species which vary only in size of flower. All are yellow, but O. *cinaeus* and 'Fireworks' have also colourful spring foliage before the 40 cm stems produce their yellow cups. 'Yellow River' remains popular and 'Highlight' is taller at 60 cm. All this type have shallow roots and benefit from dividing and replanting every 2-3 years.

OMPHALODES

Omphalodes species are good carpeters in well nourished soil. Pictured is Omphalodes verna.

These are carpeting plants showing kinship with *Myosotis*, but these below are fully perennial and good hardy carpeters in any fertile soil.

O. *cappadocica* is evergreen, with ribbed grey-green leaves, and has sprays of bright-blue flowers in Spring. 15 cm.

O. *cappadocica* 'Anthea Bloom' is very free-flowering in sky-blue, 10 cm. These flourish with minimal attention for several years with slow spread, but O. *verna*, seen in both blue and white, is more rampant and does not retain its leaves beyond Summer.

It flowers briefly in April, 10 cm. Both are best divided in early Autumn and all respond to an occasional light mulch.

O. *luciliae* is a charmer, but not outdoors in wet cold winters. In an alpine house the sprays of sky-blue flowers above silvery-blue foliage are a rare sight in Spring. 20 cm.

Bottom left: *Onopordum acanthum* is a close relative of the 'globe artichoke'.

Below: *Onosma taurica* forms dangling, light-yellow flowers from May until July.

ONOPORDUM

Onopordum acanthum. This close relative of the globe artichoke is a stately plant with large, silvery, very jagged basal leaves. Strong stems to 130 cm end in scaly knobs and large, tufty, rosy-violet flower-heads. It is for light soil and a warm spot.

ONOSMA

The best known of this small genus for well-drained soil is O. *taurica*. It has hairy narrow leaves of grey-green, forming a mound from a tap-root. The flowers are light yellow and tubular, dangling from 25 cm stems, May to July. Seed is the only means of continuity when plants are exhausted. A pink-tinged species of similar growth is O. *alborosea*.

OPHIOPOGON

These are closely related to *Liriope* and have
evergreen grassy foliage and short spikes of tiny
purple flowers in Summer.
The most outstanding is *O. planiscapus* 'Nigrescens'
for the 10 cm foliage is almost black. It makes a
slow spread from underground shoots and can be
left alone for years except for an occasional
mulching of peat. The green *O. planiscapus* is useful
only for ground cover, and in the narrow green
leaves of *O. japonicus* nestle tiny spikes of white
flowers 10 cm. The variegated form Minor is less
hardy.

*ORCHIS

Orchids form a very successful family of plants,
and one can find them all over the world. Some
have evolved quite intricate pollination methods,
which has lead to a fascinating range of flower
shapes and sizes.
All our wild orchids are terrestrial, having fleshy
roots that extract their food from the soil. (Many
of the greenhouse grown species and varieties are
epiphytic, meaning that they get their nourishment
from the air and rain, and from humus in bark
crevices). They generally do best in moist, humous
soil in partially shaded areas, and are very hardy.
However, most wild varieties are now protected
and should not be dug up.
The genus *Orchis* has some truly magnificent plants.
Typically, the flowers grow in the first half of
Summer, in dense spikes, and are characterised by
a striking lip. The plants are increased by division,
by removing the so-called pseudobulbs, which are
thickened shoots able to grow up into completely
new plants. They can also be grown from seed.
Orchis elata nowadays is called *Dactylorhiza elata*.
This species has pale green leaves and violet,
spotted flowers. Height 75 cm.
Orchis foliosa (now *Dactylorhiza foliosa*) looks like
O. elata, but stays smaller (45 cm), has shiny green
leaves, and red-violet flowers. They need winter
protection.
Orchis militaris and *Orchis morio* are of similar
shape, and increase easily by self-seeding.
Orchis fuchsii has a good, light-purple variety,
'Bressingham Bonus' (height 45 cm). This species is
also listed nowadays with the name *Dactylorhiza
maculata* spp. *fuchsii*.
Also worth mentioning is the variety of orchids,
Pleione, somewhat reminiscent of daffodils, and
with a fine inflorescence. The best known, and most
hardy, is *Pleione limprichtii*, with lilac-pink flowers
and a spotted lip. Other cultivars like *P.
bulbocodiodes* (pink, red-lipped), *P. formosana* with
several varieties, and *P. forrestii* (yellow with red)
are not very hardy and are therefore less suited
to the garden.

Ophiopogon planiscapus
'Nigrescens' has peculiar,
almost black foliage. It is a
slow spreader.

Pleione limprichtii is a beautiful,
pink-flowering, very hardy
little orchid.

Dactylorhiza foliosa is a close
relative of the *Orchis* genus. It
needs a good covering in order
to over-winter well.

ORIGANUM

Origanum vulgare, the culinary marjoram, is also available in several decorative varieties, including a golden-leaved form.

Origanum scabrum ssp. pulchrum flowers in July-August. It likes a rather dry and sunny position.

Osmunda regalis, 'the royal fern', must have a humus-rich soil to thrive.

Osmunda

There are in total 14 species of Osmunda, but only 3 of which are winter-hardy in our climate. The plants can reach an incredible age, with some known to have become several hundred years old.
Besides O. regalis, only O. cinnamomea (from America and Asia, up to 1.5 m tall) and O. claytoniana (from the same origin and very similar) are suitable for our gardens.

ORIGANUM

The alpine species are for very well-drained soil and a sunny place, but those suitable as frontal perennials are easy to grow in any soil as well as being more robust. They are distinctive for having Nepeta-like flowers in late Summer.
The most attractive need a very well-drained soil and resent winter wet.
O. x hybridum has woolly grey-green leaves from a compact root and wiry sprays carrying rosy-purple flowers July to September, 15-20 cm tall.
O. scabrum pulchrum is quite sturdy, forming clumpy plants on which appears a profusion of pale-pink, green-tinged bracts in late Summer, 15 cm.
The large hop-like flowers of O. rotundifolium are creamy green on 12 cm stems. All are long-lived where suited and can be divided in Spring.
O. laevigatum is a distinctive plant for later Summer, 50 cm. Wiry stems with small leaves carry myriads of tiny pinkish-purple flowers. The roots are somewhat woody but long-lived and dividable in Spring.
O. vulgare is the culinary marjoram, but it has several variations of decorative value with thereabouts-evergreen foliage. The golden-leaved form is very colourful till its nondescript flowers come at about 15 cm; but if cut off, the clumps colour up again. It is good as edging for a frontal position. One or two green-leaved, bluish-flowered kinds are in existence and worth looking out for, under the names 'Herrenhausen' and 'Nymphenburg'.

ORUBUS – see LATHYRUS

OSMUNDA

Osmunda regalis. This is the imposing 'royal fern'. In some shade or sun, given dampish humus soil, it makes a fine specimen clump with deeply incised fronds, attaining over 100 cm.
Slight variations have purplish stems and fronds or differences in the size and shape of secondary foliage.

OSTEOPSPERMUM

This is the most recent name for what was Dimorphotheca. Only the species O. jucundum (syn. O. barbariae) has pretension to hardiness, but it is worth the trouble of taking autumn cuttings. These planted in Spring will soon grow, with outstanding leafy stems carrying rayed daisy-type flowers in shades of pink to magenta, height about 25 cm and continuing from June till October.

OURISIA

None of these is fully hardy, but some are worth protecting in cold districts.

The largest and hardiest is O. macrophylla. Given a cool situation and humus soil, it gives a very bright display of pure-white flowers on flattish heads and 30 cm stems, May-June. There is a pink cultivar named 'Loch Ewe' of similar height and O. canbyi is another white, all forming dark green mats.

O. coccinea has small 10 cm sprays of scarlet flowers in Summer above crinkly light-green mats, but is hardy only in mildest regions. The same goes for a few other species, all preferring humus soil which does not dry out.

Ourisia macrophylla is quite hardy and has white flowerheads during May-June.

Oxalis adenophylla is a long-lived and very hardy species with bluish-green leaves and pink flowers in Spring.

OXALIS

This is a very large genus of dwarf species which includes some good plants, some that are not hardy and some which, though pretty, are pernicious weeds. Most of them have small lobed leaves — one being confused with shamrock.

My advice is to decide in advance which to have, and reject the weedy ones which should never be on sale, although O. inops (syn. O. depressa) might be. Pretty though it is, it should be avoided. And have nothing to do with the yellow-flowered O. corniculata.

O. acetosella is the native stubwort with drooping white or pale-pink flowers. By itself it can be controlled, but if allowed to find a host in which to reside, it will be more than tenacious.

O. adenophylla grows from a scaly bulb which erupts in Spring with a cluster of bright-pink flowers 5 cm high before going back to dormancy. It needs gritty soil and sun.

O. enneaphylla is a gem, on the lines of adenophylla, but with silver-grey crinkly leaves and outsize white or pink-flushed flowers, 5 cm. Both these flower in May, June, and the latter is best in peaty soil.

O. articulata (syn. O.floribunda) is the old favourite with shamrock leaves and masses of bright-pink flowers on 15 cm stems. It will grow from little tubers as a clump in any sunny position and has no vices, flowering for several weeks May-July.

O. lobata calls for patience to induce its rich golden flowers. It grows from tiny bulbs which produce a short spell of green leaves in Spring, but with patience the flowers will appear in Autumn. It is best grown in an alpine house.

O. magellanica is less demanding. It forms a modestly expanding mat of dark-green leaves after dormancy, studded with tiny stemless white cups, preferring a cool moist position.

PACHYSANDRA

Pachysandra terminalis 'Green Carpet' is one of the better varieties of this shrubby, evergreen species.

* PACHYSANDRA

Two species of this genus are reliable evergreen ground coverers. *P. procumbens* forms creeping stems and brown-green leaves which turn into bronze in Autumn. It is May-flowering with fragrant brown-white flowers. This species has little spread.

P. terminalis, is best as a ground-covering plant with leathery green leaves. Flowering is not very impressive (green flowers). It is good for shady sites, and is increased by cuttings and division.

PAEONIA

Paeonies are not only amongst the most-loved of perennials but are also the longest-lived. They should be planted for permanence.

Paeonies need an open situation and good deep soil — regardless of texture or alkalinity. They do in fact like lime, and flower best if given a top dressing of fertiliser in late Summer or early Autumn when new feeding roots begin again. This, too, is the best planting time, and nursery-grown plants, not newly cut-up divisions, will give best results.

Paeonies can be divided, but it calls for skill with a knife and one should not expect flowers in the first season. Planting depth is important. The pinkish crown buds, on which next season's growth depends, should be settled at no more than one inch below surface after firming round the plant. The largest-flowered paeonie are the *P. lactiflora* varieties which flower in June. These are mostly doubles of which *P.* 'Festiva Maxima', *P.* 'Sarah Bernhardt' and others are good examples.

Below left: Paeonia 'Bowl of Beauty' has huge rose-pink flowers.

Below: Paeonia mlokosewitschii is a single-flowered, bright-coloured species.

A vast range of varieties exists apart from those basic colours of red, pink and white, some having merging shades and others with a deeper centre. There are some fine single and semi-double varieties in this range, of which *P.* 'King Arthur' is a good example, with its gold centre on a dark-red background.

P. 'Bowl of Beauty' has huge flowers of rose-pink in which the creamy centre stands out, and *P.* 'Defender' has massive blood-red flowers.

Some white varieties shade towards creamy-yellow in the centre, but the self-coloured single *P. mlokosewitschii* is a glistening colour. This is a much-sought-after plant despite its difficult name, not only because of its colour but because it flowers in April-May before any others.

Other earlier paeonies include the limited range of *P. officinalis*-mostly doubles in pink, white and red, flowering in May at 90 cm.

Then there are the one or two brilliant *P. lobata* (syn. *P. peregrina*) varieties, single salmon-red in the 2 feet high *P.* 'Sunshine', and the single red *P.*

PAPAVER

x *smouthii* and the deep-pink *P. arietina*, of which the red 'Northern Glory' is a splendid variation. Several other species exist which would not be easy to come by, but there is a welter of named varieties of the main group *P. lactiflora* in existence.

Well-grown plants of paeonies may be more expensive to buy, but when one considers the returns over a period of many years, then they become a very good investment.

PANICUM

Panicum virgatum. This grass has upright, wiry stems, well clothed with foliage reaching 100 cm or more. It has thin purplish plumes above and gives good autumn colour. One variation is *P. virgatum* 'Strictum', having a stiffer habit, and 'Rubrum', having brownish-purple tints — all with non-invasive growth and for ordinary soil in sun. Flowering time is June-August.

PAPAVER

The oriental poppies, *(Papaver orientale)*, dominate the genus and provide the garden in early Summer with brilliant colours. Their huge flowers may appear blowsy to some, but are nothing if not gorgeous.

Of the many varieties in cultivation, several new introductions in recent years have ousted some of the older ones. There are enough available to represent every shade from white through pink,

Double forms of *Paeonia lactiflora* in all kinds of available shades.

Right: *Panicum virgatum* 'Strictum' is a quite tall (100 cm), upright growing grass, with elegant flower plumes and a nice autumn colour.

Left: *Papaver orientale* is the best-known species of this genus with varieties in many bright shades.

PAPAVER

Papaver nudicaule is the species of 'Iceland Poppies' with single flowers.

All Parahebe species are rather shrubby, but can be divided. Pictured is P. lyallii 'Miss Willmott'.

Blood-red flowers come on leafy 120 cm stems, but the also-erect scarlet 'Marcus Perry' is 100 cm. Other sturdy varieties are 'Black and White', 70 cm, 'Glowing Embers' with ruffled petals, orange-red, 110 cm, 'Midnight' orange-rose, 75 cm, and 'Perry's White', 90 cm. There are a few species worth growing having smaller flowers. P. heldreichii (syn. P. spicatum), P. lateritium, P. pilosum and P. rupifragum have in common lots of base foliage, and a bright display of single poppies in shades of orange-scarlet, varying in height from 40-70 cm for several weeks. All may be raised from seed, but not so the little P. 'Fireball', which may well be a species. This has double orange — scarlet flowers on 20 cm stems, May-July. Unlike others, it spreads enough to need occasional curbing.

Two diminutive species of poppy are worthy of note, in spite of being short-lived.
P. alpinum (syn. P. burseri) grows like a miniature Iceland poppy (P. nudicaule) with single flowers rising from a blue-green tuft to 12 cm from May to August. This comes only from seed as a miniature in white, yellow and orange shades.
P. myabeanum makes a mound of lobed greyish leaves and has a long succession of soft, light-yellow flowers, 10 cm. Seed is the only means of reproduction of both the above, and they often self-sow.

PARADISEA – see ANTHERICUM

PARAHEBE

These are the sub-shrubby kinds — half way between the Hebe and Veronica which used to be the overall name.
P. catarractae makes low mounds of dark-green shiny leaves and pale-lilac flowers in early Summer, 25 cm. The form 'Diffusus' is dwarf at 15 cm and more desirable. 'Tiny Cat' is a pretty miniature with lilac-blue flowers at 5 cm.
P. lyallii is more upright at 15-20 cm with near-white flowers, and 'Miss Willmott' is of similar height with pinkish-lilac flowers. The taller ones respond to trimming with shears after flowering, but P. x bidwillii is too small to need this, being only 5 cm, of bronzy leaves and white flowers. Parahebes can be divided and combine agreeably with most dwarf Penstemons and dianthus.

PARONYCHIA

These mat-forming, sun-loving alpines are grown for their silvery foliage, flowers being insignificant. P. capitata (syn. P. nivea) has silver-grey mats and more silvery bracts. P. kapela ssp. serpyllifolia is more compact, also silver grey.

Paronychia
Of this genus there are about 40 very similar species in the temperate and subtropical zones. In the course of the years the plants can cover large areas of rock, which creates an amazing sight. The growth is slow but continuous, and they need little care as long as the soil is well-drained and they are in the full sun.

salmon and lilac, to claret and red with a few parti-coloured and double-flowered. But all have the disadvantage of leaving a bare patch after flowering.
If cut hard back, new base foliage may be induced, but another dodge is to have adjoining groups of subjects which make a spread when the poppies are over.
Another fault, inherent in some varieties, is that of being top heavy, having large flowers and weak stems. The few upright ones are mentioned below.
Papavers have deep fleshy roots and prefer light soil as well as full sun. They resent wetness and may rot during Winter in wet conditions. They can be increased from root cuttings in early Spring, but few come true from seed.

One of the finest for colour and stem strength is 'Goliath', now proved identical with the old 'Beauty of Livermere'.

PATRINIA

This is a small genus of umbellifers of value for late flowering.

P.gibbosa is rarely seen. The 45 cm stems carry heads of tiny greenish-yellow flowers, August-October, above broad basal leaves. It has a slow spread from permanent roots and prefers a cool position.

P. palmata (syn. *P. triloba*) makes a good spread of delicately lobed leaves and gives a long succession, July-October, of golden yellow flowers on 15 cm branching heads: a very desirable plant for moist humus soil and part shade.

Patrinia palmata flowers over a long period – July-October – with golden-yellow flower heads.

Below: *Paronychia serpyllifolia* is a compact, mat-forming plant with silvery foliage.

* PELLAEA

Pellaea atropurpurea is a fern with shiny-black leaf stems and greyish-green leaves. It is not very hardy, but good for sunny spots in the rock garden, otherwise for the alpine house.

Peltiphyllum peltatum is a nice flowering species that spreads steadily.

PELTIPHYLLUM

Peltiphyllum peltatum, is called the 'Umbrella plant' from the size and shape of its leaves up to 40 cm across on single stalks up to 90 cm high. The leaves follow flowering in Spring as rounded heads of small reddish-pink, clustered and starry flowers. Roots are thick rhizomes near the surface and in good moist soil make a steady but not invasive spread. Its big leaves however need space and it is a good waterside plant. A dwarf (35 cm) form exists in 'Nanum', but is much less spectacular.

PENNISETUM

Pennisetum compressum forms flower plumes above the grey-green, arching leaves. It prefers sunny, rather sheltered sites.

PENNISETUM

This is an important group of long-lived, non-invasive grasses, some of which form large clumps. They are easy to grow in a sunny position but need forks for division.

P. compressum (syn. P. alopecuroides) makes a hefty permanent clump with narrow, arching blades of grey-green up to 40 cm long. Above, in sunny climes, come erect plumes of buff flowers. A few variations are more reliably flowering such as 'Woodside' and 'Hammelin'.

P. orientale is most attractive with its long display of pokery purple-green flowers from July onwards. These are barely 30 cm tall and the plant's habit is low and tufty and slow to make large clumps.

PENSTEMON

Although this large and varied genus contains many highly desirable members, very few are wholly reliable where cold or damp winters prevail. The majority are dwarf enough to be classed as alpines. The low semi-shrubby kinds need a sunny spot and well-drained soil.

P. alpinus forms clumps of broad leaves and has 20 cm spikes of light-blue flowers in May-June.
P. barrettae is of similar height with blue-purple tubular flowers, and P. virens has small but intensely deep-blue flowers on 15 cm spikes above green-leaved mats. These three are non-shrubby and can be divided or reared from seed. The shrubby kinds may also come from seed but are better from cuttings after flowering.
The erect-growing P. heterophyllus 'Blue Gem' has very showy sky-blue spikes to 20 cm. This comes only from seed.
P. edithae has large purple-rose flowers on low 25 cm bushes.
P. pinifolius grows erectly with narrow leaves and sprays of scarlet flowers, 20 cm. A yellow form now exists.
P. roezlii is low-growing at 15 cm with deep-red flowers, effective in or on a wall.
P. scouleri has light-lavender flowers, 20 cm, and the cultivar 'Six Hills' has large, soft-lilac flowers, 10-15 cm. Shrubby penstemons respond to top dressing with sandy soil in which new roots can form, but it is advisable to sometimes replant more deeply or take cuttings if they appear to be losing vigour. Several other species are in cultivation.

Of the taller-growing kinds, the most widely grown are hybrids, but the doubtful species of P. campanulatus is reliably hardy. It grows somewhat bushily to 30 cm and has a long succession of lilac-blue tubular flowers. The variety 'Evelyn' is a true

Penstemon pinifolius forms sprays of scarlet flowers and is rather upright in growth.

P. *campanulatus* cultivar. It has slender spikes with narrow leaves up to 70 cm and pure-pink flowers, July-September, but will not survive severe winters.
P. *deustus* and P. *virens* are mat-forming with thin spikes to 15 cm of deep blue.
P. *digitalis* is fully hardy and reasonably long-lived. The 60 cm leafy stems carry mauve flowers June-August and the form 'Purpurea' has purplish leaves.
P. *diffusus* makes low mounds and has 25 cm flowers of light- and lilac-blue, June-August.
P. *fruticosus* is best in the hybrid 'Katherine de la Mare', with plenty of deep-green basal leaves and many 40 cm spikes of lilac-pink, June-September. It would be pointless to give the parentage of the many hybrids which are not reliably hardy in cold regions but are easy to protect or renewed from autumn cuttings. All are in the 50-80 cm height range and flower profusely from June onwards. 'Garnet' is wine-red, 'Firebird' blood-red, 'Hewells Pink' has a white throat, 'Pink Endurance' clear-pink, P. x *rubicunda* tall, large-flowered red, 'Ruby' free-flowering red, 'King George' blood-red large-flowered, 'Sour Grapes' purple-mauve, 'Snowstorm' pure-white.

All are best in sun and well-drained soil; but as almost all are natives of North America, with its wide climatic range, it is scarcely possible to adapt all the many species to North European gardens. It is none-the-less a fascinating genus.

Penstemon hybrids, available in many shades, flower from June onwards, but not all are winterhardy.

Penstemon scouleri has lilac or lavender coloured flowers in June-July.

Perovskia abrotanoides is a shrub, but it blends in well with perennials.

PEROVSKIA

The 'Russian sage' is one of the few shrubs which fits in with perennials. This is because the flowers come on new growth, enabling a hard cut-back of old stems in Spring. It has small greyish leaves on the thin stems and narrow tapering spikes up to 120 cm from July onwards. Flowers are small but very effective, making good foil for yellows and reds.
P. *atriplicifolia* is the main species, with 'Blue Haze' the best form, and there is also P. *abrotanoides* with slightly larger grey leaves and paler-blue flowers.

Pennisetum
In total there are some 50 species of annual and perennial grasses in this genus. They all need warmth, sun and well-drained soil. Besides the species mentioned, P. *incomptum* is a plant suitable for larger areas. It develops big clumps and reaches a height of 1.5 m. The purple flower spikes appear from July and they are suitable for cut flowers. The inflorescence turns yellow later.

165

PETRORHAGIA

Petrorhagia saxifraga does well in sunny, dry soil. It will flower all Summer.

Right: *Phalaris arundinacea* 'Picta' is an elegant, but not evergreen, tall grass.

Phlomis samia is a strong-growing plant with unusual clusters of hooded flowers on tall stems.

Phlomis
These plants with their conspicuous inflorescence are still decorative after flowering, because the dried flower stems with their particular seed capsules stay on the plant for a long time. Species such as *P. samia*, with their evergreen rosettes of leaves, form a real ground cover and weeds do not get a chance amongst these plants.

PETRORHAGIA

Petrorhagia saxifraga is native in Southern Europe and the Near East. 30 cm high, the species flowers in shades of pink, June-September. 'Alba' is white, 'Alba Plena' is a double variety and somewhat smaller (20 cm), 'Pleniflora' rose-red, 'Rosette' dark-pink (double). Increase is by seed, double forms by division. It is a plant for sunny, dry soil.

PHALARIS

Phalaris arundinacea 'Picta' is well known as the 'gardener's garters' grass. It romps and should not be planted in company with slower-growing plants. The variegated blades are 40 cm long but are not evergreen.

PHLOMIS

Phlomis samia has other names, *P. russelliana* and *P. viscosa*. They stand for a strong-growing plant with large evergreen basal leaves and sturdy stems up to 130 cm carrying clusters of soft-yellow, hooded flowers. It is a statuesque plant worth growing and is easy and long-lived in any soil, preferring sun.
P. tuberosa is less attractive, but interesting with its rosy-lilac flowers amid ample leafage. Both flower June-August. An improved cultivar has recently been introduced.

PHLOX

The best known of the taller kinds come under *P. paniculata*. They make a vital contribution towards colourful gardens in late Summer, at a time when yellow would otherwise predominate. Every shade of pink, red, purple and lavender-blue, as well as white and orange-scarlet, is to be seen in the vast number of varieties now in existence; and by judicious planning for colour effect, using phlox between other subjects, perfection in contrasts can be obtained.

They prefer good light soil and are least happy on alkine clay, though in this they respond to the addition of peat, sand or compost. They also respond to mulching in Winter so that their feeding roots can benefit and a better Summer display will ensue. Nursery-grown plants from root-cuttings will invariably do better than divisions, because the one pest which sometimes affects them — eel-worm — is a risk either from division or green-cuttings. Badly affected plants should be dug up and burned and it is not safe to replant on the same spot with phlox for at least 3 years. Symptoms are shrivelled and distorted stems during the growing period.

Personal choice is the guide

Phlox can be planted at any time after September up to late April and their fibrous roots should be well spread in freshly-dug and enriched soil, spaced at about 18 inches (45 cm). In my time I have grown about 250 named varieties; and though many old ones have been superceded, a few are still unsurpassed. I can but recommend readers to take notes of what they see displayed, since with such a wealth of variety and colour, personal choice is the guide.

Mention can be made of two with variegated leaves: 'Nora Leigh' is very showy, but the lilac flowers are less so: 'Harlequin', conversely, is less colourful of leaf but has good purple flowers. Other border phlox, less often seen but well worth growing, include the few *P. maculata* varieties. They have more slender stems above shallow fibrous roots and narrower leaves. 'Alpha' has large cylindrical heads of warm pink, 'Omega' is white with a red eye, and 'Rosalinde' is carmine-rose, all reaching 100 cm and flowering July-September.

That fine plantsman Georg Arends of Ronsdorf made a cross between the blue species *P. divaricata* and a *P. paniculata,* coming under *P. x arendsii*. They are not often available but are deserving. 'Anja' is reddish purple, 'Hilda' lavender and 'Susanne' white with a red eye, all 40 cm and Summer flowering.

P. divaricata itself is light violet blue, best in *P. divaricata laphanii* with slow-spreading mats and a show of flowers on 25 cm stems in May-June, preferring some shade and humus soil. Another

Above: *Phlox paniculata* hybrids, mainly flowering in shades of red, are very useful for good colour combinations in the garden, during late Summer.

Phlox subulata and its varieties are rich-flowering, spreading, dwarf plants.

PHLOX

Above left: *Phlox stolonifera* uses self-rooting rosettes to spread.

Above right: *Phlox amoena* prefers a sunny position and is mat-forming.

Left: *Phlox maculata* hybrids, like this blue-tinted one, are less well known than their *paniculata* sisters, but well worth growing. They easily reach up to 100 cm.

Below: *Phlox douglasii* varieties produce neat, close-growing mats.

Phlox
In nature there are about 60 known species of *Phlox*. They all come from North America. Very few are annuals. This genus offers many possibilities of combinations with other plants. One thing all phloxes have in common: they cannot stand drought and severe Winters. A somewhat sheltered and shady place is often better than an open spot in the full sun.

worth-while phlox is *P. pilosa*, only 30 cm, with deep-pink flowers. It is more reliable than the somewhat similar *P. ovata*.

Alpine phlox
In alpine phlox the cultivars far outnumber the species. The easiest and most popular kinds come under the species *P. douglasii* or *P. subulata*, both being carpeters and capable of rooting as they spread. They are invaluable for making a bright display in Spring and early Summer and especially effective on a slope, needing no special soil or attention, given good drainage and a mainly sunny position.
Those under *P. douglasii* have a colour range from white to lilac, pale-blue and pink, with close-growing mats of small leaves and flowers and generally of neat habit, height 5 cm.
In *P. subulata* some brighter colours including crimson-red, are available amongst the twenty or so cultivars in existence. Most of them have a quicker spread than *P. douglasii* and flower at about 8 cm high.
Few alpine phlox need shade and peaty or acid soil, although *P. adsurgens* prefers such conditions; it has small leathery leaves and heads of soft-pink flowers. This is not an easy plant, in contrast to *P. amoena* which is undemanding in a sunny position. Its growth is more tufted though still mat-forming with magenta-pink flower heads and there is also a pretty variegated-leaved form.
P. stolonifera spreads quickly with blue, pink or white flowers with self-rooting rosettes or runners with rounded leaves. It flowers in Spring at 10 cm and is best in cool soil and some shade, from cuttings or division.

PHORMIUM

These are handsome foliage plants but liable to suffer in severe winters. Where these occur, it is essential to protect with ample litter, but they still cannot be recommended for northern climes.
The tallest and freest to flower is the New Zealand Flax, *P. tenax*, having yellow flowers in Summer to 300 cm on strong stems.
P. cookianum is reasonably hardy, half the height of *P. tenax*, and flowering consistently in any sunny

Phuopsis stylosa is an easy to grow, somewhat stark, spreading alpine species, flowering from June until August.

PHUOPSIS

Phuopsis stylosa (syn. *Crucianella stylosa*) is a very easily grown, long-flowering plant, but it spreads too quickly to be amongst choicer alpines. It will grow more or less anywhere except in deep shade with narrow light-green foliage and dense heads of deep pink. But for its lolling habit and strong odour when damp, it would make a good permanent edging.

PHYGELIUS

These South African natives fall just short of being fully hardy but are easy to keep alive with litter. They need sun and have strong, slow spreading roots, and flower for a long time from July to October in any reasonable soil.
P. aequalis has dark-green oval foliage and branching 60 cm spikes of coral-red lipped tubular flowers. This is less hardy and less vigorous than 'African Queen' which has slightly larger and

position. The broad-bladed leaves stand well up to 130 cm, of greyish-green hue.
The purplish-leaved form 'Purpurea' is most effective but a little less hardy, whereas the more highly variegated forms are more tender still. Several are now in circulation, all very desirable, in heights down to a mere 20 cm, all clump-forming and long-lived in warm climates. None is fussy as to soil so long as it is well drained.

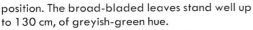

Several varieties of *Phormium* grown together. They need well-drained soil, and as they may suffer in severe winters, a mulch of litter is advised for protection.

PHYGELIUS

Phygelius capensis tends to shrubbiness and can reach 120 cm in a warm position.

Physalis alkekengi var. *franchetii*, the 'Chinese lantern' produces bright orange 'balloons' that retain their colour when dried.

Phyllostachys species and varieties may grow 4-15 m tall. They can be very showy for their colours, but need plenty of space and warm sites.

Physalis
P. franchetii is officially a subspecies of *P. alkekengi*. A second subspecies *P. alkekengi* ssp. *alkekengi* is also cultivated, but is less attractive. Unlike *P. franchetii* (from east Asia), *P. alkekengi* originates from south-east Europe. This plant reaches 30-60 cm and develops inconspicuous, yellow-white flowers.

brighter flowers as well as being taller at 80 cm. Even more vigorous is 'Yellow Trumpet', though the colour is nearer to creamy-primrose.

It is unfortunate that all the above were given different cultivar names which are not valid. The names 'Devon Cream', 'Fanfare' and 'Devil's Tears' apply to those correctly given above.

P. capensis is more shrubby, but only if grown against the shelter of a wall. It has small, rounded, shiny leaves and short spikes of bright-reddish tubular flowers.

It flowers less freely in amongst border perennials.

* PHYLLOSTACHYS

All 50 species of this bamboo genus come from China. The plant needs higher temperatures during the growing season (May-August) than others like *Sinarundinaria*. Therefore they provide less general opportunities in the garden. They need a sunny but moist site. Some good species are contained in the following:

P. aurea will grow up to 10 m and can stand 20 degrees C. frost. It is rather stiff, upright growing.
P. nigra with its cultivars are also hardy.
P.n.'Borgana' has distinctive spots on the green blades (4-15 m).
P.n.'Henomis' perhaps is the most beautiful with bending green blades which stay green even if the stalks get older. (5-16 m).
P.n.'Nigra' and *P.n.*'Punctata' get black blades (spotted in the case of 'Punctata'). They are very showy and grow to 5-10 m.
P. viridis, variety 'Robert Young', has golden-yellow blades with green stripes. A beauty growing 6-15 m.
Increase by division.

PHYSALIS

Only one of these can be recommended and then to grow more or less by itself, for it is decidedly rampant below ground. It is the 'Cape gooseberry' or 'Chinese lantern', much valued for its little pointed balloons of bright orange for indoor decorations when dried. Inside the bag is a gooseberry-type fruit which is edible, but the plant has a rather untidy habit at about 70 cm in the best form *P. franchetii*.

The time to cut physalis is when the leaves begin to fade, for it is then that the 'lanterns' begin to take their colourful tint. Stems should be cut close to the ground and by tying up a few in a bunch and hanging them upside down in a dry airy place, the colouring and drying process will complete itself. After a few weeks they can then be brought indoors to stand in a vase without water, or used for winter decoration in a variety of ways, one of which is to open the lanterns.

PHYSOSTEGIA

Plants which are easy to grow cannot often be termed distinctive, but this is true of physostegia. Spike-forming plants are moreover very helpful in breaking up any tendency to uniformity in a border or bed, and these with their long-flowering habit fill such a need. They are, however, subjects that thrive in good soil which does not dry out severely; and though this produces fuller, taller spikes, it also involves the need, after a year or two, to thin out some of their roots or to replant. The variety P. 'Vivid' is the latest to flower – in September, the 30-45 cm spikes coming from quick-spreading underground shoots and which need curbing or setting back into position in Spring. P. 'Rose Bouquet' grows 75 cm and is lilac-pink, July-September, when the 90 cm deep-pink spikes of P. 'Summer Spire' taper up to flower on slender spikes. These two, and the pretty white P. 'Summer Snow', also 90 cm, are less rampant than P. 'Vivid' but grow with vigour in any ordinary soil. They are easily divided in Spring.

The name 'obedient plant' comes from the fact that when the little tubular flowers arranged in rows on the spike are pushed aside, they stay put without snapping off or springing back.

PHYTEUMA

Although these are related to campanula, they do not have bell-shaped flowers. Relatively few of the 30-or-so species in cultivation are likely to be seen or offered, and most of them are alpines with tiny blue flowers in clusters. They have distinctive blue flower-heads with sharply pointed petals.

The best known P. comosum (syn. Physoplexis comosa) is a good little plant, only 8 cm, and happy in a crevice between rocks. It has lilac-blue flowers, as has the taller P. orbiculare, both being easy to grow.

P. scheuchzeri has deep-purple flowers on 20 cm stems. All flower in Spring and early Summer and are best perpetuated by seed.

Physostegia varieties are available in heights between 30 and 90 cm and in shades varying from white and pink to lilac and red.

The taller species have narrow spikes above deep-green basal leaves.

P. campanuloides, with the generic name of Asyneuma sometimes used, is quite a pretty summer-flowering plant, 60 cm tall, violet-blue, but P. spicatum of similar height appears in light, pale blue and deep blue, above heart-shaped foliage. They are easy to grow and, whilst not startling, add interest for several weeks in Summer.

Phyteuma scheuchzeri flowers in Spring and early Summer. Its deep-purple flowers make a good show.

PHYTOLACCA

Phytolacca
There are 35 species of this genus, some of which are trees. They occur mainly in tropical and subtropical regions. It is very attractive to make a group of some of the species described in a somewhat shady place. The beautiful foliage stands out best in this way. In the old days juice from the fruits of some species was used as a dye, including use in food products, even though rather poisonous.

Phytolacca americana, the 'Virginia Poke weed' may grow up to 130 cm. The berries are its main attraction.

Plantago major 'Rosularis', the rose plantain, has coloured leaf-rosettes instead of flowers.

PHYTOLACCA

Phytolacca americana (syn. *P.decandra*) is also known as 'Virginia Poke weed' and grows to 130 cm in any soil, robust and leafy. The flowers are white but the deep-red berries are more appealing though poisonous.
P. clavigera has the same height and habit, also white, but the berries are shining black and equally poisonous. The stems turn bright red in Autumn. Both are for late Summer and both are liable to self seed.

PIMPINELLA

Pimpinella major 'Rosea' is somewhat like a refined cow parsley, though less clumpy in habit. The flowers are quite pretty, pale pink on 60 cm stems, June-August, and thrive in any but dry poor soil.

* PLANTAGO

This genus is spread worldwide. Wild species include ribwort and hoary plantain. Some are worthy for special collections in the garden, e.g. *P. major* 'Rosularis', the rose plantain. The flowers have been replaced by rose-like green rosettes of leaves. It needs loamy or sandy soil.
P. nivalis is a species for the rock garden, but needs winter protection against wet conditions. Greenish flowers appear in July — August and increase is by seed.

PLATYCODON

This is a distinctive campanula relative known as the 'balloon flower'. This comes from the way the petals are joined together; and, if pinched just before they open of their own accord, they will make an audible pop. They are fleshy-rooted plants, long-lived in any reasonable soil and sun, but do not emerge in new growth till April. They are excellent for frontal border positions, and flower from June for many weeks.
P. grandiflorum varies in height from 35-50 cm and in colour from white to shades of blue. There is a pale pink named 'Mother of Pearl', but this is hard to come by as are the double white and blue. Most often offered is the dwarfer *P. grandiflorum* 'Mariesii', but even this varies a little from seed, from 30-40 cm.

Stocks are mostly raised from seed and this is why the dwarfest form *P. g.* 'Apoyana' was only 15-20 cm when first introduced but seems now to be more often 30 cm.

Spring division is a means of keeping any special form true, but calls for care as the roots of old plants are congested and brittle.

* POA

Poa annua is the most common grass in the world, but there are other species in culture.

P. glauca has stiff leaves and bluish spikes, 20-35 cm tall, and is good for alpine conditions.

P. colensoi is winter-green, 20 cm. The leaves are an astonishing blue. Others like *P. badensis* are less important.

Increase is by division.

PODOPHYLLUM

Podophyllum emodi (syn. *P. hexandrum*) is fleshy-rooted and needs moist humus soil and shade. It has handsome lobed, umbrella-type leaves and sparse, fleeting, pale-pink flowers in Spring. These turn into bright red fruits, the size of a hen's egg, which last for a few weeks.

Height is 40 cm, a little more in the 'major' form. The roots are slow to spread but *P. peltatum* is more vigorous. Leaves are large and handsome, 45 cm high; and the creamy, nodding flowers are followed by pinkish fruits.

POLEMONIUM

The folk name 'Jacob's ladder' comes from the way the leaves are dissected as lateral rows on each side of the midriff; strictly, it applies only to the species *P. caeruleum*, but though a pretty old-timer, it is rather short-lived and persists by being very free to seed. None of the other and more desirable species is difficult to grow, given a sunny position. *P. caeruleum* itself has light-blue, yellow-centred, cup-shaped flowers 1 cm across in early Summer on 60 cm stems. The form *P. x richardsonii* is a little taller and deeper in colour.

P. 'Dawn Flight' is pure white above light-green foliage and very attractive, 75 cm.

P. carneum has pinkish flowers but even the variety

Above: *Platycodon grandiflorum* 'Mariesii' is mainly grown from seed.

Left: *Polemonium* 'Dawn Flight' is a white-flowered variety of 'Jacob's Ladder'.

Below: *Podophyllum emodi* forms bright-red fruits, about 5 cm tall, after flowering.

POLEMONIUM

Polemonium foliosissimum is one of the tallest growing (up to 100 cm) of this genus, with a long flowering period from May to September.

Shrub-like *Polygala* species need a little shade, rather moist soil and generally dislike lime.

Polygonatum
There are about 30 species in this genus and they all originate from the temperate regions of the northern hemisphere. Practically all are woodland plants. Therefore they combine well with for instance ferns, shade loving grasses, *Rodgersia aesculifolia* and *Podophyllum*. The plants stand out well in large natural gardens in particular.

'Pink Dawn' is well short of pink. It is dwarf at 25 cm and long-lived, as are two other hybrids of *P. reptans*. One is 'Sapphire', sky-blue, 30 cm, and the other 'Blue Pearl' only 20 cm, both flowering May-June.

The tallest I know is *P. foliosissimum*. It is also the finest, being long-lived and long-flowering from late May to September, given fertile soil.

The flowers are deep mauve with yellow stamens on strong 100 cm stems; but although I have never known it to set seed, good sized plants are not difficult to divide, best in early Spring.

P. pulchellum (or *pulcherrimum*) grows with lots of evergreen basal foliage and has stiff 50 cm spikes of almost sky-blue flowers; a vigorous but compact plant which flowers from late Spring for several weeks.

Seed or division increases stock.

POLYGALA

Where happy in limy soil and full sun, *P. calcarea* makes a bright display of blue flowers only 5 cm high in late Spring. It makes deep-green, but not widely-spreading, mats. Other species below are inclined to be shrubby and lime-hating. They like peaty soil, a little shade, or a north aspect.

P. chamaebuxus is the best known, making a mound 12 cm high with small leathery leaves and creamy-yellow bicolour flowers.

The most spectacular is *P. chamaebuxus* 'Purpurea' ('Grandiflora') for the flowers are carmine with a yellow keel.

P. vayredae has a prostrate habit with narrower leaves and purple-red flowers, also yellow keeled. Both flower in early Summer and cuttings are better than attempted division.

POLYGONATUM

This genus includes the well-known and much-loved Solomon's seal, but there are others on similar lines well worthy of note. All prefer some shade; and once settled down they are best left alone for several years, expanding steadily just below surface.

They do not like hot and very dry situations and pay for added humus and occasional mulching.

P. giganteum may also be listed as *P. commutatum* or *P. canaliculatum*, but the first name is preferable because the plant is the tallest, with graceful stems up to 150 cm. It has glaucous foliage and the little clustered wiry bells dangle from the strong arching stems in early Summer.

P. falcatum is an unreliable name, apt to be

confused with *P. japonica*. For lack of certainty I give it to a dwarf leafy species 20 cm high with erect stems and a fairly vigorous spread. Although equally unsure of the validity of *P. multiflorum,* I believe this is the original Solomon's seal growing to about half the height of *P. giganteum*. It has a pretty form with variegated leaves, brighter than that of *P. odoratum*, which has louvred leafy 30 cm stems as if to shield the dangling, slightly scented little bells. The green-leaved form of both species lacks nothing in charm. *P. verticillatum* is not exciting. Its wiry stems reach 130 cm with narrow leaves and tiny purplish-green flowers. The dwarfest is the seldom-offered *P. hookeri*. This creeps below ground where shady and cool and sends up sheathed stems only 8 cm high bearing tiny ivory flowers May-June. Division of the above is best in late Autumn.

POLYGONUM

This highly distinctive genus has a vast range of species, from mat-forming to some over 200 cm tall. Some are first-rate garden subjects, free to flower and reliably perennial.

It includes some choice subjects as well as a few which should be avoided for being perniciously weedy. *P. capitatum, P. cuspidatum* (also known both as *Reynoutria japonica* and as *Fallopia japonica*), *P. compactum,* and *P. sachaliense* should be black-listed for gardens and the tall whites of *P. weyrichii, P. molle, P. paniculatum* and *P. rude* should only be used in a wild garden or as space fillers. That warning given, it can be said that a number of others are fully garden-worthy. Almost all polygonums are too tall to consider as alpines.

P. affine and its variations flower at only 15-20 cm but have rather too vigorous a surface spread. They are good for ground cover or a bank, having fingery leaves not unsightly when faded, and erect pokery spikes in Summer — sometimes in Autumn also.
'Darjeeling Red' is less bright than the pure-pink 'Dimity' or 'Donald Lowndes', but the latter is faulted for sometimes dying out in patches.
Two others are to be recommended as alpines.
P. tenuicaule has masses of pale-pink, small pokers in Spring, only 12 cm, from clumpy growth, but *P. vacciniifolium* is valuable for Autumn. It makes twiggy, spreading mats covered in 10 cm little pink pokers but needs a warm position.
The others mentioned also prefer sun but will take some shade. Ordinary soil suits.
P. amplexicaule, in contrast, makes a massive bush of summer growth up to 150 cm in good soil, but

Polygonatum species vary in height from 8 cm to 150 cm, but all have bending stems with dangling bell-shaped flowers.

Polygonum affine varieties are all good ground-coverers, and are available in pink or red colours.

POLYGONUM

Polygonum amplexicaule 'Arun Gem', sometimes called *Persicaria amplexicaulis* var. *pendula*, has clear-pink dangling spikes, 35 cm long.

Polygonum bistorta 'Superbum' forms light-pink 90 cm pokers.

is an easy, long-lived plant, making large clumps of tough roots. Flowering begins in June and continues till Autumn, with masses of thin pokers topping the leafy bush.

P. a. 'Atrosanguineum' is deep rosy-red, less bright than the variety 'Firetail'. Shorter forms are now available. At 90 cm 'Taurus' has blood-red flowers. 'Inverleith' is a vigorous crimson at 60 cm and 'Arun Gem' has clear-pink dangling spikes, 35 cm. All are for Summer into Autumn, and all require space in which to show their luxuriance.

P. bistorta itself is inferior to *P. bistorta* 'Superbum' which has finger-thick erect 90 cm pokers of pure light-pink in early Summer from vigorous clumps. This is best where not dry and it applies also to *P. campanulatum*, a very useful space filler with no vices. Its light-pink flowers come as clusters above dense leafy summer growth, from July till frost comes. It makes a marvellous subject for a bank or pondside.

P. carneum grows compactly and gives a good display May-July of pink pokers up to 50 cm.

P. millettii is one of the choicest and most distinctive. Given good moistish soil, above its clumpy base of narrow deep-green leaves come 30 cm pokers of deep red for many weeks.

P. macrophyllum is also very desirable for similar soil. Its long wavy-edged leaves arch over and are a perfect backcloth to the clear-pink 40 cm pokers above.

The trio of choice species for rich cool soil in sun or part shade is *P. sphaerostachyum*. The short bright-pink pokers begin in May and continue all Summer on leafy light-green stems if given a mid-season cut-back of any fading 60 cm stems.

P. regelianum also deserves to be known. It makes sturdy clumps with large basal leaves and has a long succession of pure-pink pokers to about 90 cm.

Finally comes rather an oddity. It is *P. viviparum*, and the white or pale-pink spikes above narrow basal leaves at 30 cm fade to reveal purplish seed. These germinate in situ and soon colonise weedily.

POLYPODIUM

There are two species of this fern suitable for gardens.

P. interjectum is native in Europe. The leaves can measure 60 cm if the site is right (under shrubs in deep moist soil).

The variety 'Cambricum' was found in 1743 in Wales: bright-green, leaf undersides bluish. 'Cornubiense' (found in 1867 in Cornwall) is dark green. It gives undivided leaves sometimes, which have to be removed. 'Omnilacerum' is a form of 'Cambricum', with less broad leaves. There are

Polypodium 'Cornubiense' may form undivided leaves, which should be removed.

more varieties, all slightly differing.
P. vulgare is the native form which can differ
greatly. In moist conditions the leaves can be up
to 60 cm, in other places they just reach 5 cm.
Several varieties, like 'Bifido-grandiceps', are
smaller than the species, with typically formed leaf
ends. Increase is by division.

POLYSTICHUM

These are the 'shield ferns'. The 'hard shield' is P.
polyblepharum (syn. *P. braunii*) and grows strongly
from a stout central stock with erect fronds to 45
cm. Though not evergreen, the one-season's growth
remains until new fronds come.
P. setiferum and its many variations of the 'soft
shield' are evergreen. Fronds of some arch over to
form dense green hussocks of intricate form and
grace. Variations are too complex to list and
describe, but they have a distinctive year-round
appeal.
All are easy to grow in shade and are drought
resistant.

POTENTILLA

Apart from the popular shrubby kinds, *P. fruticosa*,
there is a wealth of perennial or herbaceous
species and cultivars in heights ranging from
stemless mats of alpines to 60 cm border types. All
are easy to grow, given sun and good drainage,
and the vast majority are long-lived. Only one or
two alpines have an invasive habit. Those having
no below-ground spread, i.e. tufty or mat-forming,
are best divided and replanted every 3 years to
maintain flowering vigour.

P. aurea forms green prostrate mats with ample
golden flowers in Summer, and there is a double-
flowered form of this, both being 5 cm.
P. alba is white, more tufted and 15 cm tall.
P. cinerea (syn. *P. tommasiniana*) quickly forms a
grey-silver mat with a show of yellow in Spring.
P. eriocarpa is also mat-forming with grey-green
foliage and light-yellow flowers for most of the
Summer and makes somewhat invasive mats as
does the rather similar *P. cuneata*. Both are apt to
invade.

The silver-leaved tufts of *P. nitida* have rose-pink
flowers 5 cm in early Summer, and the tiny green-
leaved *P. tabernaemontani* 'Nana' has yellow
flowers for most of the Summer.
P. ternata (syn. *P. chrysocraspeda*) has larger green
tufts and yellow flowers for many weeks, but *P.*

Polystichum polyblepharum is a
strong growing, but not
evergreen, shield fern.

Potentilla x tonguei forms
crimson-blotched, light-orange
flowers on clumpy plants.

POTENTILLA

Potentilla aurea forms green prostrate mats with many golden flowers in Summer.

Potentilla nepalensis 'Miss Willmott' is one of the most widespread varieties of this species.

Pratia treadwellii is a mat-forming species for half-shaded places.

Pratia

A genus with about 20 species in Asia, South America, New Zealand and Australia. Practically all are small creeping plants which flower between July and August. Winter protection is absolutely necessary. They are suitable for both peaty soil and moist parts of the rock garden. Snails love them!

aurea 'Aurantiaca' is orange buff, both 8 cm. P. x tonguei is outstanding for its prostrate sprays from clumpy plants of crimson-blotched, light-orange flowers from June till Autumn. To round off the list there's P. fragiformis (syn. P. megalantha), 20 cm high, which has bright yellow flowers above silky, silvery foliage in early Summer.

As border perennials the majority available are hybrids. They are nothing if not colourful. P. argyrophylla has some variations of this sturdy, silver-leaved species. It is itself clear-yellow, but P. atrosanguinea has blood-red strawberry-type flowers on 45 cm sprays. 'Flamenco' is even more brilliant, but with green leaves.

All flower June – August. The old favourite 'Gibson's Scarlet' is shorter but longer in flower, and identical with 'Congo'.

Many other hybrids exist but some have become rare. Happily, the early, silver-leaved 'Yellow Queen', 30 cm, is still around, as is the sumptuous double 'Gloire de Nancy' with its large flowers of suffused orange. Mahogany-red 'Mons. Rouillard' is somewhat similar, and the fiery-orange of 'Wm. Rollison' is quite startling. These are in the range 40-50 cm, but 'Blazeaway' with its double flame-orange flowers is 30 cm with grey-green strawberry-type leaves, which applies to all these hybrids.

P. nepalensis has two well-known variations in the pink 'Miss Willmott', but may well be superceded by the clearer-pink 'Helen Jane', which so far has proved more reliable. 'Roxana' is pinkish-orange suffused, and 'Firedance' is yellow with a red centre, but apt to revert to yellow overall.

The nepalensis kinds are best from seed and do not readily divide. Both these and the other hybrids above are inclined to be less than erect when flowering, but this is no fault to remedy with supports; This would spoil the overall effect and is unnecessary. All are under 60 cm and cover a long period of Summer.

P. warrenii (syn. P.recta) is taller and upright, with clustered flower heads topping 70 cm stems in June-July.

P. thurberi is a newcomer and this too grows erectly to 30 cm with good foliage and small but rich-crimson flowers in early Summer.

POTERIUM – see SANGUISORBA

PRATIA

The only species likely to be available is P. treadwellii. This forms prostrate mats and has stemless white flowers followed by purple berries. It prefers a cool, semi-shaded place where not dry or exposed, divided in Spring. P. pedunculata has tiny pale blue flowers, but is apt to invade.

PRIMULA

Experts have divided this vast and varied genus of over 500 species into 30 groups, designed to classify botanically, but for the purpose of this book they must be covered according mainly to height – as between alpines and the taller ones which are either shade or moisture lovers.

Dwarf primulas

Some of the dwarfer kinds are adaptable to sun or partial shade, others prefer full shade, and some are best in an alpine house.

Readers interested in growing a wide range of primulas would do well to make a study from more detailed information than is possible in this context, and authoritative books on this very complex genus are available.

The dwarf kinds include, of course, the primrose and oxlip, as well as auriculas. Some with resemblance to primrose in habit are known as 'petiolares' and these are difficult to grow in other than a cool northern or western climate and are rarely offered in catalogues. I have almost given up trying to grow them in East Anglia with its low rainfall and humidity.

Many dwarf primulas, including variations on the primrose, enjoy stiff or heavy soil. This applies also to oxlips and cowslips.

Shade is not essential, nor is soil richness. Hybridists have produced some fascinating double-flowered ones in many shades of colour, and tissue culture appears to have given them more vigour.

Some old favourites, including 'Wanda' and the ever popular 'Garryard', now come under *P. x pruhoniciana* and some specialists offer a wide range of these and the doubles and the *P. auricula* types. These also prefer strong soil and mainly sunny positions. They are distinct for having rounded leaves often powdery, and clusters held on open heads. They tend to grow out of the ground as the rosettes lengthen and need to be set in more deeply every few years. All the above are easily divided and this is best done soon after flowering.

Also dwarf, but preferring shade and humus soil, are a few species and varieties with flowers setting closely on the plant.

The hybrid 'Johanna' is one of them and has bright-pink flowers in March, April. In this group are some of the difficult species, such as the soft-mauve *P. edgeworthii* and the light-blue *P. whiteii*. These 'petiolares' are connoisseur plants for those able to grow them, but 'Johanna' is not difficult.

Later in Spring comes another group of woodlanders, mostly growing from 10-15 cm. *P. cortusoides*, and *P. heuchrifolia* have deep lilac-pink flowers above soft basal foliage.

These and many more can be raised from seed and are not very long-lived, but the *P. sieboldii* varieties are good perennials and slowly spread

Primula vialii is unique for having dense poker-like spikes, flowering crimson, then turning to violet when fully open.

Primula

Most primulas occur in the northern hemisphere. Some species were found in South America, southern Asia and Africa. There are annual and biennial kinds and even semi-shrubs, but the majority are perennials.

Primula veris is one of the smaller species, in this case with bright-yellow, scented flowers.

PRIMULA

Primula beesiana is a 'candelabra' form which can reach over 1 m.

Primula rosea 'Delight', has pink flowers at 15-20 cm.

Primula denticulata, the 'drumstick' primula.

Primula x bullesiana is one of the well known hybrids within the 'candelabras'.

below the surface. Given shade and light rich soil they are a joy in April, May, with loose heads of quite large flowers in white, light and deep pink, and pale blue at 15 cm above soft basal leaves. 'Snowflakes', 'Geisha Girl', 'Mikado', 'Cherubim' and the pale-blue 'Seraphim' fit these colours. Many other woodland species exist but are usually available only from specialists, if at all.

The easiest to grow are popular enough and of these the 'drumstick' *P. denticulata* always appeals for early Spring in white, mauve and pink. They do not need shade, nor does *P. rosea*, also easy where not dry, having intense-pink flowers at 15-20 cm in the c.v. 'Delight'.

Both these come readily from seed, but old plants may be divided.

For May, June, such as *P. alpicola* in creamy white and pale violet are good perennials, flowering at about 30 cm, but the yellow and scented *P. sikkimensis* is somewhat taller.

Candelabras

What are generally known as 'bog primulas' do better in more open soil rather than where tight and saturated. They thrive in both sun and partial shade and come in a wide range of colours, often carrying whorls of flowers up the stem which suggest the group name of 'candelabra'. Not all candelabras, however, are specially in need of moisture, though none will flourish where dry.

P. cockburniana has whorls of orange-scarlet flowers, shorter than most at 45 cm. This and the rich crimson *P. pulverulenta* are not long-lived but come well from seed.

P. japonica is best-known of the candelabras and is seen in pink, white and red up to 60 cm.

For a good yellow, *P. helodoxa* is unsurpassed, also 60 cm, though heights may vary according to soil richness. Many more exist, including the worthwhile orange *P. bulleyana* and the purple-red *P. burmanica*, but crosses have given some excellent mixed strains. These in a massed group are showy indeed with an entrancing colour range. All are seed raised, but two outstanding hybrids 'Rowallane' and 'Inverewe' are sterile and increase by division. They grow lustily to 70 cm in salmon-orange shades.

June is the peak month for these taller primulas, but the 90 cm tall, strong-growing *P. florindae* will keep on much longer and will take more moisture than most others. It has heads, not whorls, of pure yellow.

P. secundiflora is rosy crimson and powdery.

P. viallii is unique for having dense pokery spikes. These come from a small fibrous-rooted plant. Well-grown plants may reach 60 cm, but are equally bright if shorter, having crimson buds turning to violet when fully open.

PRUNELLA

These are easy growing, mat-forming plants good for frontal positions. From a green base come stumpy spikes in June-July and sometimes later if cut back.

Three under the name 'Loveliness' give pink, lilac and white, 25 cm tall.

P. incisa, 15 cm, has deeply-cut leaves and reddish flowers, not very different from *P. x webbiana*. 'Little Red Riding Hood' is the brightest of these. Spikes are only 12 cm on vigorous green mats. All are shallow-rooting and divide freely, doing well in sun or any but dry sandy soil.

PTEROCEPHALUS

Pterocephalus parnassi used to be under the *Scabiosa* genus, but is still an attractive alpine. It soon spreads into a soft, greyish-leaved mat and sends up 10 cm stems carrying lilac-pink pincushion flowers.

These do not come all at once but continue somewhat sparsely over several weeks in Summer. It needs sun and good drainage and is not for coldest regions.

PULMONARIA

These are amongst the most valuable of easy-growing plants for spring flowering – some show even in March. They are adaptable to all but dry sunny positions and will flourish in quite deep shade, giving good ground cover between shrubs etc. They divide readily – best in early Autumn. All but *P. angustifolia* are thereabouts evergreen. This has narrow leaves arching out as the first flower sprays appear in March, small, bright blue and bell-shaped. There are several other named cultivars: 'Azurea', 'Munstead' and 'Mawsons' are blue, but the white forms are less attractive. Of the other species, *P. officinalis*, *P. rubra* and *P. saccharata*, many hybrids have appeared. Some, such as 'Bowles Red', are rather coarse-growing with large rough leaves. 'Highdown', rich blue, is also robust at 30 cm; but the most attractive are those which make a long-lasting mound of overlapping leaves after the pink, blue or white flowers have finished.

'Sissinghurst White' is popular, but 'Pink Dawn' has highly decorative leaves spotted white. 'Red Start' is really red, and 'Highdown' a strong growing blue.

P. saccharata is the species which gives this variegated foliage, 'Argentea' being more silvery than green. 'Margery Fish', 'Mrs. Moon' and others make up a splendid range for those able to accommodate these worthy, undemanding plants.

Prunella x *webbiana* 'Loveliness' is available in three different colours: pink, lilac and white.

Pterocephalus
There are about 25 species of shrubs, annuals, biennials and perennials in this genus and they originate from the Mediterranean to central Asia.
P. parnassi (syn. *P. perennis*) can cover stones and walls completely within a few years. The difference with *Scabiosa* is in the inflorescence. *Pterocephalus* has 12 or more flowers together, *Scabiosa* only 5.

Left: *Pterocephalus parnassi* may be found listed under *P. perennis*.

Below: *Pulmonaria* 'Pink Dawn' is a well known hybrid with white-spotted leaves.

PULSATILLA

PULSATILLA

This is now a separate genus from *Anemone*, of which the best known is the 'pasque flower'. *P.vulgaris* is now seen in several variations from the original purple-mauve. In the wild it grows in limy soil and I find it flourishes better in very sharp drainage and poor soil in conditions which are rich or heavy. In Spring come goblet-shaped flowers of a hoary appearance, which develop into attractive winged seed heads. Foliage is ferny all summer; and though plants do not spread, they become a fair size and long-lived where suited. They do not divide successfully and seed should be sown as soon as ripe. Heights vary from 20 to 30 cm and they are at their best in April, May. Colours are white, several shades of mauve, lavender, purple, pink and ruby red. Once planted as youngsters, they should be left alone.

P. alpina also has lacy, greyish foliage and large white cup flowers in Spring at 40 cm, but the yellow form *P. alpina* 'Sulphurea' is superb. So is *P. caucasica* which may well be a geographical form of *P. alpina*. This is rare, and equally demanding of perfect drainage to encourage its somewhat tardy growth and its lovely soft-yellow flowers.
P. vernalis is also rarely seen and highly prized. White and yellow stamened goblet flowers stand above low lacy greenery in Spring, laced with golden and purple hairs.

Pulsatilla

There are about 30 *Pulsatilla* species, all in the northern hemisphere and as far north as the arctic. They flower between March and July. Some species such as *P. vernalis* hate lime, others for instance *P. vulgaris* need some lime. Therefore cultivation is different and the species cannot be simply interchanged.

Above: *Pulsatilla vulgaris* 'Rubra' shows just one of the many shades available.

Below left: *Pulsatilla* species should be left undisturbed, once planted.

Below: *Pulsatilla alpina* 'Sulphurea' is a superb variety.

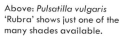

PYRETHRUM

Pyrethrum coccineum (syn. *Chrysanthemum coccineum*). I make no excuses for keeping the old name for this group which is distinctive enough to remain separated from *Chrysanthemum* to which it has now been assigned. The main genus is well-known for the range of cultured daisy-type flowers in Summer, single and double, including some rich colours, and excellent for cutting.
All grow with delicate carroty foliage above clumpy fibrous-rooted plants and will often flower a second time if cut hard back in July. At one time and another I have grown over 50 varieties, but now the range is more limited. They can be raised from seed as a mixture and division is best in early Spring or right after flowering.
Height varies: 60-80 cm.
Colours of the single-flowered are white and many shades of pink including salmon and red. Doubles are less vigorous but in smaller colour range and 60-80 cm is the usual height. Lately, some dwarfs have appeared, only 20-30 cm tall, under the names 'Laurin', single red, 'Pink Petite' and 'Red Dwarf', semi-double red. They do not lack vigour and make attractive frontal groups.

P. parthenium is the 'feverfew' with an astringent smell in the leaves, reputedly good for headaches. It has a golden leaved form, but neither is more than a biennial, seeding itself. These and the double white button-flowered 'White Bonnet' grow to barely 60 cm in June-July, but 'White Bonnet' is also short-lived and much inferior to one we grew 60 years ago, now happily with us again. It is 'Snowflakes' and is a good perennial with firm upright stems to 75 cm, and masses of pure white double buttons above the leafy, bushy habit. Cutting back in August after flowering ensures new basal growth. The c.v. named 'Rowallane' is rather weak.

RAMONDA

These, along with the related *Haberlea*, are best grown in north-facing crevices and even vertical walls, and resent being on the flat. They are long-lived with broad, flat rosettes of darkly-evergreen leaves, and flowers come in short sprays, 8-10 cm, in Spring and early Summer.

Only three species exist, *R. myconi* (syn. *R. pyrenaica*) being the best known, and has open-petalled purple-mauve flowers, though white and pink forms have appeared occasionally from seed, which is the only means of increase. The other two species, *P. nathaliae* and *P. serbica*, are rarely offered; and in any case, differences are only slight.

RANUNCULUS

The buttercup family includes treasures as well as weeds.

The wild meadow species is *R. bulbosus* and has a variation which is a good garden plant far removed from weediness. It is *R. bulbosus* 'Speciosus Plenus' which makes a neat, leafy clump and has fully double glistening flowers of good size, yellow with just a hint of green, only 25 cm high, June-July. Although easy in any but poor dry soil, more care is needed for the delightful double form of *R. aconitifolius* — known from olden times as 'fair maids of Kent' (or France). This likes rich soil, fairly moist, and branching stems carry masses of pure-white button flowers, fully double, up to 60 cm in early Summer.

There is a taller more robust single-flowered in *R. planatifolius* which flowers at 120 cm where moist. A double is also seen in another wild species, *R. acris*. This is not at all fussy and has a steady but not invasive spread. The 60 cm stems carry an array of bright yellow flowers in early Summer.

Pyrethrum 'Red Dwarf' only grows to 30 cm. It is a semi-double late- Spring-flowering variety.

Above: True double pyrethrums are perhaps the most showy of this genus. They may also be offered under the name *Chrysanthemum*. Many of these can be rather short-lived.

Above: *Ramonda myconi* are long-lived alpines for semi-shaded positions.

Right: *Ranunculus montanus* 'Molten Gold' forms yellow flowers in Spring.

RANUNCULUS

Ranunculus acris is available in a double or single-flowering type. They are steady spreaders, but not too invasive, flowering in early Summer.

R. repens has a double yellow form but creeps, rapidly rooting as it spreads, and is best avoided. All the above are best divided in early Autumn. There are relatively few dwarf species in cultivation and R. amplexicaulis has pointed glaucous leaves and 25 cm sprays of pure-white flowers in early Summer. They are finest in the form 'Grandiflora'.

Also glaucous, but grassy-leaved, is the very attractive R. gramineus. It gives a long display of shining yellow buttercups in early Summer, and is only 25 cm tall from tufty plants.

R. gouanii is also tufty but green leaved and this too is yellow, only 15 cm.

Smaller still is R. montanus 'Molten Gold', with yellow flowers above the green, 8 cm in Spring. It needs frequent division and loses foliage later in Summer.

All these dwarf kinds prefer light soil and mainly sunny positions.

RAOULIA

These are mat-forming alpines coming mainly from New Zealand. They grow in sun and well-drained soil but are resentful of winter wet and severe frosts. Those below are the hardiest and are grown for their close silvery foliage.

R. australis is the best-known, with silvery mats of no height at all composed of tiny hard rosettes and occasional yellow flowers.

R. hookeri is slightly larger and makes a good silver pad.

R. tenuicaulis, though less silvery-grey-green also spreads well as a carpeter.

In mild districts, all three are useful ground coverers over spring alpine bulbs.

REINECKEA

Reineckea carnea. This is synonymous with Liriope hyacinthiflora. It makes evergreen spreading tufts of deep-green bladed leaves and has tiny spikes of pink flowers in Spring.

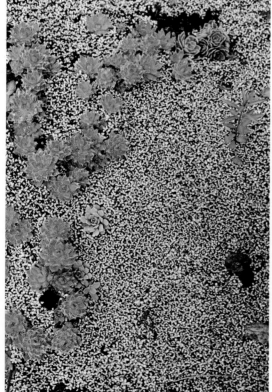

Below left: The main attraction of Raoulia australis is its formation of flat, silvery mats.

Below: Reineckea carnea is a pink-flowering, carpet-forming evergreen.

Reineckea

This genus with its one species (R. carnea) was not only classified under Liriope, but also under Sansevieria. The plant reaches a height of 30 cm.

Out of the pink racemes you will find red berries develop. Reineckia will make large carpets quite quickly in a suitable place. Given a sufficiently warm and sheltered site and well-drained soil, it provides a good ground cover under shrubs.

Rhazya orientalis is not easily obtainable, but its blue periwinkle-type flowers during Summer make it worth growing.

RHAZYA

Rhazya orientalis. This resembles *Amsonia* but is shorter and less vigorous. The 45 cm wiry stems with green willow leaves branch out and carry small blue periwinkle-type flowers June-August. It does not divide easily and seed is scanty, and its appeal keeps it in short supply.

RHEUM

The ornamental species of rhubarb are well worth growing, though some of them need ample space. *R. alexandrae* has leaves of modest size – rounded and smooth, and with a compact rootstock. In May come stems carrying curious but charming papery yellow bracts on spikes up to 90 cm tall, which stay effective for several weeks. Ordinary good garden soil suits this unusual plant, as it does the more massive but imposing *R. palmatum*. One should go for either the 'Rubrum' or 'Atrosanguineum' forms, since these are deep pinkish-red when their 180 cm spikes open out in late Spring. The first leaves, too, are brightly coloured from early April till flowering time – pink, red, purple, but after flowering, fading to green. These rheums have such a wide spread when leaves develop, that an established plant needs a 120-150 cm diameter spacing.

R. 'Ace of Spades' is less massive and has white spikes to 130 cm in Spring above long-lasting jagged base leaves.
R. 'Kialense' is an interesting dwarf only 30 cm tall, with miniature leaves and lots of brownish-red flowers on loose sprays during early Summer. Plants are clumpy and vigorous.
R. delavayi is also a miniature with more erect spikes, but plants lack vigour and hardiness. 15 cm. Division of rheums is best in Autumn or very early Spring.

Rheum palmatum is a very imposing ornamental rhubarb with medicinal values.

RODGERSIA

Left: *Rodgersia aesculifolia* is, as the name indicates, chestnut-leaved. It needs good moist soil, and a somewhat sheltered position is best.

Below: *Rodgersia tabularis* has broad umbrella-like leaves. Creamy-white flowers appear on stalks up to 150 cm.

RHODIOLA – see SEDUM

RODGERSIA

These have become deservedly popular for their handsome foliage as well as for flowering. They are fully hardy but need good moist soil and prefer some shelter in positions exposed to fierce winds, otherwise shade is not essential. The roots spread as rhizomes close to the surface but are not invasive.

Most of the species have large, deeply divided leaves like an out-stretched hand up to 30 cm across on stems up to 80 cm high. Above come strong spikes carrying a flowering plume, June – August.

Once well established, clumps benefit from a little annual mulch, but division is quite easy.

The species *R. aesculifolia* (chestnut leaved), *R. sambucifolia* (elder leaved), *R. podophylla*, *R. pinnata* and *R.* 'Purdomii' do not differ greatly. The latter flowers at 90 cm whilst the others may go to 120 cm in good moist soil. Hybrids have occurred, but with one exception all are creamy white.

R. pinnata 'Superba' is pink with reddish stems and 'Irish Bronze' is notable for the hue of its leaves. *R. pinnata* 'Elegans' is elegant indeed and is the tallest and freest to flower of a creamy shade. *R. tabularis* is quite distinct and has broad umbrella-type leaves up to 100 cm on single stalks and above come creamy-white spikes up to 150 cm.

Romanzoffia

There are 4 species of this genus which originate from the region of Alaska and other parts of northern America. They are low perennials with more or less kidney-shaped foliage. They are not very rich in flowering, but they are a real acquisition for lovers of alpines. They can stand moderate shade and moist soil. Sometimes the foliage dies down after flowering and new growth appears again towards the end of the Summer.

Romanzoffia unalaschkensis is a mat-forming alpine, preferring a cool position.

ROMANZOFFIA

Romanzoffia unalaschkensis. This formidable name is for a mat-forming alpine rather like a mossy *Saxifraga*. It has 5 cm stems carrying waxy white flowers in early Summer. It is best in a cool position and divided after flowering.

ROMNEYA

The 'Californian tree poppy' is semi-shrubby; and though cut back by frost in northern climes, the deep roots usually sprout again. These are not subjects to grow close to other perennials; and, if suited in the stony, well-drained soil they demand, they will spread far and wide below ground. Although untidy in some respects, the pure-white poppy flowers nestling amid bluish foliage are appealing; but having planted pot grown plants in a carefully selected site, they are then best left alone.

R. coulteri is the best known and will attain over 200 cm with white flowers 8 cm across, bright with yellow stamens.

R. trichocalyx is less tall and has even larger flowers; and in both, flowering keeps on from July till Autumn.

Romneya coulteri, the 'Californian tree poppy', is a tall semi-shrubby perennial. It flowers beautifully, but is a rather vigorous spreader.

Below: Roscoea auriculata is a fine species with rich, violet-purple flowers on 40 cm stems and deep-green foliage.

ROSCOEA

In recent years these have become decidedly popular. They are quite unlike any other perennial, having curiously attractive hooded lipped flowers on stem-sheathed leaves. The roots are fleshy as vertical thongs, rather brittle and holding orange-coloured sap. They appear above ground rather late in Spring but soon run up to flower. Any well-drained soil in sun or part shade suits them and with care they are very easy to divide in early Spring.

R. alpina, though dwarf enough as an alpine, is apt to spread itself rather too quickly. It has pinkish flowers on 15 cm stems in June-July.

R. auriculata appears to be the same as R. purpurea. It grows freely but compactly and has deep-green foliage and violet-purple flowers on erect 40 cm stems in Summer.

R. procera (syn. R. purpurea var. procera) may be a form of this, but it is much finer and larger leaved with larger, richer, violet flowers on 50 cm stems: a splendid plant, flowering June – August.

R. cautleoides is the earliest to flower, light yellow, but growth is less leafy.

R. cautleoides 'Kew Beauty' is very beautiful with its large primrose-yellow flowers above handsome foliage in June-July.

R. humeana grows stockily with large leaves and stiff stems carrying lilac-purple, yellow-throated flowers in Summer, 30-40 cm.

R. 'Beesiana' may be a hybrid of R. humeana. It has massed leafy stems and parti-coloured flowers lilac, cream and violet, 30 cm high.

Roscoea cautleoides is the earliest flowering species within this genus.

RUDBECKIA

R. 'Goldquelle' is outstanding for its erect bushy habit, well clothed with deep-green leaves, and set with fine double chrome- yellow flowers from early August into October. The height is little more than 90 cm and it is a far tidier plant than the tall, floppy R. 'Autumn Sun', (syn R. nitida 'Herbstonne') but even this will reach 150 cm or more.
All these rudbeckias will divide in early Spring and will flower for longer in good soil, not too dry, than where starved.

See under Echinacea for what is still sometimes called R. purpurea – the 'purple cone flower'.

Rudbeckia laciniata 'Goldquelle' shows a perfectly erect, bushy growth, with deep-green leaves and double-yellow flowers in late Summer and Autumn.

Rudbeckia fulgida 'Goldsturm' will flower all Summer and Autumn.

Rudbeckia

There are about 30 species of *Rudbeckia*, some of which are annuals. Of the perennial species in particular, the tall kinds have been very succesful in gardens for many years. Species such as *R. fulgida* were seen everywhere. Once in the garden however, they were difficult to get rid of. Because these kinds are so rampant, people have become somewhat careful, and nowadays varieties such as 'Goldsturm' are preferred.

RUDBECKIA

For long flowering and general reliability, the rudbeckias rank highly for adding brightness in the garden in late Summer and Autumn, even though all are in shades of yellow.
R. deamii will flower in great profusion from late July into October with its black-centred rayed flowers. The height is 60-75 cm, a little taller than the deep-yellow R. 'Goldsturm' which in good soil will flower for an even longer period. These supercede the old R. speciosa and there are taller, grey-leaved species in R. subtomentosa and R. mollis which grow 90-120 cm, flowering July-September.

The foregoing rudbeckias are mat-forming with a shallow-rooting outward spread. Nearly all such plants deteriorate after 2-3 years. The remedy is to replant using only the outer, more vigorous growth in enriched soil.

RUTA

Ruta graveolens Jackman's Blue Rue'. Although this rue is half way to being a shrub, it fits in with other perennials near the front where its shapely 40 cm bushes can be appreciated. The lobed leaves are distinctly bluish and evergreen; and above, at 70 cm, come clusters of yellow flowers. Severe frosts may damage the upper growth but if cut back in Spring it will fill out again from the base. Full sun is much preferred and increase is from cuttings.

SAGINA see Arenaria

SALVIA

This is another large genus with great variations, and it is the only one I know which has red, blue and yellow flowered species. Unfortunately, a number are not hardy except in warm climates. Almost all prefer sun but otherwise they are not fussy as far as soil is concerned.

S. ambigens (syn. *S. guaranitica*) makes a stately bush of deep greenery topped with an array of light blue flowers up to 130 cm for a long time in later Summer. The clumpy roots are close to being fully hardy and they divide easily in Spring. This is a charmer for fairly moist or rich soil.
S. argentea makes a wide base of large, felted, almost white leaves, and sends up branching stems of white hooded flowers in Summer to about 80 cm. It is not long-lived but comes freely from seed.
S. azurea is tender but has narrow grey-leaved spikes up to 200 cm in late Summer and Autumn. These carry sky-blue flowers and in mild regions make a superb display.
S. blepharophylla is also tender, but vigorous enough to keep alive in Winter in warm districts. It makes a mat of small green leaves and has 30 cm spikes of brightest red for many weeks after June.
S. bulleyana has yellow flowers with a maroon base.
Bright green puckered leaves set these off; and with the flower spikes only 40 cm tall, it makes a neat and unusual subject.
S. farinacea is popular, in sunny climes, for its long season of blue flowered spikes on a grey-white bushy habit. 60 cm.
S. glutinosa makes a sturdy bush. Although the flowers are but pale yellow, it is lusty and leafy as well as being hardy.
S. haematodes makes a splendid show of blue flowers on 100 cm spikes in early Summer. It comes freely from seed as some compensation for its lack of longevity. The hybrid between this and *S.* x

Ruta graveolens 'Jackman's Blue Rue' is a semi-shrubby perennial with bluish evergreen leaves, and yellow flowers during May-July.

One of the varieties of *Salvia farinacea*. This one is 'Victoria'. A popular species for sunny positions.

SALVIA

Above: *Salvia officinalis*, Sage, is a well known kitchen herb, but the variegated forms like this 'Tricolor' also have ornamental value.

Left: *Salvia nemorosa* is one of the best spiky perennials, with rich, violet-blue flowers from June to August.

Salvia

This is an enormous genus which comprises more than 300 species. They occur practically all over the world in the temperate and subtropical zones. A number of species such as *S. argentea* are beautifully silvery-haired. Such plants mainly like dry conditions. They make nice combinations with many shrubs and perennials such as *Echinops*, *Santolina*, *Nepeta*, *Perovskia* and *Lavandula*.

superba, named 'Indigo', is long-lived with showy spikes of deep blue.

S. involucrata is another tender species but the form named *bethellii* is worth caring for. It makes a brightly green bush up to 130 cm, bright with quite large carmine flowers in later Summer and Autumn.

S. jurisicii forms a tufty base to its 45 cm spikes, lilac-blue, and is reasonably hardy.

S. nemorosa is more often listed as just *S. superba*. It is one of the very best spiky perennials and makes such a contrast to the yellows, with long tapering spikes of rich violet-blue from June to August. The height is about 120 cm, but there are named cultivars of similar colour and habit, but less tall. 'Lubeca' is 70 cm, 'East Friesland' 60 cm, and 'May Night' 40 cm and earlier to flower. All these flower longer if faded spikes are removed, and all are hardy, increased by division.

S. pratensis has 80 cm branching spikes in blue and occasionally pink forms but is not spectacular, nor is the 120 cm *S. verticillata*, with a more bushy habit, and deep blue flowers.

S. uliginosa is distinct not only for being very late to flower, but for its preference for moist soil. In northern climes it is not reliably hardy, but the 160 cm spikes with small light-green leaves carry an array of sky-blue flowers in Autumn.

It is safe to say that those salvias which are long-lived with an expanding root system are safe to divide, preferably in Spring, whilst the others are best raised from seed.

Sanguinaria canadensis, the 'blood root', needs some shade and light soil in order to flourish.

SANGUINARIA

Sanguinaria canadensis, the 'blood root', so named for the red sap in its fleshy root, always excites attention. In Spring come scalloped glaucous leaves; and at about 15 cm, large white poppy-type flowers are revealed. The fully double form is even more appealing but its display is rather brief.

Requirements are for light soil with sand and peat, but it is not a lime hater, nor need full shade be given.

SAPONARIA

SANGUISORBA

Syn. *Poterium*. These are vigorous spiky plants with deeply cut fingered leaves. They have tough but dividable roots and will grow in any reasonable soil in sun.

P. canadensis grows to a stately 200 cm, with white 'bottle brushes' on erect branching stems in late Summer.

P. obtusa has thicker 'bottle brushes' held at an angle above a very leafy vigorous base.

P. magnificum 'Album' may be a variant on this, but it soon makes a massive plant. Both are about 100 cm in flower for July-August.

P. sitchensis has narrower reddish pokers on more elegant spikes; and though less leafy, it is more compact in growth.

SANTOLINA

These are strictly shrubs, but are soft-wooded and dwarf enough to enhance perennials with their shapely bushes of grey or green throughout the year.

S. chamaecyparissus (syn. *S. incana*) seldom exceeds 60 cm and may be clipped to preserve shapeliness. Yellow button flowers appear in Summer on short stems. There is a seldom-seen dwarf form *S. chamaecyparissus* 'Nana' about 25 cm, but it is less hardy.

S. virens (syn. *S. rosmarinifolia* and *S. viridis*) is bright green with yellow flowers. It is easy to grow and root from cuttings and needs only a sunny place.

SAPONARIA

Saponaria officinalis, also known as 'bouncing Bet' and 'soapwort', is a rapid spreader below ground and generally untidy. But it does produce 75 cm stems which carry single or double flowers in white and two shades of pink in late Summer. The best of the saponarias are alpines, although *S. x lempergii* 'Max Frei' is only 30 cm, having a mounded floppy habit and pink flowers June, July. True alpines must include the 'Bressingham' hybrid which forms an almost flat pad covered by brilliant deep-pink flowers in early Summer. It demands perfect drainage with some humus and a mainly sunny place. It can only be increased from cuttings and has a slow spread.

The best-known and easiest dwarf species is *S. ocymoides*. It makes a fair surface spread from a compact rootstock and carries a bright display of pink flowers only 10 cm high, June-August. It also obliges by being easy from seed.

S. x olivana is also a hybrid with low tufts and quite large pink flowers in Summer, 5 cm.

Above: *Santolina chamaecyparissus* is a semi-shrubby species.

Above right: The flowers of *Sanguisorba obtusa* are thick 'bottle brushes'.

Above: *Saponaria x olivana* forms low tufts and has pink-flowers in Summer.

Saponaria ocymoides is a spreading dwarf species, displaying bright pink flowers on 10 cm stems.

Santolina

Several of the 10 species of this genus of shrubs are not sufficiently winter-hardy to survive severe Winters. All originate from the Mediterranean. Once settled (for instance in the rock garden) they have a tendency to expand and develop into large bushes. The plants can be pruned well and are therefore sometimes grown as a small hedge. They make a good combination with other plants which like full sun and drought.

SATUREJA

Satureja montana, Winter Savory, is a kitchen herb, (eaten with beans), with very attractive tiny flowers.

SATUREJA

This is a small genus which has become somewhat mixed up with *Micromeria*. They are mostly dwarf with small flowers and aromatic foliage and easy to grow in sun and well-drained soil. All may be increased by division, best in Spring.

S. illyrica (may be listed as *Micromeria*) makes a low shrubby plant with small deep-green leaves and short spikes to 30 cm of deep blue in Summer.

S. montana makes a mound up to 30 cm high and is covered in late Summer and Autumn with tiny blue flowers.

There is a dwarfer variation as well as one somewhat taller with lighter-blue flowers. All should be clipped back in Spring.

S. repanda is white-flowered in late Summer, coming on a green carpet, though not evergreen.

S. subspicata grows into a tight, grey and somewhat prickly hummock barely 5 cm high, with pink flowers nestling therein in late Summer.

Saxifraga trifurcata is one of the 'mossy' Saxifrages, forming low green mounds with white flowers in April-May.

Saxifraga

A very variable and large genus with more than 350 species. The flowering times differ greatly. It is possible to have flowering *Saxifraga* from the early Spring till October. However, most species flower between March and June. They are not only free-flowering plants, but their rosettes of leaves very often are decorative too. Ideal plants for the rock garden, they need little care and are hardly ever troubled by pests or diseases.

SAXIFRAGA

The best way to deal with this genus is to divide it into four groups;
1. partial shade preferred
2. cool shade
3. mainly sun, not too dry
4. sun

This large and diverse genus is also best divided into groups in keeping with cultural requirements based on natural habitat. The easiest to grow in ordinary soil other than in hot dry positions are the 'mossy' Saxifrages, **Group 1**.

These have green rosettes forming a low mound or carpet, almost invariably green and having sprays of open, bell-shaped flowers in April to May. Colours obtainable vary from white to cream and many shades of pink through to blood red, and plants vary in height from 5 to 20 cm in named cultivars. They are best replanted every two to three years to restore neatness and vigour.

Group 2 has similar cultural requirements and includes the ubiquitous London Pride *S. umbrosa* (now *S. urbium*) which is valuable for shady places giving good evergreen ground cover and a show of small, deep-pink flowers on 25 cm stems. This has dwarfed cultivars, such as *primuloides* 'Elliott's Variety', a neat miniature with evergreen rosettes and flowers 10 cm high.

Saxifraga x urbium is a hybrid for cool shade. It is an evergreen ground-coverer, with deep-pink flowers.

The white S. *cuneifolia* is pretty and there is one form with variegated rosettes.

S. *aizoides* 'Atrorubens' is a slow growing, green carpeter, having brownish-red flowers in Summer, 5 cm.

A cross between this and S. *primuloides* named 'Primulaize' is charming for its 8 cm sprays of deep carmine from June to September. This is best in shade and peaty soil, as is the handsome S. *fortunei* and its variations.

These are shallow-rooting, clump-forming plants and make a fine canopy of large, handsome leaves from Spring till October when they erupt into showers of starry white flowers to 25 cm. The type is green leaved, coppery-green underneath, but 'Wanda's Variety' has reddish-purple leaves, while 'Rubrifolia' is coppery red. The last two flower above the leaves about 20 cm tall. Although not quite 100 per cent hardy in cold areas, they are easily protected with leaves from November to March to ensure survival and they appreciate a spring application of a peaty top-dressing.

In this group must be placed the early-flowering S. *oppositifolia*. They prefer some sun provided moisture is not lacking.

They form mats of dark sessile foliage and the terminal flowers are little cups of intensely bright pink, only 2 cm above ground in March to April. They root down as they spread and are quite evergreen. Replanting is best in early Summer when moist.

Group 3 is of cushion-forming Saxifrages, known as Kabschias. With a few exceptions, these are slow growing; and although they need well-drained soil, many preferring gritty or scree conditions, they dislike being in full sun all day. The easier, faster-growing kinds have sizeable low mounds of mostly green or grey-green rosettes with flowers in white or yellow shades showing colour often by March and continuing through April, at 5-10 cm tall.

S. x *apiculata* is the best known with primrose-yellow flowers, with a white form 'Alba', with S. *haagii* and 'Gold Dust' deeper yellow, and 'Elizabethae' soft yellow. There are very many Kabschias in the slower-growing range, most of them being silver-leaved cultivars, having white, pink and near-red flowers as well as shades of yellow. The tiny close-packed rosettes are hard to the touch, some with such stemless flowers as to be virtually at ground level, others having short stems up to 10-12 cm as a clustered flower spike. The range includes choice connoisseurs' items which are grown in scree soil, troughs or in an alpine house. The best known of proven worth are S. *burseriana* 'Gloria' for a white, 'Cranbourne' and 'Jenkinsae' for light pink, 'Megasaeflora' and 'Bridget' for deep pink, 'Grace Farwell' or 'Winifred' for a near

Saxifraga arendsii hybrids are mat-forming, mossy plants producing many flowers during May. They are available in shades of red, pink, white and yellow.

Right: *Saxifraga* 'Gold Dust' is cushion-forming and rich-flowering in semi-shaded positions.

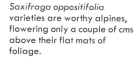

Saxifraga oppositifolia varieties are worthy alpines, flowering only a couple of cms above their flat mats of foliage.

Saxifraga fortunei 'Rubrifolia' is suitable for shade, and peaty soil.

Below: 'Jenkinsae' is a beautiful, hardy, pink-flowering hybrid from *Saxifraga burseriana* x S. *lilacina*.

SAXIFRAGA

The typical rosette-forms of the Aizoon Saxifrages.

'Tumbling Waters' is one of the most impressive Aizoon Saxifrages, flowering at 60 cm from a huge rosette.

Right: The 'pincushion' form of the heart of a *Scabiosa caucasica* flower.

A good example of *Scabiosa caucasica*.

Below: *Scabiosa graminifolia* 'Pincushion' is a hardy, long-lived, pink flowering variety.

red, 'Faldonside' lemon-yellow, and 'Valerie Finnis' primrose-yellow. All flower February to April.

Group 4 is of 'encrusted' or Aizoon Saxifrages. These make rosettes mostly silvered, varying in size from under 1 cm diameter to 20 cm or more with long, radiating leaves. The smaller ones are cushion-forming, for gritty but not poor or very dry soil. They like lime as do most Saxifrages, and in the wild are often found growing in chinks and crevices in limestone mountain regions.
The largest *S. longifolia* grows only in the Pyrenees in mainly vertical positions. The Aizoons are easier to grow outdoors than the more precocious Englerias. Flower spikes arise from the centre of mature rosettes and are usually in spray formation with a large number of small individual flowers in white (some spotted pink) and various shades of pink. A few are light yellow, such as the green-rosetted *S. aizoon* (syn. *S. paniculata*) 'Lutea' and the cultivar 'Esther'. Both are 20-25 cm tall and generally this group flowers in May and June. Whites predominate, from the tiny *S. cochlearis* 'Minor' at 10 cm, to the magnificent 'Tumbling Waters' at 60 cm from a huge rosette. In between is the pretty 'Southside Seedling' with spotted flowers at 30 cm, 'Dr. Ramsey', 20 cm, white, and 'Kathleen Pinsent', shell-pink, 15 cm.
All these Saxifrages are best from cuttings of individual rosettes taken after flowering.

SCABIOSA

Most of these sun-loving plants are outstanding for having a long flowering season. They all need well-drained soil; and although the majority may be readily divided in Spring (never in Autumn), many germinate freely from seed. They are lime tolerant but grow best in temperate climatic zones.

The dwarf kinds growing 15-30 cm are excellent for frontal positions with taller perennials, but are not out of place as alpines.

Both the species below are dwarf and mounded with the typical pincushion-type flowers over a long period. *S. alpina* (now listed as *Cephalaria alpina*), however, is not very long-lived, though it reproduces easily from seed, and old plants will rejuvenate by division. The light blue flowers come on 12 cm stems held erectly above the green tufted plants. The mounded habit of *S.* 'Butterfly Blue', with flowers 25 cm tall, is remarkable for seldom being out of flower.
S. graminifolia is not only very long-lived but has a wealth of narrow basal foliage of silvery hue, making a broad mound of 15 cm high just above which come lavender-blue flowers from June to September.

There is a pretty pink-flowered cultivar named 'Pincushion', and both are very good plants, dividable in Spring.

The best-known perennial scabious is, of course, the blue S. *caucasica* which is so useful for floral decoration. A good many varieties have been raised and introduced, and of these S. 'Clive Greaves', unlike many, has stood the test of time, both for constitution and colour. There are deeper blues such as S. 'Moerheim Blue', and paler ones as in S. 'Moonstone', as well as two good whites in S. 'Miss Willmott' and S. 'Bressingham White'. All grow to 75-90 cm, flowering from June to September.

If dead flowers are cut, or others used for indoor decoration, it lengthens the flowering period. These scabiosa must have well-drained soil and they like lime. They are best planted or divided in Spring and losses may occur as plants become old and woody after 3-4 years.

From seed, S. *caucasica* comes in variable shades. Where grown other than as single plants, it is good practice to divide a third of one's stock every year, beginning when the original plants are not more than three years old. It is when dividing old stock that planting losses may be heavy, and by this means one has always younger, healthier plants to go at. If there is any menace at all from slugs, they will go for S. *scabiosa* during the dormant season and one should use slug bait, sharp ashes or lime around the plants.

S. *columbaria* grows somewhat untidily to 60-70 cm but it scarcely detracts from its display of blue pincushions, June — September.

S. *ochroleuca* is of similar habit but the flowers are light yellow.

S. *lucida* is neater and dwarfer with lilac-pink flowers.

S. *minoana* is greyish-leaved and mounded, having flowers on 50 cm stems bearing pink flowers. This unusual species needs a warm dryish spot.

SCHIZOSTYLIS

Schizostylis coccinea. This can be a joy to those who garden in very temperate climes. The flowers come in Autumn and often into December like small delicate gladioli or montbretia. Roots will wander over the surface in the light humus-rich soil they prefer. They do not like hot dry conditions but are tolerant of some shade.

The original species has given way to improvements, and colours range from red, salmon-pink, light pink, but rarely white. Much larger flowers and stems up to 60 cm are seen on the red 'Major', the pink 'November Cheer' and 'Salmon Beauty', than on the older 'Mrs. Hegarty' and others. 'Snow Maiden' is the rare white. These plants are not difficult to protect in Winter with leaves or litter.

'Clive Greaves' is one of the best of the *Scabiosa caucasica* varieties, trustworthy and flowering from June to September.

Schizostylis coccinea 'Major' forms larger flowers than the species, on tall stems up to 60 cm. Winter protection is needed.

SCILLA

Scilla
The species of this genus of bulbous plants are ideal for naturalizing. They combine well with, for instance, Cyclamen, Primula, Daphne, Helleborus, Doronicum, Dicentra and snowdrops. Most species (for instance S. hispanica, S. nonscripta and S. sibirica) flower early in Spring and die down very soon after flowering. They will then easily be lost to sight amongst other plants. Most species give good cut flowers.

Above left: The bulbous Scilla peruviana forms dense flower heads with violet-blue or white flowers in early Summer.

The complete name of this easy, Spring-flowering plant is Scopolia carniolica ssp. hladnikiana.

Scrophularia aquatica 'Variegata' is worth growing for its brightly-coloured foliage.

SCILLA

Scilla peruviana. This bulbous plant is distinctive for having leaves above ground for most of the year – unlike other bluebells. Nor are they deep in the ground, but increase as a compact cluster. The flower heads are dense in early Summer, reaching 40 cm, and violet-blue in colour. A white form exists and both grow happily in quite dry situations and ordinary soil in sun.

SCOPOLIA

Scopolia hladnikiana. It may be difficult to pronounce the name, but the plant is easy to grow in any fertile soil, sun or shade. Its main feature lies in the yellowish potato-like flowers in early Spring, on 45 cm stems, followed by the rather rough leaves. Roots have a steady spread though not invasive, and divide readily.

SCROPHULARIA

Scrophularia aquatica 'Variegata'. This brightly variegated form of the figwort is worth growing even if its flowers are of little consequence. The stiff flowering stems are best cut back if only to prevent seeding, since seedlings would be green leaved. The yellow-splashed leaves are evergreen from a basal clump which has fibrous roots.
It likes a fairly moist soil and makes a fine subject for contrasting.
Increase is from division or cuttings.

SCUTELLARIA

These have small flowers in abundance in shades of blue, but the taller species are undeservedly neglected. Most of them are easy to grow, but the dwarfest S. indica (syn. S. japonica or S. indica var. parvifolia) is somewhat tender. It is a charming plant only 8 cm tall, mat-forming with soft grey-green leaves and tiny spikes of deep lavender flowers for much of the Summer.

S. hastata, however, romps away, with its small fleshy roots inclined to invade, and has many 15 cm sprays of mauve-blue flowers in June, July. Much the same may be said of S. scordiifolia, except that the 15 cm spikes have violet-blue flowers and roots that resemble maggots.

S. baicalensis is not a spreader but has compact fleshy roots and branching stems carrying deep blue flowers at 30 cm for many weeks, June-September.

S. canescens (syn. S. incana) has ash-grey foliage of an erect bushy habit with most attractive 90 cm terminal spikes of light lavender-blue. It likes a sunny place and good light soil, July-August.

S. canadensis is less refined but more vigorous. The light blue flowers on 100 cm stems come in June – July.

Scutellaria baicalensis is a nice, compact growing, long-flowering species.

Scutellaria indica, the smallest of all Scutellarias, is a rather tender, mat-forming plant with deep-lavender flowers.

A pleasing combination of different sedums.

SEDUM

The name 'stonecrop' strictly applies to one species, S. acre which, with a few others such as S. album and S. dasyphyllum, should be avoided for being a nuisance amongst choicer plants, although S. album murale is useful as a wall plant.

Many sedums are evergreen carpeters, rooting as they spread, and with very few exceptions all are easy to grow in well-drained soil and sun – some, like the true stonecrop, needing virtually no soil at all. Others form clumpy growth, dying back in Winter after a show of yellow or pink-to-red flowers.

S. ewersii has near-prostrate growth with glaucous foliage and heads of pink flowers in July to August at 15 cm, and 'Weihenstephaner Gold' makes a fine show of deep yellow from June onwards above dense green leaves.

S. middendorfianum is also deep yellow and neater growing at 10 cm, as is the purple-green leaved S. oreganum (syn. S.obtusatum) at 8 cm and the powdery grey-purple mounded forms of S. spathulifolium only 5 cm in June to July.

S. spurium makes spreading carpets with little nuisance value and has heads of glistening pink-to-red flowers, June to August, at 8 cm.

All make good foliage foil and in some, notably 'Purple Carpet' and 'Ruby Mantle', the leaves themselves are purple-maroon in colour, attractive almost all the year round. The cultivar named 'Green Mantle' does not flower but makes a close,

SEDUM

Sedum album can become a nuisance amongst choicer plants.

Sedum spectabile varieties form large plate-heads of flowers which attract butterflies and other insects.

Sedum
Many of the 500 or so *Sedum* species are suitable for the garden. There are numerous kinds available, and it is always possible to find some special ones. There are evergreen and deciduous species. Practically all originate from the northern hemisphere, although some occur in the middle of Africa. The main flower colours are white, yellow and pink-to-red. The plants hardly ever give problems. They grow well even in small containers and boxes.

evergreen, trouble-free carpet through which bulbs and some dwarf shrubs can grow.

Amongst the smaller growing sedums which die back in Winter to a compact rootstock are some that make a charming display in late Summer at about 18 cm tall. These are *S. lidakense* and *S. pluricaule* and *S. cauticola*. The latter is a lighter pink.
The variety 'Ruby Glow' is very showy at 15 cm and 'Vera Jameson' is of similar height with glistening deep-pink heads: both flower July to September.
S. tatarinowii is a more compact and upright species with flesh-pink flower heads.

S. pulchellum needs special mention because it flourishes only in good moist soil. It is also outstanding for its glistening pink cockscomb flower-heads from a light green mat-forming plant from July till Autumn, barely 8 cm tall.

The plants above are a selection from the best of this large genus, most of which are so easy to grow that they can be moved or divided for replanting at almost any time of the year.
Though mostly associated with rock gardens, there are some excellent sedums which deserve full marks amongst the dwarfer herbaceous plants. There are enough kinds to cover the whole season,

Sedum spurium is also available in a yellow-flowered variety.

Sedum spurium 'Dragon's Blood' is an outstanding deep-red variety of this overwhelming flowering species.

for *S. rhodiola* (syn. *Rhodiola rosea*) flowers in Spring. It has a fleshy root and tufty yellow flowers above blue-grey imbricated stems to make a neat clump effective for a long time though only 25 cm high.

S. heterodontum is a fine but little-known plant of similar habit with bronzy foliage and burnt-orange-coloured heads in April.

S. aizoon is a summer flowering yellow, and the best form is the orange-coloured *S. aizoon* 'Aurantiacum', which grows to about 30 cm with a coppery tinge to the leaves. Also in July-August there is the brilliant 25 cm *S.* 'Ruby Glow' with headed flowers above glaucous foliage. This theme is magnified when the large plate-heads of pink above 'ice-plant' foliage open in September in the *S. spectabile* varieties such as *S.* 'Brilliant'. These do not differ greatly in colour, and all are about 40-45 cm high, with the 25 cm diameter heads glistening and attracting bees and butterflies. The ultimate is *S.* 'Autumn Joy', for this has even larger plate-heads, on stems almost 60 cm tall. The colour is light pink at first and by October has changed to a salmon shade till in early November it fades to russet. This is one of the finest plants ever introduced.

All these sedums are easy to grow and are dividable in Spring when old.

Sedum kamtschaticum flowers in August-September, but remains beautiful for a long time after that, as the orange-tinted veins retain their colour.

Sedum spathulifolium flowers in June-July at a height of 5 cm on top of a grey-purple mounded plant form.

SELINUM

Selinum carvifolia is next of kin to S. tenuifolium and may be confused with it. Both species are not often available, although they are tall growing, nicely flowering, elegant plants.

SELINUM

Selinum tenuifolium. This was given an RHS award as long ago as 1881, but is still a comparatively rare umbellifer, radiating branching leaves of delicate greenery; above, erect stems carry broad heads of tiny white flowers up to 120 cm in Summer. It is a most elegant plant; but although seedlings need nurturing, its fleshy rootstock does not readily divide.

It grows in ordinary well-drained soil in sun or part shade.

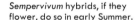

Sempervivum hybrids, if they flower, do so in early Summer.

SEMPERVIVUM

The name 'houseleek' applies to a species S. tectorum after it was seen growing on tiled roofs, and it is said to have some value against lightning damage. All form rosettes, which expand as others begin to grow from beneath the lower layer of fleshy leaves. They are fascinating plants to grow and are very adaptable to pot or pan culture as well as to many other positions where soil is well drained. They will grow quite well in old ashes and rubble: the best colourings come when grown in semi-arid soils. In richer, moister soils they are apt to grow too lush and lose colour, as well as compactness. The smallest are those with 'spider web' filaments in the rosette, from which the specific name S. arachnoideum is derived. It has silver-grey rosettes 1 cm in diameter and deep-pink flowers on 4 cm stems.

All sempervivums, if they do so at all, flower in early Summer, but in very few cases does this add to their attraction. Sometimes the flowering rosettes die out afterwards, but the gap is usually filled by new ones.

Two good and slightly larger forms of S. arachnoideum are seen in S. a. laggeri S. guiseppii and 'Jubilee', all pink flowered. Those with small rosettes in silver, green or tinged purple will fill crevices very neatly or a low hummock gradually expands where space permits, and they can be left to themselves for years to give year-round interest as do all sempervivums.

Those with more colourful rosettes — in shades of green towards mahogany and bronzy purple and

Sempervivum 'Commander Hay' forms large, colourful rosettes.

crimson — are legion. In total, sempervivums run into several hundreds, each differing in some respect and thereby making them attractive to collectors.

A few of the larger-growing, colourful species and cultivars such as 'Alpha', 'Beta', 'Commander Hay', 'Mahogany', 'Othello', 'Rubin', *S. marmoreum* 'Rubrifolium', 'Triste', and 'Noir' can be recommended, but in recent years a host of new varieties has arrived from the USA to widen still more the range available.

Sempervivum arachnoideum var. *laggeri*, a beautiful small rosetted, pink-flowered plant that gradually spreads if left undisturbed.

Right: The brown-purple rosettes of *Sempervivum* 'Othello'.

Various Sempervivums in mainly blue and green shades of foliage.

Red and maroon coloured Sempervivums grown together.

Sempervivum
In its natural habitat this genus of some 30 species is much smaller than *Sedum*. However, the number of hybrids and garden varieties is enormous. This means that there is tremendous confusion as to the right names. Many varieties received the name of a species, which later-on proved to be wrong, but which still remains regularly used. The natural species originate mainly from Europe and south-west Asia.

SENECIO

Senecio species belong to the *Aster* family, showing the same, (mostly yellow), type of flowers.

SENECIO

Until the Ligularias were extracted as a separate genus, there were over 500 species of *Senecio*. Very few, however, are good garden plants and some, such as 'ragwort', are weeds.

Of the dwarfer kinds, *S. abrotanifolius* is just worthy of inclusion. It makes a somewhat sprawling mound of greenery, narrow leaved and with 30 cm heads of orange flowers in early Summer. Both this and the much smaller *S. tyrolensis*, along with the 30 cm *S. adonidifolius*, are easy in any soil and sun, and frequent replanting is required to avoid them becoming ragged-looking.

S. cineraria is the grey-leaved plant, effective for contrasting as well as for bedding. Such as 'White Diamond' has silvery-white leaves, large and finely cut, and the yellow flower-heads are somewhat superfluous. It falls short of being fully hardy and needs a sunny place.

S. doronicum is very different. It forms a clumpy herbaceous plant with green leaves and has large, orange-gold daisy flowers on erect 40 cm stems in early Summer. It likes sun and any fertile soil. *S. pulcher* is both rare and distinctive, for the flowers are quite large of bright rosy magenta in Autumn on 45 cm stems. It is slow to make a sizeable plant and, though hardy, requires deep, rich, well-drained soil in full sun.

Also autumn flowering is *S. tanguticus* (syn. *Ligularia tangutica*) which is totally different. The roots spread quickly in most soils and produce 130 cm upright stems topped with clusters of small yellow daisies. Though attractive for late flowering, it needs to be curbed.

Senecio congestus is a rather rare species for moist soil.

Serratula tinctoria is a tall growing species, (up to 100 cm), flowering in late Summer.

SERRATULA

This is another neglected genus, at least two species being of value for late flowering. They are all herbaceous perennials, having a bushy habit well clothed in deep green foliage. All are easy to grow in sun and may be increased by division. *S. macrocephala* grows neatly from clumpy plants and has 30 cm branching heads carrying purple fluffy flowers in late Summer.

S. shawii – (*S.* syn. *seoanei*) – is shorter at 20 cm and has its violet-purple flower-heads in Autumn. *S. coronata*, *S. quinquifolia* and *S. tinctoria* are in the 80-100 cm range. All are purplish except for a white form of the latter, but all rather coarse amid other choicer late summer perennials.

SESLERIA

Sesleria caerulea. This is a more-or-less evergreen grass with narrow bluish blades and buff flowers about 20 cm high.

SHORTIA

This genus of shade-loving and very choice plants now includes *Schizocordon.* Its shiny evergreen leaves in slow-growing tufts become bronzed in Autumn, having short sprays of waxy pale-pink flowers in early Summer.

The species *S. galacifolia, S. soldanelloides* and *S. uniflora* are all rarely offered and are slow if not difficult to establish, demanding cool, peaty but gritty soil.

SIDALCEA

Almost all these pretty, spiky-flowered plants in cultivation are hybrids. They are related to the hollyhock and have shiny basal foliage above a fairly shallow root system, but large plants are easily divided. It is important to cut them back after flowering to encourage new basal growth, otherwise they flourish in any well-drained soil and sun.

S. 'Rose Queen' is one of the older varieties, reliably perennial, growing to 120 cm and flowering from June to late August.

S. 'William Smith' is distinctive for its warm salmon-pink shading and S. 'Croftway Red' is the deepest pink — nearest to red. Both these grow to about 90 cm, but S. 'Rev. Page Roberts' and S. 'Elsie Heugh' are light satiny pink, with slender 120 cm spikes.

S. 'Wensleydale' is of similar habit, with sizeable rosy red flowers and S. 'Loveliness' is a shell pink only 75 cm high.

S. 'Oberon' is also 75 cm and even more attractive as a light pink, as is the newer 'Mary Martin'.

Sesleria
This is a genus of clump forming grasses of which the blue colour is conspicuous. The flowering times differ greatly. There are very early flowering species, but none flower in the interim period. This is, in fact, an advantage which can be used in composing a border. *S. caerulea* for instance flowers as early as the end of March, whereas *S. autumnalis* (not described) flowers in September.

Right: *Sesleria caerulea,* a small grass with bluish blades.

Left: *Shortia uniflora* is a rather difficult evergreen species with special requirements as to site and soil.

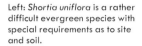

Below: *Sidalcea* 'Elsie Heugh', a pretty satiny-pink, spiky-flowered hybrid up to 120 cm tall.

SILENE

Silene acaulis may be left to itself, once planted. It will form close mats covered with flowers in late Spring and early Summer.

Silene maritima is available in single and double-flowered white varieties and pink shades.

Sisyrinchium bermudianum, an easy to grow, violet-blue flowering plant with iris-like foliage for sunny sites.

SILENE

Almost all the cultivated species are alpines and are generally easy-to-grow plants in any well-drained soil, although S. acaulis may be seen growing where quite damp in the wild.

The best in this close mat-forming species is S. acaulis 'Pedunculata' with a display in Spring and early Summer of small, clear-pink flowers. S. alpestris forms deep-green tufts and sends up 20 cm sprays of white flowers, which in the double form 'Plena' are much more effective for the early summer display.
S. maritima is also available in a double white form 'Plena' as well as the single, and in the pale pink 'Rosea'. This makes compact, glaucous-leaved plants and has prostrate sprays of quite large flowers in Summer 2-3 cm across. This type is especially good for walls, but S. schafta makes very little spread and forms a neat, green-leaved plant with 15 cm spikes of bright pink from July to September.
The more vigorous and reliable S. schafta 'Robusta' has larger flowers from a steadily expanding plant, flowering continuously from July to October, in a similar colour and height.
These are all quite reliable plants, dividable in Spring, but S. schafta comes best from seed. These associate agreeably with campanulas.

SISYRINCHIUM

These have bladed iris-like foliage but all those below are fibrous rooted, with no rhizomes. They are all easy to grow, preferring sun and have no fads except when dividing. Some, such as S. bellum and S. bermudianum, have open violet-blue, yellow-centred flowers on 12-15 cm stems in Summer. 'North Star' is similar, but white.
S. californicum and S. brachypus are yellow-flowered at 15 cm with broader leaves.
S. idahoensis flowers freely at 25 cm, deep blue, whilst the white-flowered S. macounii is quite dwarf at 10 cm.
S. striatum is the tallest with broad iris-like leaves and sprays of yellow at 60 cm. This is adaptable to sun or shade and will even grow in paving crevices from self-sown seed. There is a variegated form but it flowers sparsely and has a short life in my experience.

SMILACINA

Smilacina racemosa. This relative of Solomon's seal has creamy-white fluffy flowers on the tips of arching 60-70 cm stems in May, June, slightly scented. Its leafage is freshly green for a long time and the roots spread slowly to become large clumps where suited in light fertile soil. Though some shade is preferred, and limy soil is not, it will adapt to sun.

S. stellata is much dwarfer and much inferior, with small whitish flowers, 25 cm. It has invasive tendencies in light soil.

Smilacina racemosa has scented flowers in May-June. It is a close relative of 'Solomon's seal'.

Soldanella

The 10 species of *Soldanella* are all native of Europe. Although they like moist soil, they should not have too much shade, because this decreases their flowering ability. Another danger for *Soldanella* is that snails eat the flower buds, which are already formed in the Autumn. You need to take measures against the thieves! Buds and flowers of *Soldanella* are also rather sensitive to night-frost.

Soldanella alpina can form spreading evergreen clumps, flowering lavender-blue in April-May.

SOLDANELLA

These charming spring-flowering plants sometimes baffle would-be cultivators. They demand well-drained but not dry gritty soil, rich in humus, and shade – preferably not under trees. They form spreading evergreen clumps where happy, with a low canopy of deep green, circular leaves and dainty, lace-edged stalks.

S. alpina is lavender-blue spotted crimson only 6 cm high, but not so free to flower as *S. montana.* This has a more vigorous spread and ample rounded foliage beneath the 10 cm lavender-blue flowers.

S. pindicola has more heart-shaped leaves with lilac-lavender flowers on 12 cm stems. *S. minima* is similar but only 8 cm tall.

Division is best in early Autumn or early Spring, and older plants benefit from a little top dressing to assist their shallow rooting system.

SOLIDAGO

Facing page: *Solidago* 'Crown of Rays' is a dwarf 'golden rod', only 60 cm high.

Solidago
True species of this genus, which originates from North America, are rarely available. They are mainly varieties which you find in nurseries and garden centres. There are more than 100 species many of which have the tendency to spread quickly over much larger areas of the garden than provided for. Such species are therefore only suitable for large and natural gardens. They can however be very beautiful.

Below: x *Solidaster luteus* is a 60 cm high, yellow-flowered cross between *Aster ptarmicoides* and *Solidago canadensis*.

SOLIDAGO

The 'golden rods' have undergone a great change in recent years, with the taller, weedier kinds being ousted by the more discerning gardeners for those that are more compact and give a better show.
S. 'Leraft' was the first of this new race, growing only 75 cm tall and flowering in July-August.
S. 'Golden Shower' is slightly taller and in their varying shades of yellow and shape of the plume, 'Golden Mosa', 'Golden Gates' and 'Lemore' (a lemon-yellow) can be recommended.
For something dwarfer, S. 'Crown of Rays' is leafy with prominently lateral spikes, only 60 cm high, and 'Peter Pan' of similar habit, 110 cm.
Amongst the dwarfs, late flowering, S. 'Laurin' makes a wide foliage and flower spread, but 'Queenie' and 'Golden Thumb' form little bushes barely 30 cm high. Both have somewhat golden-green leaves and deep-yellow flowers, making them ideal for frontal positions, where compactness counts.
S. 'Mimosa' is about the best of the taller kinds with handsome plumes in late Summer on strong 180 cm stems.
Of the species, S. *caesia* can be well recommended. It has wiry stems arching a little, and abundant dark greenery, ending in narrow sprays of deep yellow in late Summer.
S. *vigaurea* 'Praecox', however, flowers in June-

Solidago caesia is one of the best species for late Summer flowering.

July, with effective yellow plumes on 100 cm stems. Such old, rather tall and weedy varieties as 'Golden Wings' are best avoided. Solidagos appreciate good soil, and division of old plants is an easy matter in Spring.

x SOLIDASTER

x *Solidaster luteus* is a cross-breed between *Aster ptarmicoides* and a *Solidago*, 60 cm high, with narrow long leaves. It is well branched with yellow flowers in July – September, good for cut flowers. Increase is by division.

SPEIRANTHA

Speirantha gardenii. This seldom-seen little plant has narrow evergreen leaves and 10 cm sprays of tiny white flowers.
It spreads slowly but needs cool, humus-rich, lime-free or neutral soil and is summer flowering.

STACHYS

Stachys lanata is widely used for its silvery felted leaves.

Left: *Stachys macrantha* produces lilac-pink flowers in June-July.

Below: *Stipa pennata* shows some resemblance to oat grass. Good for sun and rather dry soil.

STACHYS

This name now includes what were known as *Betonica* There is nothing difficult about any of the *Stachys*.

S. lanata is not one of these, for as 'donkeys ears' it is seen in many a garden, popular for its rapid surface spread of felted silver leaves and 50 cm sprays of small pink flowers. These are not very attractive and in the variety *S.* 'Silver Carpet' there are none, and the plant lives up to its name as a first-class ground-covering subject, capable of growing between shrubs, withstanding drought, and can be planted at almost any time. 'Cotton Boll' flowers freely and is so named because of its long-lasting seed heads.

S. byzantina is even more vigorous, with green larger leaves and lilac pink spikes.

S. macrantha makes neat 60 cm bushes with bright lilac-pink flowers of good size in June and July, and the variety *S. macrantha* 'Robusta' is earlier and stronger growing.

S. spicata 'Robusta' is very erect and spiky, flowering bright pink to 60 cm, and *S. spicata* 'Densiflorum' has tightly packed spikes at 45 cm. These are two excellent long-flowering but little-known plants, clumpy but compact; and there is a charming dwarf white *S. nivea* ('Stricta Alba') which grows only 20 cm, flowering a long time. All these grow in ordinary soil and can be divided.

STIPA

One of the most elegant of tall grasses is *S. gigantea*. It makes large clumps of narrow silvery foliage and in early Summer come 200-250 cm plumes of oat-like flowers which remain effective for many weeks, waving in the breeze.

Other stipas are less tall, less effective and less reliable.

S. barbata has feathery sprays on 50-70 cm wiry stems.

S. pennata is like a much-refined oat grass. Both have narrow green blades and all three are best in sun and well-drained soil.

S. splendens is referred to under *Lasiogrostis*.

STOKESIA

Stokesia cyanea is a small but very distinctive genus with large cornflower-type flowers having quilled centres. They have a long flowering period and make excellent frontal plants at about 30 cm high, June-August. The basic is light blue, but a deeper blue is seen in the 40 cm 'Wyoming'. 'Blue Star' is large-flowered light blue, and though a white is not uncommon, the pink form is rare.
All have leathery strap leaves and grow in any reasonable soil, best in sun.
Increase is by seed or division.

STROBILANTHES

Strobilanthes atropurpureus grows into sturdy, leafy bushes each season from a tough clumpy plant. The violet-mauve flowers are not large, but plentiful, and continue for several weeks in late Summer.
In good soil the growth attains about 130 cm and increase is by seed or division: an unusual but worthy plant.

STYLOPHORUM

Stylophorum diphyllum. Though very different, this too deserves to be more widely grown. Fleshy, green, dissected leaves appear in Spring, topped soon after with handsome yellow poppy-like flowers for several weeks on 30 cm stems.
Light soil and sun are preferred or some shade, and the somewhat fleshy roots are best divided in early Autumn.

SYMPHYANDRA

These closely resemble campanulas; and although showy, I have found none to be reliably perennial, and have had to raise them from seed as they resent division.
S. hofmannii is monocarpic but makes a show of light-blue bells.
S. wanneri is the best-known species and is longer lived than most. The indented deep-green rosettes send up 30 cm sprays of deep blue in Summer.

The cornflower-type flowers of *Stokesia cyanea* (syn. *S. laevis*) are to be seen from June-August.

Stylophorum diphyllum is a creeping plant, flowering in June-July.

Symphyandra wanneri is the most reliable perennial species of this genus.

SYMPHYTUM

Symphytum x uplandicum is one of the comfreys with ornamental value.

Symphytum grandiflorum, a good ground-covering plant and rapid spreader, with white flowers in Spring.

Synthyris missurica displays beautiful small blue flowers in early Summer. The compact plant has leathery green leaves.

SYMPHYTUM

The comfreys have yielded some good garden plants as well as the well-known herb. All but one are very easy to grow in sun or shade; and if a few are somewhat coarse, they have their uses.

S. caucasicum is an excellent wild-garden subject with its large hairy leaves and 80 cm branching spikes in early Summer, displaying little, blue, bell-shaped flowers. But for being a spreader it would be a good border perennial.

S. grandiflorum has a rapid surface spread and makes good ground cover with dangling creamy-white flowers in Spring, 20 cm high. The variegated form is much more showy and will brighten up bare places in the shade of trees and shrubs.

S. 'Rubrum' is the exception in that it needs good deep soil, not dry or too shady. It expands slowly with spear-shaped leaves, and has 40 cm stems carrying deep-red tubular flowers. It may well be a hybrid, as is S. x uplandicum.

The green-leaved type is not very different from comfrey
(S. officinale), but the variegated form is outstanding. The large leaves are brightly splashed with pale yellow; and if the purplish flowering stems are cut back, plants will produce large showy leaves until Autumn.

Care should be taken with the roots or, if severed or damaged, they will sprout and grow with all-green leaves.

SYNTHYRIS

Many more species exist than are in cultivation. They have sprays of mainly blue flowers in Spring and early Summer, coming from compact plants which do best in cool, humus soil and part shade.

S. missurica has green leathery leaves, and the 25 cm sprays of small blue flowers in early Summer are very showy.

S. stellata (syn. S. reniformis) is more demure and flower in April-May. The azure-to-gentian-blue flowers on 15 cm stems are cheerful.

Increase is by seed or divison.

Synthyris

The species (there are 15 wild species) of this genus show their fresh green foliage until Winter if they like their position. This will only be the case if they are allowed to stay in the same place for many years.

Originally they are woodland plants which combine well, for instance, with Trillium.

TANACETUM

All tanacetums have been listed with *Chrysanthemum* according to the newest scientific information. The species names have stayed the same.

Only three 'tansies' are worth including.

T. herderi makes dense mounds of silvery filigree foliage and heads of yellow unpetalled flowers in Summer, about 25 cm.

T. vulgare 'Crispum' grows strongly with parsley-like foliage and leafy spikes up to 120 cm, with yellow tansy flowers in Summer.

T. densum ssp. *amani* keeps close to the ground with quick-spreading silvery leaves. The flowers are small and yellow, but not very free unless semi-starved and in full sun. They are only 15 cm tall, and apt to die out in patches with the need for replanting.

Tanacetum (now *Chrysanthemum*) *densum* ssp. *amani* is one of the 'tansies' with rapid ground-covering habits. Its main feature are the silvery leaves.

TANAKEA

Tanakea radicans. This is another plant for moist lime-free or neutral soil with shade and humus. It makes a slow spread of rounded evergreen leaves and has 15 cm sprays of dainty white flowers. It belongs to the *Saxifraga* family.

TELEKIA

This genus is closely related to *Inula*. Two species are important for gardeners.

T. speciosa (syn. *Buphthalmum speciosum*), 150cm high with big leaves and yellow flowers in June — August, and ideal for naturalizing. Increase is by division. *T. speciosissima* (syn. *Buphthalmum speciosissimum*) 20-30 cm, with yellow flowers in July-September. Increase is by seed.

Left: *Tanakea radicans* is a member of the Saxifrage family. It is a plant for shady sites, in soil with plenty of humus.

Right: *Telekia speciosa* may be listed as *Buphthalmum speciosum* and is a tall plant, (up to 150 cm), with yellow flowers in June-August.

TELLIMA

Teucrium
A genus with more than 100 species. They occur all over the world in temperate and subtropical regions.
T. chamaedrys 'Nanum' is sometimes used for low hedges instead of *Buxus*. This kind is very similar to *T. chamaedrys*, but the plant is evergreen and does not form suckers.

Left: *Tellima grandiflora* is the answer for dry shady corners where other plants hardly survive. The evergreen leaves give good ground cover.

Below: *Teucrium* 'Ackermanii' forms greyish mounds, topped by deep-red spikes.

Teucrium chamaedrys forms shapely, pink-flowered bushes.

TELLIMA

Tellima grandiflora is a useful plant for an odd corner or in fairly dry shade. The leaves closely resemble *Heuchera* — soft and evergreen, and give good ground cover, but the 50 cm flower sprays are pale greenish-buff.
The form 'Purpurea' is more colourful in the leaf. Both are trouble free except for occasional self seeding.

TEUCRIUM

These are not spectacular but some add variety to the rather sparse range of later-flowering alpines.
T. 'Ackermanii' has short clustered spikes of deep red on greyish mounds and both *T. polium* ssp. *aureum* and *T. aroanium* form silvery mounds with insignifcant flowers. All three are about 10 cm high.
T. pyrenaicum spreads steadily into a mat with soft hairy leaves and heads of hooded cream and lavender flowers, 10 cm in Summer.
T. scordium 'Crispum' is of interest for making 25 cm mounds of pretty, crinkled leaves, but the flowers are of no account.
T. subspinosum is only 5 cm in a tight hummock of spiny silvery foliage set with minute pink flowers. This is late-flowering and all are best in light soil.
T. chamaedrys 'Nanum' makes a compact, shrubby evergreen bush of deep green with short spikes of deep pink in late Summer at 25 cm.
T. chamaedrys itself is more upright and makes shapely 45 cm bushes with deep-pink flowers if given an annual trim with shears.
They are easy to grow in any soil.

THALICTRUM

This genus varies in height from under 5 cm to 200 cm. The smallest, *T. kiusianum* is a first-class species given well-drained, but not dry, peaty or humus-rich soil with shade. The roots are very small and shallow but capable of spreading to form a loose mat of pretty leaves of purple-green through which comes a long display of fluffy lilac flowers only 5 cm high from June to Autumn. Old plants fall apart for replanting, best done in Spring.
T. coreanum is a little larger in all its parts, and is clump-forming with lilac 'powder-puff' flowers on 10 cm stems.
T. orientale is a rare, slow-growing little gem. It has wiry 15 cm stems bearing large deep-pink flowers. All these dwarf species like a humus rich soil which does not dry out and are partial to some shade.

The most entrancing but difficult to grow is the mauve-flowered
T. diffusiflorum with 30 cm branching stems and 'maidenhair' leaves, with rich lilac flowers. It is easier to keep in northern climes.

Of the taller species, *T. dipterocarpum* (correctly *T. delavayi*) is the best-known. This also likes rich soil and carries myriads of lavender yellow-centred flowers on often-tangled branching stems up to 150 cm.
'Hewitt's Double' is less tall and prefers some shade, but the single white *T. dipterocarpum* 'Album' is unusually attractive. 'Hewitt's Double' will not come from seed, as will the other two.
T. angustifolium carries yellow fluffy flowers on strong 180 cm stems in July, August. All flower in later Summer. Neither this nor the others below need fussing.
T. aquilegifolium is earlier with more rounded heads in shades of mauve to purple and white, height 100-130 cm in June.
T. minus has greenish flowers and masses of 'maidenhair fern' leaves.
T. flavum ssp. *glaucum* and *T. speciossissimum* are said to be synonymous. All have attractive foliage, strong 150 cm stems and heads of yellow flowers.
T. rochebrunianum is of somewhat similar growth, but more elegant, and has 120 cm stems with lavender-purple flowers in July, August.
All these will divide from old clumps.

THERMOPSIS

These are closely akin to lupins, but are long-lived given sun and well-drained soil.
Unfortunately, the one most likely to be listed is in my view the least desirable. It is *T. montana* and has an invasive spread. The 80 cm spikes of yellow come in early Summer, but make a less pleasing

Thalictrum delavayi. On well fed soils it should provide numerous lavender flowers on tall stems.

Thalictrum dipterocarpum is another tall species of this genus, displaying myriads of flowers.

Thermopsis caroliniana forms erect 100 cm stems with yellow-flowering spikes.

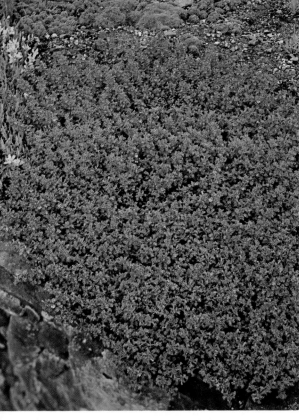

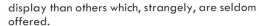

Thymus 'E.B. Anderson' may be listed as *Acinos alpinus* ssp. *meridionalis*. It is a green leaved, low mounded type of plant, flowering lavender-mauve over a long period.

display than others which, strangely, are seldom offered.

T. lanceolata has erect 120 cm stems with narrow leaves and fine spikes of butter-yellow flowers, June – August.

T. mollis is not quite so tall and has fuller spikes, and *T. caroliniana* is somewhat similar.

All three are yellow and have deeply penetrating roots, and none divides at all well. Seed-raised plants are best.

THYMUS

No collection of alpines should leave out thymes. Although a few are not quite hardy in cold climes, the majority include some indispensables, both of carpeting and erect-growing kinds, and many have aromatic foliage.

The true lemon-scented *T.* x *citriodorus* is bush-forming at 15 cm, but the green-leaved type is unworthy when there are both gold, 'Aureus', and silver, 'Silver Queen' or 'Silver Posie', or variegated forms.

The brightest gold is now 'Archers Gold' which, unlike some, appears so far not to revert to green in patches. Flowering is not conspicuous.

There are also creeping, mat-like thymes with colourful scented leaves named 'Golden Dwarf' and 'Doone Valley', the latter being deep green, speckled with gold in the mass.

The closer creeping thymes include the May-to-June-flowering grey-leaved *T. praecox* (syn. *T. doerfleri*) of which the cultivar 'Bressingham Seedling' is extra good. They flower at only 5 cm, as do the most colourful variations of *T.drucei*

Left: *Thymus* x *citriodorus* 'Aureus', is one of the gold-leaved varieties of this lemon-scented species.

Below right: *Thymus drucei* 'Coccineus' produces masses of flowers in June-July.

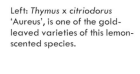

Thymus

All over the temperate zones of Europe and Asia *Thymus* species occur. There are more than 300. There are also a large number of hybrids and varieties which are often difficult to distinguish from each other. The small, low species are especially important for the garden. They are often very suitable for the rock garden where they will make a nice combination with low *Campanula* species. The majority of the ground covering species can stand very dry soil. They also make a suitable combination with various small bulbous plants.

Thymus x *citriodorus* 'Archer's Gold' is the brightest golden-leaved variety available.

Thymus x *citriodorus* 'Silver Queen', a silver-variegated, scented form.

Thymus 'Doone Valley' is a gold speckled, deep green x *citriodorus* variety with scented leaves.

(formerly *T. serpyllum*). 'Elfin' makes tiny mound pads of deep green and has pink flowers to match. A firm favourite is *T. drucei* 'Coccineus' with masses of near-red flowers June to July, and *T. drucei* 'Major', a little paler but larger. The cultivars 'Annie Hall', flesh pink, 'Snowdrift' or 'Albus', white, and 'Pink Chintz' clear pink, complete the colour range, but the form 'Minus' is a mere film of green with pink flowers at 3 cm, and *T. lanuginosus* has a grey woolly appearance. All these are excellent paving plants and do not object to being trodden upon. The smaller forms of *T. drucei* will allow bulbs to come through their mats.

If trodden on or bruised, *T. herba-barona* gives off a strong caraway-like scent from its deep green foliage. This, too, has a creeping habit, as has *T. montanus (syn. T. pulegioides)*, a vigorous green species, very free with its 7 cm heads of pink from July to August.

A few thymes are not fully hardy in cold districts, and *T. cilicicus*, *T. ericifolius (syn. Micromeria varia)*, *T. membranaceus* and *T. micans (syn. T. caespitosus)* are best grown in scree or an alpine house. All are low mounded and sub-shrubby, but the hardier sub-shrubby kinds are well worth growing.

The name 'E.B. Anderson' has been given to a low mounded type, (correctly known as *Acinos alpinus* ssp. *meridionalis*), with deep-green leaves and a long display of lavender-mauve flowers at 8 cm. *Thymus nitidus* is more shrubby, quite erect at 20 cm and grey leaved. It has clear-pink flowers from June to July, and there are very good forms in the more compact 'Peter Davis' and 'Valerie Finnis'. Of similar growth but with almost too vigorous a spread for small gardens is the bright pink 20 cm 'Porlock' flowering in May to June.

All thymes are best divided after flowering where not dry or in early Spring.

TIARELLA

These are like miniature heucheras, making mostly evergreen mounds of carpets. They like some shade and are excellent for ground cover between shrubs.

T. cordifolia is best known and makes a dense leafy carpet, even in deep shade, the leaves being ivy-shaped but light green. A mass of tiny flowers on 15 cm sprays comes in early Summer.

T. c. collina is of a more clumpy growth and, with abundant leafage, is always attractive.
In May to July it sends up a profusion of 25 cm sprays of pearly-white flowers. Both these are easy to divide in early Autumn.

T. wherryi comes best from seed, and is not always long lived. It is, however, very long-flowering with 25 cm creamy-white sprays from slightly golden-green foliage.

T. polyphylla and *T. trifoliata* are also long-flowering and with good foliage cover all year with small white flowers on 15 cm stems.

Tiarella cordifolia, a pretty ground-covering, rich-flowering plant that will tolerate deep shade.

TOLMIEA

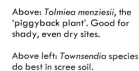

Above: *Tolmiea menziesii*, the 'piggyback plant'. Good for shady, even dry sites.

Above left: *Townsendia* species do best in scree soil.

Left: *Trachystemon orientalis* is a spreading plant for shady positions, with deep-blue flowers.

Below: *Tradescantia virginiana* cultivars, like this 'Isis', flower for several months.

TOLMIEA

Tolmiea menziesii is the 'pickaback plant', so named from the way baby plants are formed in the base of the leaves. It spreads well even in fairly dry, deep shade, to give dense evergreen ground cover, and has short sprays of greenish flowers.

The form 'Taffs Gold' is more colourful in the leaf, but short of true gold.

TOVARA

Tovara virginiana has been elevated to generic status from the polygonums. The habit is bush-forming of summer growth, each pointed leaf having a dark midrib. Thin flower-spikes at 80 cm are of no value, but the form 'Painter's Palette' is well worth growing for its multicoloured leaves, attractive from June to November.

Easy to grow, making stout clumps, it does best in sun where not bone dry.

TOWNSENDIA

The charming midget blue daisy, *T. formosa,* is best in scree soil and good for troughs, and has wide-rayed flowers with yellow centres only 5 cm high. Unfortunately, it is short-lived, but is easily reproduced from seed, sown when ripe.

TRACHYSTEMON

Trachystemon orientalis grows lustily almost anywhere but is especially useful for shady places. It spreads well with 50 cm spikes of small deep-blue flowers in Spring, followed by quite large, somewhat rough, leaves. It is shallow rooting and easy to curb.

TRADESCANTIA

Almost all in cultivation are varieties of *T. virginiana*. Though not by any means choice, the tradescantias have at least two good points in their favour. One is that they flower for a long time and the other is on the score of reliability and hardiness.

On the debit side, it must be said that they take on a rather tatty appearance after being in flower for a couple of months, and that they do not stay erect unaided when in damp or rich soil. They begin flowering in June when about 30 cm high, but by August will be 45 cm or more, with their three-petalled flowers (hence the name 'trinity flower') continuing to open on clustered heads. The foliage is rushy and glaucous green, and the plants are quite rooty, though not difficult to divide. T. 'Purewell Giant', carmine purple, T. 'Osprey', pure white, and T. 'Isis', deep blue, are, with T. 'Purple Dome', a good selection from the varieties in cultivation.

A mixed planting of 'trinity flowers' (*Tradescantia*) showing a small selection of the flowering colours available.

Tradescantia

The many varieties of *Tradescantia virginiana* are generally classified as *T. Andersoniana* hybrids. However, there are dozens of true species, a small number of which are cultivated. They all originate from America. A number of species only occur in tropical America and therefore are only suitable for us in the greenhouse. The Andersoniana hybrids combine beautifully with plants of the same habitat such as some *Iris* species. A combination with grass species, near a pond for instance, is also very attractive. The plants often seed themselves easily.

Tricyrtis formosana, a sturdy plant with many brownish-mauve flowers. This one is hard to tell apart from the form or species *stolonifera*.

TRICYRTIS

The so-called 'toad lilies' have become more popular as their value has been more fully appreciated. They are reliably perennial and have a modest spread in the rich soil they prefer, but are adaptable to any hot dry conditions, preferring some shade in the sunnier climes. All have bell-shaped or reflexed petals and most have interesting spots within.

T. formosana grows sturdily to about 80 cm and in late Summer has a display of open-headed flowers prettily spotted in a brownish-mauve. The form T. f. stolonifera is very similar but spreads more quickly. Both have pointed deep-green leaves.

T. hirta has slightly hairy leaves and the near-white flowers are spotted lilac. This too is 80 cm tall and late-flowering, as is T. macropoda. The colour impression is greeny yellow and purple spotted, coming on strong stems, but T. latifolia is nearer to yellow with reddish-purple spots.

Heights vary somewhat in keeping with soil, moisture and richness, and some interesting hybrids are just beginning to widen the colour range of these charming plants.

TRIFOLIUM

Trifolium
Of the hundreds of species of clover only a few are suitable for the garden. Most of them – however beautiful they sometimes are – behave as uncontrollable weeds.
Some species can be seen in botanical gardens as specialities, such as *T. alpinum*, an alpine which only grows well under very special circumstances, and is not suitable for the average garden.

Above left: *Trillium grandiflorum* 'Plenum', the American 'wake robin'.

Left: *Trillium sessile* is available with pure white or purple flowers.

Below: *Trollius* species, 'globe flowers' will thrive in drier soil, provided it is rather heavy.

TRIFOLIUM

Trifolium pannonicum. Although this is a species of clover, it is a very handsome perennial with no fads or faults. Leafy stems rise to 70-80 cm with fine clover heads of creamy yellow, June – August. It is deep-rooting and happy in sun and any good soil.
Increase is by seed or division.

TRILLIUM

These are amongst the most exciting spring subjects and demand is still in excess of supply. They are not difficult, given good humus and well-drained soil with some shade, but are slow to expand.
Most kinds take five years to flower from seed and almost as long for a single flowering crown to become large enough to divide. But however long they remain in one position, flowering becomes progressively more profuse. In other words, they are long-lived. All flower between late March and well into May. All have three-petalled flowers and three lobed leaves.
T. cernuum has rather small nodding flowers at 40 cm, tending to be hidden by the luxuriant leaves.
T. chloropetalum is the name best applied to the 40 cm greenish-yellow flowers which sometimes appear with *T. sessile* (q.v.) *T. erectum* is also 40 cm but has deep-purple flowers with reflexed petals. There is a pure white named *T. erectum* 'Albiflorum'.
T. grandiflorum is the American 'wake robin' and is invariably popular with its large pure-white flowers on 30 cm stems. The most sought after is the double *T. grandiflorum* 'Plenum' with sumptuous white flowers almost like a camelia, 5 cm across or more where well grown.
T. grandiflorum 'Roseum' is as rare as it is charming.
T. nervosum is a smaller-flowered single and *T. ovatum* is the earliest to flower with large white flowers which turn pink with age.
T. sessile is exceedingly handsome with its upright maroon flowers above a wealth of marbled leaves, up to 50-60 cm. It is the most robust and least fussy as to soil. Trilliums are best divided in early Autumn.

TROLLIUS

It is surprising how well these moisture lovers will flourish even in soil which has a low water table. The key is soil quality, but they do better in heavy than in light, sandy soil which quickly dries out. As 'globe flowers', such a description as 'glorified

buttercups' does not do them justice. They have a very fibrous-rooted and clump-forming habit and will often flower a second time if cut back in July and fed. Division is safe in March or after flowering if moist. All are bone hardy.

Named cultivars are mostly on offer and there are variations on *T. europaeus* which in the wild is canary-yellow. Improvements have larger flowers and richer colours, the deepest being 'Fire Globe', paling slightly in 'Orange Princess' and 'Salamander'. 'Goldquelle' is medium yellow as is the vigorous free-flowering 'Bressingham Sunshine'.

T. europaeus 'Superbus' and 'Canary Bird' are pale but glistening-yellow, whilst 'Alabaster' is more of a primrose-yellow, but it lacks the height and vigour of others at 45 cm. Others may attain 70-80 cm where well suited.

The later-flowering *T. ledebourii* (syn. *T. chinensis*) seems to have become scarce. It is distinctive for having rich-orange flowers with prominent stamens, flowering at 80 cm in June, July. Two undeservedly neglected varieties are *T. stenopetalus* and *T. yunnanensis*, both of which are about 60 cm high, and have more-open flowers of bright yellow, June-August. They do not expand into large clumps as do the cultivars but are worth a little extra fussing.

A few dwarf kinds are also worthy, though again not in plentiful supply. *T. acaulis* carries golden yellow flowers on only 10 cm stems, and *T. pumilus* has finely divided leaves with clear-yellow flowers on 15-20 cm stems, most often listed as 'Wargrave Variety'.

TROPAEOLUM

These are climbers which die back every year after giving a brilliant display of tubular flowers.
T. polyphyllum tends to sprawl rather than climb, trailing its slender long stems with blue-grey leaves. Its flowers are like small nasturtiums of brilliant yellow in June, July, but it is not easy to establish and needs to be planted deeply in a sunny position and light soil.
T. speciosum is a wayward climber, and if it settles in will even romp up hedges and conifers, giving a long display of bright-scarlet flowers. It likes cool, humus soil but its long trailing stems reach for light and sun.
T. tuberosum has substantial roots like small artichokes, but they need protection from frost. In a sunny place with a fence or pea sticks on which to climb, it makes masses of greenery and orange-red flowers if the free-flowering form named 'Ken Aslet' is acquired.

The dwarf *Trollius pumilus* has nicely divided leaves with clear yellow flowers on stems only 20 cm high. It may be listed as 'Wargrave Variety'.

Trollius ledebourii has orange flowers in June-July. It is a rather tall species, (80 cm), which may also be found under the name *T.chinensis*.

Tropaeolum polyphyllum is not an enthusiastic climber. Its long, trailing stems will bear brilliant yellow flowers in June-July.

Tunica saxifraga (often called *Petrorhagia*) is available in single and double, white and pink varieties. The species itself is pink-flowered.

TUNICA

Tunica, (also now known as *Petrorhagia*), are dainty little plants, allied to gypsophila, and very useful for late flowering.

The single-flowered pink species, *T.saxifraga,* is rather short-lived but comes easily from seed, to give a display of small, open, pink flowers above narrow leaves, from July onwards.

Much more showy and choice, for gritty soil, are a double white 'Alba Plena' and the double pink 'Rosette' which can be divided in Spring.

All are about 15 cm in height.

Urospermum dalechampii. Though not very long-lived, the species will provide you with pleasing yellow flowers, year after year, if you allow it to self-seed.

UROSPERMUM

Urospermum dalechampii has large rayed flowers like a much refined dandelion of clear lemon-yellow for many weeks, June — September. Stems little more than 30 cm and a background of grey-green foliage make this a most useful and attractive dual-purpose plant. It much prefers sun but is not fussy as to soil, and if life span is only 3-4 years, self seeding keeps up the supply.

Below left: *Uvularia grandiflora* is a beautiful Spring-flowering, Solomon's seal-like plant with yellow bell-shaped flowers.

Uvularia

There are only 4 species of *Uvularia*, all of which are natives of North America. They are plants for keen gardeners and they add a very decorative element to the garden. They combine well with, for instance, *Smilacina*, *Polygonatum*, *Tellima* and *Waldsteinia*, near shrubs and in other humus rich and shady places. A combination with ferns and other shade-loving plants is of course highly suitable.

UVULARIA

Uvularia grandiflora is another charmer for Spring. Its habit is like that of Solomon's seal, with slow below-ground spread, and in April and May come leafy arching sprays up to 60 cm, dangling butter-yellow flowers of bell shape. It is a woodlander for humus-rich soil but ideal for a north-facing or shady peat bed. Increase is by division of large plants in Autumn. A slightly dwarfer species with stem-clasping leaves is *U. perfoliata*.

VALERIANA

The taller species are well short of being good garden plants though easy enough to grow. Both *V. alliariifolia* and *V. pyrenaica* grow to about 100-120 cm with deep-green base leaves and wide heads of pale-pink flowers in early Summer. Both self seed to make up for a short life, but do not keep to their appointed spot.

Of the dwarfer kinds, the pale-pink flower heads of *V. montana* come on 15 cm stems in May, June, but *V. saxatilis*, even paler, is 10 cm. Other dwarf species exist but are seldom seen: and though the two above make compact clumpy growth, and do not self seed, their flowering is rather brief.

VANCOUVERIA

Of the three species, *Vancouveria hexandra* (syn. *Epimedium hexandrum*) is the most likely to be available, but even so it is uncommon.
As a very close relation to the epimedium, its dainty foliage is not evergreen but makes a pretty foil to the spidery white flowers on 15 cm sprays in Spring.
Its preference is for shade and light humus soil and old plants divide readily in Autumn.

VERATRUM

These majestic plants also like shade, but moist, deep, rich soil is the prime essential. All have handsome sheathed foliage and given a suitable site will make long-lived clumps, attractive apart from the flower spikes. These are spire-like, made up of myriads of small florets in Summer, and what they lack in colour is made up in overall stateliness. They are best from seed even though this is a slow process, because they resent being divided.
V. album grows to a stately 200 cm in rich, moist soil, the spikes being bare-stemmed but with a mass of leafage below. The flowers are not pure white but densely packed to give a greenish-white appearance.

All four species in cultivation are much alike in growth: but in the rarely-seen *V. californicum,* the clustered greenish ivory flowers tend to droop from the 180 cm spikes.
V. caudatum has brownish-green spikes and very large leaves whilst *V. nigrum*, the best known, is indeed close to being black-flowered on tapering 200 cm spikes, though with a hint of maroon.

V. viride is not so tall at 130 cm, and the spikes carry a dense array of deep apple-green. If dividing old clumps is attempted, it should be done in Autumn. Young seed raised plants are more reliable than divisions.

Valeriana montana, a dwarf pink-flowered species forms clumpy plants and does not seed itself like the taller ones.

Above: *Vancouveria hexandra* needs partial shade and well fed soil to be happy.

Veratrum nigrum has amazing, almost black flowers during Summer on 200 cm spikes. A very appealing species.

VERBASCUM

Verbascum chaixii grows easily up to 100 cm and more, showing its yellow flowers on erect spikes in June-July.

Verbascum phoeniceum is a very variable species. It can have flowers in white, pink and purplish shades, and is less long-lived than most of its hybrids.

Below left: Verbascum olympicum is one of the 'mulleins'. These tall plants are really biennials, but have given rise to perennial hybrids.

Verbascum
Almost all Verbascum species are biennials. The few perennial species are not very long-lived either, particularly if they are in too rich soil. They are plants for sandy soil, preferably with some lime. The species hybridize easily, which has resulted in a large number of hybrids.

VERBASCUM

These two are spike-forming plants, but grow best in poorish soil and need full sun. Roots go deep and most of them may be propagated from root cuttings in Winter, as with papavers and anchusas. Many of those in cultivation are hybrids bred from the more colourful but short-lived kinds, but they are fully worthy because they fit in so well with the flat or round-headed perennials.

The species V. chaixii grows to 100 cm or so with small yellow flowers on erect, firm spikes in June, July. The white of this is not a clear colour, having a mauve eye, and it tends to self seed.

V. densiflorum (syn. V. thapsiforme) is a better yellow, growing to a leafy 120 cm.

V. phoeniceum is the short-lived parent of many hybrids and is itself variable, having 80-100 cm spikes above flat basal leaves in white, pink and purple. It seeds freely but is more or less biennial. Of the hybrids, the two 'Cotswolds' — 'Queen' and 'Beauty' — have orange, yellow and purple tints, not markedly different, and growing to 120 cm. They are reasonably long-lived, as is the 200 cm 'Pink Domino'. V. x 'Hartleyi' is tall and large-flowered, biscuit-yellow and mauve, 'Gainsborough' is clear yellow with woolly grey leaves. A few others have come and gone but the 60 cm 'Golden Bush' is a long-lived cross from different parents. It has thin spikes on branching stems and small yellow flowers for many weeks, June — September.

Dwarf verbascums

Apart from the 'mulleins' V. olympicum and V. pannosum (syn. V. longifolium), both yellow and tall biennials, there are two dwarfs which are not out of place amongst alpines.

The species V. dumulosum makes a mound of felty grey leaves and has 20 cm spikes of yellow flowers. Though not for cold wet regions, it will survive most winters on a south-facing wall top, or it makes a good alpine-house plant for a large pan.

V. 'Letitia' is a cross between V. dumulosum and V. spinosum and has more twiggy growth with smaller leaves. Dainty spikes of yellow flowers are of quite a good size and they continue for several weeks. At 30 cm or so it is an excellent dual-purpose plant, but it needs full sun and sharp drainage to winter successfully. Its parent, the V. spinosum, is small-flowered of similar height, and the cultivar 'Golden Bush', 60 cm, already mentioned, is of this parentage.

VERBENA

Very few of these are hardy, but the tall *V. bonariensis* is reasonably so and though not very long-lived it comes freely from seed.

The 130 cm stems are wiry and erect with a few dark-green leaves branching outwards to terminate in clusters of small, violet-blue, fragrant flowers, during August-October. It needs to be as a group for best effect.

V. corymbosa is a sprawler but has similar foliage and larger flower heads, also fragrant and deep blue in later Summer.

V. hastata is fully hardy and very erect at 100 cm. The flowers are small, purple-blue in candelabra formation, lasting a long time, July — September. None is soil fussy and all are best in sun.

VERNONIA

Vernonia crinita is one of the last perennials to flower. It has stiff leafy stems up to 200 cm, topped by bunched fluffy heads of deep purple. A useful background subject, interesting but not striking, it is easy to grow in sun where not too dry, and makes a large dividable plant.

VERONICA

This is another large and varied genus which includes both alpines of virtually no height to perennials up to 200 cm. In general, they are easy to grow in any soil, and almost all respond to increase by division or form cuttings rather than from seed.

One or two of the dwarf kinds are best avoided as invasive, in particular *V. filiformis* and the damp-loving 'Brookline', which has the curious name *V. beccabunga*. Both are romping creepers difficult to eradicate.

Dwarf veronicas

Taking first the dwarfest or alpine kinds, *V. armena* is very attractive but seldom seen. From a somewhat woody rootstock comes a low mound of lacy leaves and a brave show of bright-blue flowers May-July. A pink form is rare and is more particular as to sun and good drainage.

V. cinerea has grey leaves with much the same habit as *V. armena* and a good spread, covered in Spring with sky-blue flowers, mounding to 8-10 cm.

V. filifolia (not the weed *V. filiformis*) expands slowly into a mat of minute ferny foliage only 8 cm high, with light-blue flowers.

Verbena bonariensis is the hardiest perennial of all *Verbena* species and very worthy for its violet-blue fragrant flowers in Autumn.

Vernonia

The perennial species of Vernonia all originate from North America. There are also *Vernonia* species in South America, but these are mainly trees and shrubs. In total there are more than 500 species. It is therefore particularly surprising that only one species is grown in our gardens, and this very rarely.

Right: *Veronica spicata* is available in pink, blue and white flowering shades.

Below: *Vernonia crinita* is an Autumn-flowering, tall-stemmed, striking species.

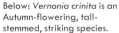

VERONICA

Above: The flowering spikes of *Veronica virginica* 'Alba', an elegant and tall-growing species.

Above left: *Veronica incana* forms silvery mats with violet-blue flowers in June-July.

Left: *Veronica gentianoides* is a late Spring-flowering species up to 45 cm.

Below: A large group of tall Veronicas make a striking effect.

V. x guthrieana is mat-forming but has 12 cm spikes of blue, May-July.

V. pectinata 'Rosea' or 'Rubra' has greyish hairy leaves on vigorous prostrate evergreen mats, covered in late Spring with pink flowers.

V. prostrata (syn. *V. rupestris*) is a good standby, not evergreen but with a profusion of short blue spikes. A good pink form is 'Mrs. Holt'. Both are 8 cm. A minute form 'Nana' exists, but the pale-blue 'Blue Sheen' is outstanding as is the slightly taller rich-blue 'Kapitan'.

More upright growth is seen on *V. pinnata* 'Blue Eyes', giving a bright-blue display at 20 cm, May-June.

V. saturejoides is mat-forming and the blue flowers on 8 cm stems have a red eye.

V. spicata is variable in pink, blue and white, and with spikes June-August from 15 cm in the pink 'Heidekind', to 60 cm in others.

Dual-purpose veronicas

Several veronicas come in the dual-purpose category, especially those of the *V. teucrium* species. These make clumpy, deciduous plants and a bright summer display in shades of blue. 'Shirley Blue' is 20 cm, 'Crater Lake' 25 cm, and 'Blue Fountain' 50 cm, whilst 'Trehane', 15 cm, is golden leaved. It prefers cool soil and some shade.

V. gentianoides is spring flowering, light blue at 45 cm, but there is a 25 cm form 'Nana' and one with variegated leaves. It has vigorous growth with broad-leaved rosettes for sun or shade.

V. incana forms grey or silvery mats and has 40 cm spikes of violet-blue, June — July. Hybrids of this and *V. spicata* have given the delicate pink 'Minuet', grey-leaved, 35 cm, and the deeper green-leaved 'Baccarole'; also the German raised 'Red Fox' and 'Blue Fox', both 30 cm. Other hybrids of the same parentage are the 'Saraband'-grey leaved, deep blue — and the lighter 'Wendy', both 50 cm.

V. longifolia also has variations, but all have quite full spikes on clumpy habit, late to make new growth in Spring, in the 45-75 cm height range, flowering July-September. 'Lavender Charm' and 'Icicle' are two modern varieties, 60cm high.

V. perfoliata is distinct for its glaucous stem leaves of leathery texture, and china-blue flowers on twiggy stems. It needs a warm sunny spot.

V. virginica is the tallest species up to 140 cm. It has slender spikes in both the type and the pink form, but the most elegant and effective is the white 'Alba', with spikes July — September making splendid contrast.

VINCA

As 'periwinkles', none is really suitable to grow in with other perennials, but they are useful in shady places as ground cover.
They have a rather brief or sparse show of flowers; and of the two main species *V. major* and *V. minor*, the compact forms of the latter are more desirable.

They also have the widest range of colour even if freedom to flower is not one of the strong points of vincas generally. The freest of the *V. minor* cultivars is the bright-blue 'Bowles Variety'; 'Atropurpurea' is a plum-purple shade which spreads more rapidly, as does the white 'Alba'. The variegated-leaved subjects are naturally brighter in foliage effect, and both the silvery 'Argentea' ('Argenteo-variegata') and the golden 'Aurea' ('Aureo-variegata') are worth having. *V. major* has leaves twice as large as *V. minor*, but is no quicker to spread. These make less of a carpet, but both the green type and the bright golden-green of *V. major* 'Variegata' are useful and attractive. Old vincas tear apart quite easily, but are not so easy to plant safely as young pot-grown plants.

Above: *Vinca minor* 'Aurea' (syn. 'Aureo-variegata').

Right: *Vinca major* is rather slow to cover the ground compared with the smaller *Vinca minor*.

Below: *Viola cornuta* 'Purpurea' (syn. *V. labradorica*).

VIOLA

Only a few of the 400 or so species are in cultivation. The vast majority seen in gardens are hybrids and of these few could be considered as truly alpine, though they lack nothing in richness of variety, colour and long flowering.

Of the species, *V. cornuta* is quite vigorous, and has a long succession of light-blue 'horned' pansy flowers, seen also in the white 'Alba' and the deep blue 'Purpurea' (syn. *V. labradorica*). All are 10 cm May-August. In this category, but with more compact growth, are the cultivars 'Nora Leigh', light blue, 'Blue Carpet', and the yellow and maroon 'Jackanapes'. 'Molly Sanderson' is quite black, and 'Moonlight' pale yellow. All are long-flowering, about 15 cm tall.
V. cucullata (syn. V.obliqua) is more in the style of a large violet (*V. odorata*) but does not run. The white flowers, 15 cm high, have a violet-blue streak in *V. cucullata* 'Striata' as has *V. septentrionalis*, both being at home where cool and shady. This applies to the very good species *V. labradorica* which has purplish, rounded leaves giving excellent ground cover even where dry, and lilac-mauve flowers, 10 cm, for a long period.
V. hederacea is not fully hardy though pretty with its violet and white flowers for most of the Summer, 7 cm. It is easy to protect over Winter.
No protection is needed for the little yellow *V.*

VIOLA

Viola

A speciality of *Viola* is that the plants often produce two different kinds of flowers. Early in the Spring sterile flowers are formed, which do not give seeds whereas, later on, flowers appear which are capable of forming seeds, and do so abundantly. Because *Viola* species have been hybridized for a long time, it is very difficult to determine the genetic origin of the many hybrids. It is certain, however, that two species were very influential: *V. altaica* from Siberia, which produces large, often bi-coloured flowers at the end of Spring, and *V. lutea* from southern and central Europe, which flowers from June onwards (yellow with black markings). Both are plants for enthusiasts and are difficult to obtain.

Above left: A *Viola cornuta* hybrid, displaying the colours most associated with pansies.

Left: *Waldsteinia ternata* is an excellent ground coverer, which will thrive in sun and shade.

Wulfenia x *suendermannii* forms mats of leathery leaves, and has blue flowers in early Spring.

biflora which, with the pink *V. rupestris* 'Rosea', will come from self-sown seeds. There are many cultivars in existence to add colour if need be, such as the rich-red 'Arkwright's Ruby', the apricot-yellow 'Chantreyland', and the soft-pink 'Haslemere'. These will come fairly true from seed as replacements for plants which soon exhaust themselves by flowering.

Some reliable hybrids of *V. cornuta* and *V. gracilis* are very worthwhile. The blue *V. c.* 'Norah Leigh', violet-blue 'Hansa' and blue and gold 'Blue Carpet', *V. g.* 'Major' and many more, exist as reliable and long flowering varieties.

VISCARIA – see LYCHNIS

VITALIANA – see DOUGLASIA

WALDSTEINIA

This splendid carpeting trailer, *W. ternata* (syn. *W. trifolia*), makes only a brief display of its bright yellow flowers in Spring, but is excellent as a ground coverer in sun or shade, especially over walls. The leaves are of 'strawberry' form, glossy and rich green, giving complete cover. It can be planted at almost any time when not in flower.

WULFENIA

These form neat tufts or mats of leathery leaves, light green in *W. carinthiaca*. This has short spikes of close-set, deep-blue flowers 12 cm tall in June and July: an easy-to-grow plant not objecting to some shade.

The smaller, rarer *W. amherstiana* has small, deep-green, slow-growing mats and arching sprays of lavender-blue, June to August. It prefers some shade and is only 8 cm high.

Division is best in early Spring.

W. x *suendermannii* is larger and showier than *W. carinthiaca*, with sprays of rich blue on 30 cm stems in early Spring.

YUCCA

Some yuccas are said to flower only once in seven years, but *Y. filamentosa* seldom misses a year given a sunny place and well-drained soil once it has become established. This is a subject for isolation where its symmetry can be appreciated; and when in flower during July and August, it is an imposing sight with its ivory bells on spikes 120-150 cm high. The sharp-pointed leaves of this species have small, drooping, loose threads along the edges; and being evergreen, the woody stem lengthens with age. Plants will, however, produce suckers from the roots which in time mature to make a single plant form a group. When planting in Autumn, a collar of litter should be placed around for protection over the first Winter, but once established it can take care of itself.

Y. flaccida also has hanging threads but the leaves are narrower. It flowers freely, ivory-white and green in the bud, and is resistant to both frost and drought. So is the daddy of them all, *Y. gloriosa*, but it flowers erratically and in time becomes untidy, taking up considerable space. Spikes attain 200 cm or more.

Y. recurvifolia must be rated highly for magnificence. Its 200 cm spikes come a little earlier than others, the white cups being more open. The sword-like leaves arch over from the central stumpy crown.

There are several yuccas with variegated leaves, but none is quite so hardy and they are much less free to flower. Given a warm position in well-drained soil, they are quite spectacular and I have known them to survive 25 degrees F.(−14°C) of frost without serious damage.

Yucca filamentosa 'Variegata' needs a warm, sheltered position in well-drained soil to survive our winters.

Above: *Yucca filamentosa* makes quite a show when flowering during July-August.

Right: *Yucca aloifolia* is grown widely in the south of Europe, but is only suitable as a tub-plant in our climate.

ZANTEDESCHIA

Zantedeschia aethiopica and its varieties will grow in any moist soil, but need some winter protection.

Zauschneria californica produces a splendid display of scarlet-red flowers from August to October.

ZANTEDESCHIA

Since the advent of *Z. aethiopica* 'Crowborough Variety', interest has led to its being grown as an outdoor arum lily. It will grow in any moist soil, in sun or shade, and it will grow in water. The need for winter protection applies to young plants and it is quite surprising how, when established, they can endure much frost. Even so, such a spectacular subject is worth covering with litter before December, when severe frosts can be expected. This is far better practice than lifting and storing over Winter.

Apart from the 'Crowborough Variety', there is the more open-flowered 'White Sail' and 'Little Gem' which at 60 cm is only half the height. There is also 'Green Goddess', but though this may appeal to flower arrangers, one has to look closely to distinguish the spathes (flowers) from the lush green foliage they all have.

All divide readily and this is best done as new growth begins in Spring.

ZAUSCHNERIA

Although needing winter protection in cold districts, these are valuable late-flowering plants which are easy to protect. They prefer light, well-drained soil in full sun in a southerly aspect. The twiggy growth, with small soft leafage, produces spikes of brilliant scarlet-red from August to October. A vigorous plant named 'Glasnevin' is hardier than the grey-leaved *Z. californica*, *Z. californica* ssp. *mexicana* and *Z. cana* (syn. *Z. microphylla*). All reach 30 cm in height.

Z. canescens is also grey leaved and any of them will add a splash of brightness when colour is dwindling.

They are increased from cuttings or careful division in Spring. They show up well with *Aster thompsonii* 'Nana' and *Aster spectabilis*.

ZIGADENUS

These are becoming less rare as their qualities are appreciated. As semi-bulbous members of *Liliaceae*, they are not difficult to grow in fertile soil and sun and have a charm of their own, with narrow grassy leaves and short spikes of open flowers, greenish, creamy or ivory white.

Z. elegans is best known, but *Z. glaucus*, *Z. nuttallii* and *Z. muscitoxicus* are all decidedly worth growing even if variations among them are not wide.

Heights range from 30-60 cm and they flower in the June-September period. They divide readily but are slow from seed.

PLANTS FOR SPECIFIC PURPOSES

and INDEX

Perennials – for dry soils

A quick guide to plants for specific purposes

The following pages provide useful plant checklists, for a wide range of applications. From these you can choose plants which are likely to meet your specific needs. There's a guide to the number of plants you'll need per square metre, too.

By cross-referencing the checklists, you can make selections like 'Which plants will give me a blue-flowering border, for my dry soil, in a sunny position?'; or 'Which yellow-flowering plants may also be good for cut-flowers, or for drying?'

Naturally these lists are not exhaustive, but they are made up from the plants listed in the A-Z part, and are here to provide you with a few extra ideas and perhaps some answers.

Perennials – for dry soils

Acaena	Eryngium	Monarda
Acanthus	Euphorbia	Nepeta
Achillea	Festuca	Oenothera
Aconitum	Filipendula	Papaver
Alyssum	Fuchsia	Perovskia
Anaphalis	Gaillardia	Petrorhagia
Anchusa	Geranium	Phlox
Anemone	Gypsophila	Physalis
Anthemis	Hebe	Physostegia
Aquilegia	Helenium	Platycodon
Arabis	Helianthemum	Potentilla
Armeria	Helianthus	Prunella
Arrhenatherum	Helictotrichon	Pulsatilla
Artemisia	Hypericum	Rudbeckia
Asperula	Iberis	Salvia
Aster	Incarvillea	Santolina
Astilbe	Inula	Saponaria
Aubrieta	Iris	Saxifraga
Briza	Kniphofia	Scutellaria
Campanula	Lamium	Sedum
Centaurea	Lathyrus	Sempervivum
Centranthus	Lavatera	Solidago
Cerastium	Leontopodium	Stachys
Coreopsis	Liatris	Teucrium
Cortaderia	Limonium	Thymus
Corydalis	Linaria	Verbascum
Dianthus	Linum	Veronica
Dictamnus	Lupinus	Viola
Draba	Lychnis	Yucca
Echinopsis	Macleaya	
Erigeron	Malva	

Perennials – for moist/wet soils

Aconitum	Hosta
Ajuga	Inula
Alchemilla	Iris
Anemone	Lamium
Aruncus	Ligularia
Asarum	Luzula
Astilbe	Lysimachia
Astrantia	Lythrum
Bergenia	Mimulus
Brunnera	Monarda
Campanula	Myosotis
Chrysanthemum	Paeonia
Cimicifuga	Polygonum
Dicentra	Primula
Epimedium	Pulmonaria
Eupatorium	Rheum
Ferns	Rodgersia
Filipendula	Sagina
Galium	Thalictrum
Geum	Tiarella
Gunnera	Tradescantia
Heliopsis	Trollius
Helleborus	Vinca
Hemerocallis	Viola
Hepatica	

Ornamental grasses – for moist/wet soils

Carex
Clyceria
Miscanthus
Pennisetum
Phalaris

Flowering bulbs – for moist/wet soils and inclusion amongst perennials

Colchicum
Fritillaria
Leucojum
Lilium

Perennials – grouped by colour

White	Height in cm
Alyssum saxatile	15-30
Anemone	30-40
Anemone japonica	50-100
Aquilegia caerulea	40-80
Arabis caucasica	10-20
Aruncus dioicus	100-200
Aster alpinus	15-25
Aster ericoides	60-100
Aster dumosus	15-40
Aster novi-belgii	50-150
Astilbe arendsii	60-100
Astilbe japonica	40-60
Bergenia cordifolia	30-50
Campanula lactiflora	50-100
Campanula latifolia	50-150
Campanula persicifolia	40-100
Centranthus ruber	60-80
Cerastium	15-25
Chrysanthenum	50-90
Chrysanthemum nipponicum	15-20
Cimicifuga racemosa	100-150
Cimicifuga simplex	120-150
Delphinium	100-200
Dictamnus albus	60-100
Dianthus plumarius	25-40
Erigeron	50-80
Gillenia trifoliata	60-70
Gypsophila paniculata	80-100
Iberis sempervirens	25-35
Iris germanica	30-60
Iris pumila	10-15
Iris sibirica	70-100
Lupinus polyphyllus	80-100
Lychnis viscaria	30-40
Macleaya cordata	200-300
Papaver orientale	60-80
Phlox paniculata	70-120
Phlox subulata	10-15
Physostegia virginiana	60-80
Platycodon grandiflorum	30-60
Polygonum campanulatum	60-100
Primula denticulata	15-45
Primula elatior	8-30
Primula juliae	5-10
Rheum palmatum	200-250
Rodgersia aesculifolia	120-150
Saxifraga arendsii	15-20
Scabiosa caucasica	50-80
Stachys grandiflora	40-70
Tradescantia andersoniana	50-60
Verbascum	80-100
Viola cornuta	15-30

Yellow	Height in cm
Achillea filipendulina	80-100
Adonis amurensis	20-30
Alchemilla mollis	40-60
Alyssum saxatile	15-30
Anthemis tinctoria	30-80
Aquilegia caerulea	40-80
Aster ericoides	60-100
Centaurea macrocephala	50-90
Coreopsis grandiflora	80-100
Coreopsis lanceolata	40-60
Coreopsis verticillata	70-90
Doronicum orientale	20-30
Echinacea purpurea	60-100
Geum	20-40
Helenium autumnale	50-100
Helenium-hybrids	100-200
Helianthus atrorubens	150-200
Helianthus decapetalus	100-200
Heliopsis helianthoides	100-130
Hemerocallis	60-80
Inula ensifolia	30-60
Inula magnifica	150-180
Iris germanica	30-60
Iris pumila	10-15
Kniphofia	60-80
Ligularia x hessei	100-150
Ligularia przewalskii	150
Lupinus polyphyllus	100
Lysimachia clethroides	60-80
Lysimachia punctata	80-100
Oenothera fruticosa	30-50
Oenothera tetragona	50-80
Potentilla	20-60
Primula bullesiana	40
Primula elatior	10-30
Primula florindae	50-70
Rheum alexandrae	70-90
Rudbeckia nitida	100-120
Rudbeckia fulgida	40-60
Saxifraga arendsii	15-20
Sedum	10-20
Solidago	30-70
Trollius europaeus	50-70
Trollius-hybrids	50-100
Verbascum	100

QUICK GUIDE
Perennials – grouped by colour

Orange	Height in cm
Alstroemeria	60-120
Chrysanthemum rubellum	70-100
Geum	30-50
Helenium	80-200
Heliopsis helianthoides	100-125
Hemerocallis	60-120
Inula orientalis	50-70
Iris pumila	10-15
Kniphofia	70-125
Ligularia dentata	100-150
Mimulus	15-30
Papaver orientale	80-100
Phlox paniculata	70-120
Primula bullesiana	30-50
Primula elatior	10-30
Rudbeckia	70-90
Trollius	50-100

Red/Pink	Height in cm
Anemone japonica	50-100
Anemone hupehensis	50-100
Aquilegia	60-100
Armeria	40-60
Aster amellus	40-70
Aster dumosus	15-40
Aster novae-angliae	70-250
Aster novi-belgii	50-150
Astilbe arendsii	60-100
Astilbe japonica	50-70
Astrantia major	30-60
Bergenia cordifolia	30-50
Campanula lactiflora	80-100
Chelone obliqua	60
Centranthus ruber	80
Chrysanthemum rubellum	80-100
Dianthus deltoides	15-30
Dianthus gratianopolitanus	10-25
Dianthus plumarius	10-20
Dicentra formosa	20-30
Geranium endressii	25-30
Geranium sanguineum	15-25
Geranium subcaulescens	10-20
Geum chiloense	40-60
Geum-hybrids	25-40
Gypsophila paniculata	30-50
Helenium	100-200
Hemerocallis	60-80
Heuchera	50-70
Iris germanica	30-60
Iris pumila	10-15
Iris sibirica	70-100
Kniphofia	60-80
Lupinus polyphyllus	100
Lychnis chalcedonica	100
Lychnis viscaria	30-50
Lythrum	100-150
Malva moschata	30-60

Red/Pink	Height in cm
Monarda	70-80
Papaver orientale	60-90
Phlox paniculata	60-125
Phlox subulata	10-15
Physostegia virginiana	60-120
Polygonum affine	20-40
Polygonum bistorta	30-100
Potentilla nepalensis	40-60
Primula bullesiana	30-60
Primula elatior	10-30
Primula juliae	5-10
Saponaria ocymoides	20-40
Saponaria officinalis	50-80
Saxifrage arendsii	15-20
Sedum spectabile	30-50
Sedum spurium	10-15
Sedum telephium	20-40
Sidalcea	60-80
Stachys grandiflora	40-80
Verbascum	100-200
Veronica spicata	20-40

Purple	Height in cm
Anemone	30-50
Aquilegia vulgaris	40-80
Aster alpinus	15-25
Aster amellus	40-60
Aster dumosus	15-40
Aster novi-belgii	50-150
Aster sedifolius	60-10
Astilbe arendsii	60-100
Astilbe chinensis	20-40
Aubrieta	5-10
Bergenia cordifolia	30-50
Delpinium	100-200
Dianthus plumarius	20-40
Dictamnus albus	60-100
Echinacea purpurea	60-100
Erigeron	60-80
Geranium platypetalum	40-70
Iris germanica	30-60
Iris pumila	10-15
Liatris spicata	40-60
Lupinus polyphyllus	100
Lythrum	60-150
Monarda	60-80
Phlox paniculata	75-125
Phlox subulata	5-15
Primula bullesiana	40
Primula juliae	5-10
Sidalcea	60-80
Silene schafta	10-15
Stachys grandiflora	40-70
Thalictrum dipterocarpum	200
Tradescantia andersoniana	40-60
Verbascum	100-200
Verbena bonariensis	150

Planting density – number of plants per square metre

With so many factors to consider, only very general advice can be given. The examples below are given as a guide.

Acaena: 12-14
Achillea: 6-8
Aconitum: 4-6
Ajuga: 10-14
Alchemilla: 6-8
Alyssum: 8-10
Anchusa: 4-6
Anthemis: 6-8
Arabis: 10-14
Armeria: 10-14
Artemisia: 4-6
Aster: 4-10
Astilbe: 6-10
Aubrieta: 8-12
Bergenia: 5-7
Buphthalmum: 8-10
Campanula: 8-14
Centaurea: 4-6
Centranthus: 6-8
Cerastium: 8-12
Chrysanthemum, tall: 6-8
Cimicifuga: 5-7
Coreopsis: 7-10
Delphinium: 4-6
Dianthus: 10-12
Dictamnus: 6-8
Doronicum: 8-10
Echinacea: 6-8
Echinops: 4-6
Erigeron: 6-8
Euphorbia: 8-12
Festuca: 12-14
Gaillardia: 6-8
Galium: 10-12
Geranium: 6-8
Gypsophila paniculata: 3-5
Hebe: 10-12
Helenium: 4-6
Helianthemum: 8-10
Helianthus: 4-6

Planting density – number of plants per square metre

Helleborus: 8-10
Hemerocallis: 4-6
Heuchera: 8-10
Hosta: 6-8
Hypericum: 8-10
Iberis: 8-10
Iris: 6-8
Kniphofia: 6-8
Lamium: 8-10
Liatris: 8-10
Ligularia: 2-4
Lupinus: 4-6
Lychnis: 8-10
Malva: 8-10
Mimulus: 10-12
Nepeta: 8-10
Oenothera: 6-8
Pachysandra: 10-12
Phlox, small: 10-12
Phlox paniculata-
  hybrids: 4-6
Potentilla: 8-10
Primula: 12-16
Pulmonaria: 10-12
Pulsatilla: 10-12
Rudbeckia: 6-8
Salvia: 6-8
Saponaria: 8-10
Saxifraga: 8-10
Sedum, small: 12-16
Sedum, tall: 6-8
Sempervivum: 14-16
Solidago: 4-6
Stachys: 8-10
Teucrium: 10-12
Thymus: 12-14
Tradescantia: 6-8
Trollius: 6-8
Verbascum: 4-6
Veronica: 10-12
Vinca major: 6-8
Vinca minor: 8-10
Waldsteinia: 10-12

Purple

	Height in cm
Verbena rigida	30-50
Viola cornuta	15-30

Violet

	Height in cm
Acanthus mollis	100
Aconitum carmichaelii	150-200
Aconitum fischeri	50-60
Aster alpinus	15-25
Aster amellus	40
Aster cordifolius	60-150
Aster farreri	50
Aster frikartii	70
Aster novae-angliae	60-250
Aster novi-belgii	50-150
Aubrieta	5-10
Bergenia	30-40
Campanula glomerata	25-60
Campanula portenschlagiana	10-15
Delphinium	100-150
Erigeron	50-80
Eryngium	100
Iris germanica	30-60
Iris pumila	10-15
Iris sibirica	70-100
Lupinus	80-100
Nepeta x faassenii	30-50
Phlox paniculata	50-120
Primula denticulata	15-40
Primula juliae	5-10
Prunella grandiflora	15-25
Pulmonaria angustifolia	20-30
Salvia x superba	50-80
Scabiosa caucasica	50-80
Tradescantia andersoniana	40-60
Veronica spicata	20-70
Viola cornuta	15-30

Blue

	Height in cm
Aconitum x arendsii	80-120
Aconitum x cammarum	150
Aconitum napellus	100
Anchusa italica	50-125
Aquilegia caerulea	40-80
Aquilegia vulgaris	40-80
Aquilegia-hybrids	60-100
Aster alpinus	15-25
Aster amellus	60
Aster dumosus	15-40
Aster yunnanensis	20-30
Aubrieta	5-10
Brunnera macrophylla	30-40
Campanula carpatica	15-45
Campanula garganica	30
Campanula lactiflora	30-60
Campanula latifolia	50-150
Campanula persicifolia	40-100
Delphinium	100-200
Echinops banaticus	80-100
Echinops ritro	50-100
Eryngium planum	80
Iris pumila	10-15
Iris germanica	30-60
Iris sibirica	70-100
Lupinus polyphyllus	100
Nepeta sibirica	70-100
Phlox divaricata	15-25
Platycodon grandiflorum	30-60
Pulmonaria angustifolia	20-30
Scabiosa caucasica	50-80
Stokesia laevis	30-40
Tradescantia andersioniana	50-60
Veronica incana	25-40
Veronica spicata	20-40
Veronica teucrium	25-40
Viola cornuta	15-30

QUICK GUIDE
Perennials – grouped by flowering time

Perennials – grouped by flowering time

White

Flowering months

3-4	Primula denticulata
3-4	Primula juliae-hybrids
3-5	Primula elatior-hybrids
4-5	Bergenia cordifolia
4-5	Alyssum saxatile
4-5	Iris pumila
4-6	Phlox subulata
5	Saxifraga arendsii-hybrids
5-6	Astilbe japonica
5-6	Lychnis viscaria
5-6	Iberis sempervirens
5-6	Polygonum campanulatum
5-6	Aquilegia caerulea
5-6	Papaver orientale
5-6	Rheum palmatum
5-6	Iris germanica
5-6	Iris sibirica
5-7	Viola cornuta
6	Cerastium
6	Arabis caucasica
6-7	Gypsophila paniculata
6-7	Gillenia trifoliata
6-7	Aruncus dioicus
6-7	Delphinium-hybrids
6-7	Cimicifuga racemosa
6-7	Rodgersia aesculifolia
6-7	Dictamnus albus
6-7	Aster alpinus
6-8	Campanula lactiflora
6-8	Campanula persicifolia
6-8	Erigeron-hybrids
6-8	Verbascum-hybrids
6-8	Stachys grandiflora
6-8	Astilbe arendsii
6-8	Lupinus polyphyllus-hybrids
6-9	Tradescantia andersoniana
6-9	Scabiosa caucasica
7-8	Dianthus plumarius
7-8	Macleaya cordata
7-8	Centranthus ruber
7-8	Campanula latifolia
7-9	Platycodon grandiflorum
7-9	Physostegia virginiana
7-9	Phlox paniculata-hybrids
8-10	Anemone japonica-hybrids
9-10	Cimicifuga simplex
9-10	Cimicifuga dahurica
9-10	Chrysanthemum serotinum
9-11	Aster ericoides
9-11	Aster novi-belgii
9-11	Aster dumosus-hybrids

Yellow

Flowering months

2-4	Adonis amurensis
3-5	Primula elatior-hybrids
4-5	Alyssum saxatile
4-5	Iris pumila
4-5	Doronicum orientale
4-7	Primula bullesiana-hybrids
5-6	Aquilegia caerulea
5-6	Viola cornuta
5-6	Rheum alexandrae
5-6	Trollius-hybrids
5-6	Trollius europaeus
5-6	Iris germanica
5-6	Hemerocallis middendorffii
5-7	Saxifraga arendsii-hybrids
6	Geum-hybrids
6-7	Potentilla recta
6-8	Oenothera fruticosa
6-8	Anthemis tinctoria
6-8	Sedum floriferum
6-8	Verbascum-hybrids
6-8	Potentilla-hybrids
6-8	Bupthalmum (Inula) salicifolium
6-8	Alchemilla mollis
6-8	Lysimachia clethroides
6-8	Lysimachia punctata
6-8	Lupinus polyphyllus-hybrids
6-8	Coreopsis lanceolata
6-8	Oenothera tetragona
6-9	Coreopsis verticillata
7-8	Inula magnifica
7-8	Inula ensifolia
7-8	Hemerocallis-hybrids
7-8	Sedum hybridum
7-8	Coreopsis grandiflora
7-8	Centaurea macrocephala
7-8	Primula florindae
7-8	Achillea filipendulina
7-9	Rudbeckia laciniata
7-9	Heliopsis helianthoides
7-9	Rudbeckia fulgida var. sullivanti
7-9	Rudbeckia nitida
7-9	Helenium bigelovi
7-9	Ligularia x hessei
7-9	Ligularia przewalskii
7-9	Ligularia veitchiana
7-9	Achillea clypeolata
8-9	Solidago-hybrids
8-9	Helenium-hybrids
8-10	Helianthus decapetalus
8-10	Helianthus atrorubens
8-10	Helenium autumnale
8-10	Echinacea purpurea
9	Aster linosyris
9-10	Kniphofia
9-11	Aster ericoides

Perennials – early flowering

Arabis
Asarum
Bergenia
Brunnera
Doronicum
Draba
Helleborus
Hepatica
Pachysandra
Primula denticulata
– juliae-hybrids
– vulgaris
Pulmonaria
Pulsatilla
Vinca minor
Viola odorata

Perennials – late flowering

Anemone japonica-
   hybrids
Artemisia lactiflora
Aster ericoides
– novae-angliae
– novi-belgii
– sedifolius
Cimicifuga
Cortaderia
Fuchsia
Helianthus
Heliopsis
Lavatera
Sedum 'Autumn Joy'
Tradescantia

Orange

Flowering months

3-4	Primula eliator-hybrids
4-5	Iris pumila
4-7	Primula bullesiana-hybrids
5-6	Trollius-hybrids
5-6	Papaver orientale
5-6	Helenium hoopesii
5-7	Trollius chinensis
6	Geum-hybrids
6-7	Hemerocallis fulva
6-8	Geum coccineum
6-8	Helenium-hybrids
6-8	Alstroemeria aurantiaca
6-9	Phlox paniculata-hybrids
7-8	Inula orientalis
7-8	Hemerocallis
7-9	Heliopsis helianthoides
7-9	Ligularia dentata
8-9	Kniphofia-hybrids
6-10	Mimulus-hybrids
8-10	Rudbeckia fulgida
9-10	Chrysanthemum rubellum

Red/Pink

Flowering months

3-4	Primula elatior-hybrids
3-4	Primula juliae-hybrids
4-5	Bergenia cordifolia
4-5	Iris pumila
4-6	Phlox subulata
4-7	Primula bullesiana-hybrids
5	Saxifraga arendsii-hybrids
5-6	Papaver orientale
5-6	Iris germanica
5-6	Astilbe japonica
5-6	Lychnis viscaria
5-6	Armeria pseudarmeria
5-6	Heuchera-hybrids
5-6	Dianthus gratianopolitanus
5-7	Heuchera-hybrids
5-7	Saponaria ocymoides
5-8	Geranium sanguineum
5-8	Polygonum bistorta
6	Iris sibirica
6	Geum
6-7	Astrantia major
6-8	Geum chiloense
6-8	Aquilegia-hybrids
6-8	Potentilla atrosanguinea
6-8	Geranium endressii
6-8	Campanula lactiflora
6-8	Astilbe arendsii
6-8	Lychnis chalcedonica
6-8	Lupinus polyphyllus-hybrids
6-8	Dianthus plumarius

Red/Pink

Flowering months

6-9	Gypsophila paniculata
6-9	Geranium 'Russell Prichard'
6-9	Geranium subcaulescens
6-9	Chelone obliqua
6-9	Malva alcea
6-9	Lythrum-hybrids
6-9	Dianthus deltoides
7-8	Stachys grandiflora
7-8	Centranthus ruber
7-8	Sidalcea-hybrids
7-8	Sedum telephium
7-8	Helenium-hybrids
7-8	Physostegia virginiana
7-8	Potentilla-hybrids
7-8	Hemerocallis-hybrids
7-8	Veronica spicata
7-8	Verbascum-hybrids
7-9	Saponaria officinalis
7-9	Potentilla nepalensis
7-9	Phlox paniculata-hybrids
7-9	Monarda-hybrids
7-9	Malva moschata
8-9	Sedum spurium
8-9	Sedum spectabile
8-9	Polygonum affine
8-9	Aster amellus
8-9	Anemone hupehensis
6-10	Dicentra formosa
8-10	Anemone japonica-hybrids
9-10	Kniphofia-hybrids
9-10	Chrysanthemum rubellum
9-10	Aster novae-angliae
9-11	Aster dumosus-hybrids
9-11	Aster novi-belgii

Purple

Flowering months

3-4	Primula juliae-hybrids
4-5	Iris pumila
4-5	Aubrieta-hybrids
4-5	Bergenia cordifolia
4-6	Phlox subulata
4-7	Primula bullesiana-hybrids
5-6	Iris germanica
5-6	Aquilegia vulgaris
5-6	Viola cornuta
5-7	Thalictrum aquilegifolium
6-7	Geranium meeboldii
6-7	Aster alpinus
6-7	Monarda-hybrids
6-7	Dictamnus albus
6-8	Lupinus polyphyllus-hybrids
6-8	Geranium platypetalum
6-8	Stachys grandifloria

QUICK GUIDE
Perennials – grouped by flowering time

Purple

Flowering months

6-8	Astilbe arendsii
6-9	Lythrum-hybrids
6-9	Delphinium-hybrids
6-9	Tradescantia andersoniana-hybrids
7-9	Echinacea purpurea
7-8	Erigeron-hybrids
7-8	Dianthus plumarius
7-8	Sidalcea-hybrids
7-9	Thalictrum dipterocarpum
7-9	Verbascum-hybrids
7-9	Phlox paniculata-hybrids
8-9	Aster sedifolius
8-9	Anemone tomentosa
8-9	Silene schafta
7-10	Verbena bonariensis
7-10	Astilbe chinensis
7-10	Verbena rigida
9-11	Aster dumosus-hybrids
9-11	Aster novi-belgii

Violet

Flowering months

2	Bergenia x schmidtii
3-4	Pulmonaria angustifolia
3-4	Primula denticulata
3-4	Primula juliae-hybrids
4-5	Iris pumila
4-5	Aubrieta-hybrids
5-6	Iris germanica
5-6	Aster farreri
5-7	Viola cornuta
5-8	Nepeta x faassenii
6	Iris sibirica
6-7	Aster x alpellus
6-7	Lupinus-hybrids
6-7	Aster alpinus
6-7	Delphinium-hybrids
6-8	Campanula glomerata
6-8	Tradescantia andersoniana-hybrids
6-8	Acanthus mollis
6-8	Prunella grandiflora
6-9	Campanula portenschlagiana
6-9	Eryngium x zabelii
6-9	Salvia x superba
6-9	Scabiosa caucasica
7-8	Veronica spicata
7-8	Erigeron-hybrids
7-8	Phlox paniculata-hybrids
7-9	Aster amellus
8-9	Aconitum fischeri
8-9	Aster x frikartii
8-10	Aconitum charmichaelii
8-10	Aster cordifolius

Violet

Flowering months

9-10	Aster novae-angliae
9-11	Aster novi-belgii

Blue

Flowering months

3-4	Pulmonaria angustifolia
4-5	Aubrieta-hybrids
4-5	Iris pumila
4-5	Brunnera macrophylla
5-6	Veronica prostrata
5-6	Campanula garganica
5-6	Phlox divaricata
5-6	Aquilegia caerulea
5-6	Iris germanica-hybrids
5-6	Aquilegia vulgaris
5-7	Viola cornuta
5-7	Aster yunnanensis
6	Iris sibirica
6-7	Eryngium planum
6-7	Veronica teucrium
6-7	Aster alpinus
6-7	Delphinium-hybrids
6-8	Campanula lactiflora
6-8	Aconitum x cammarum
6-8	Campanula persicifolia
6-8	Anchusa italica
6-8	Campanula lactiflora
6-8	Aquilegia-hybrids
6-8	Lupinus polyphyllus-hybrids
6-8	Aconitum napellus
6-9	Scabiosa caucasica
6-9	Tradescantia andersoniana-hybrids
6-9	Campanula carpatica
7-8	Echinops banaticus
7-8	Campanula latifolia
7-8	Veronica incana
7-8	Veronica spicata
7-8	Veronica longifolia
7-9	Stokesia laevis
7-9	Echinops ritro
7-9	Aster amellus
7-9	Nepeta sibirica
7-9	Platycodon grandiflorum
9-10	Aconitum x arendsii
9-11	Aster dumosus-hybrids

Perennials – flowering twice in a season

Alchemilla
Alyssum
Erigeron
Trollius

Perennials – flowering again after being cut back

Delphinium
Lupinus

Half-hardy shrubs – treated as perennials

These are plants with a shrub-like character. However, they are treated like perennials, as the top-growth on most of them is not winter-hardy.

Aethionema
Fuchsia
Hebe
Helianthemum
Hypericum x moseranum
Iberis
Lithodora diffusa
Pachysandra
Paeonia suffruticosa
Salvia officinalis
Santolina
Teucrium
Thymus
Vinca minor
Yucca

Perennials – as specimen plants

Acanthus
Aruncus dioicus
Avena sempervirens
Cortaderia selloana
Fuchsia
Gunnera
Helictotrichon
Heracleum
    mantegazzianum
Ligularia
Macleaya
Osmunda
Paeonia suffruticosa
Rheum
Rodgersia
Yucca

Perennials – tall varieties suitable for screening

Aster novae-angliae
Eupatorium
Helianthus
Lavatera
Macleaya
Rudbeckia nitida

Perennials – attractive forms (even out of flower)

Acaena
Acanthus
Achillea filipendulina
Ajuga
Alchemilla
Asarum
Astilbe
Bergenia
Coreopsis verticillata
Epimedium
Euphorbia cyparissias
Galeobdolon
Galium odoratum
Gunnera
Hebe
Heuchera
Hosta
Lamiastrum
Ligularia
Macleaya
Papaver
Physalis
Polygonum affine
Pulmonaria
Pulsatilla
Sagina
Salvia x superba
Santolina
Sedum
Sempervivum
Thymus
Tiarella
Veronica gentianoides
Vinca major

Ferns

Athyrium filix-femina
Blechnum spicant
Cyrtomium fortunei
– macrophyllum
Cystopteris bulbifera
Dryopteris filix-mas
Matteuccia struthiopteris
Osmunda regalis

Perennials – grey/ornamental foliage

Ajuga reptans-varieties
Anaphalis triplinervis
Artemisia ludoviciana
– 'Silver Queen'
– stelleriana
– vallesiaca
Avena sempervirens
Bergenia delavayi
– purpurascens
Cerastium
Festuca cinerea
Festuca glauca
Hebe pinguifolia
Helianthemum
Helictotrichon
Hosta
Leontopodium
Macleaya cordata
Santolina chamaecyparissus
Sedum kamtschaticum
– spathulifolium
Stachys 'Silver Carpet'
Thymus vulgaris
– 'Silver Queen'
Veronica incana

Ornamental grasses

Alopecurus pratensis
Arrhenatherum elatius ssp. bulbosum
Avena sempervirens
Briza
Carex buchananii
– morrowii 'Variegata'
Cortaderia selloana
Festuca capillaris
– glauca
– tenuissima
Glyceria maxima
Holcus lanatus 'Albovariegata'
Lasiogrostis
Luzula sylvatica
Miscanthus sacchariflorus
– sinensis
Molinia caerulea
Pennisetum compressum
Phalaris arundinacea
Stipa

QUICK GUIDE
Perennials – ground covering

Perennials – ground covering

	Flowering months	Suitable site	Evergreen
Acaena buchananii	6-8	sun, partial shade	*
Achillea tomentosa	6-9	sun	
Ajuga reptans	4-5	sun, partial shade	*
Alchemilla mollis	5-9	partial shade	
Antennaria dioica	5-7	sun	*
Arabis alpina	4-5	sun	*
Armeria maritima	5-7	sun	*
Asarum europaeum	3-4	partial and shade	*
Asperula odorata	5-6	partial and shade	*
Astilbe chinensis	6-9	sun, partial shade	
Aubrieta deltoides	3-6	sun	*
Bergenia cordifolia	4-5	partial shade	*
Campanula portenschlagiana	6-7	sun and shade	
Cerastium tomentosum	5-7	sun	*
Dianthus deltoides	6-8	sun	*
– plumaris	6-7	sun	*
Draba sibirica	3-9	sun	
Epimedium alpinum	5-6	shade	
Euphorbia cyparissias	4-5	sun, partial shade	
Festuca	5-6	sun, partial shade	*
Gypsophila	5-8	sun	
Helianthemum	5-9	sun	*
Hepatica	3-4	partial shade	
Hosta fortunei	7	partial and shade	
Hosta undulata	7-9	partial and shade	*
Hutchinsia	5-8	partial shade	*
Hypericum calycinum	6-9	partial shade	*
Hypericum olympicum	6-8	sun	
Hypericum reptans	6	sun	
Iberis sempervirens	4-7	sun, partial shade	*
Lamium galeobdolon	4-8	sun, partial shade	*
Lamium maculatum	4-8	sun, partial shade	*
Lysimachia nummularia	6-7	sun and shade	*
Mimulus	6-8	sun	
Nepeta x faassenii	6-10	sun	
Pachysandra terminalis	3-5	partial and shade	*
Phlox subulata	4-5	sun	*
Polygonum affine	6-11	sun, partial shade	
Prunella webbiana	6-8	sun, partial shade	
Sagina subulata	6-9	sun, partial shade	*
Saponaria ocymoides	5-6	sun	
Saxifraga umbrosa	5-6	sun and shade	*
Sedum acre	5-10	sun	*
Sedum album	6-8	sun, partial shade	*
Sedum kamtschaticum	7-8	sun, partial shade	*
Sedum spurium	7-8	sun, partial shade	*
Stachus olympica	6-8	sun	*
Thymus serpyllum	5-7	sun	*
Tiarella cordifolia	5-6	partial shade, shade	*
Veronica repens	5-7	sun	
Vinca minor	2-6	partial and shade	*
Vinca major	3-7	sun and shade	*
Viola odorata	3-4	partial and shade	*
Waldsteinia	5	sun, shade, partial shade	*

Perennials – evergreen

Acaena
Alyssum
Antennaria
Arabis
Armeria
Artemisia
Asarum
Aubrieta
Avena
Bergenia
Carex
Cerastium
Dianthus
Draba
Dryopteris
Epimedium
Festuca
Geum
Hebe
Helianthemum
Helleborus
Heuchera
Iberuis
Lamium
Lavandula
Lithospermum
Lysimachia nummularia
Pachysandra
Polypodium
Sagina
Santolina
Saxifraga
Sedum
Sempervivum
Teucrium
Thymus
Vinca
Viola odorata

Perennials – for Autumn planting

If grown in pots or containers, they can also be planted in Spring.

Alyssum
Arabis
Aubrieta
Bergenia
Brunnera
Dicentra
Doronicum
Draba
Galium
Helleborus
Hepatica
Iberis
Paeonia
Papaver
Primula
Pulmonaria
Pulsatilla
Saxifraga
Viola odorata

Perennials – for any position
– provided the soil contains a certain amount of humus

Dicentra
Matteuccia
Ranunculus aconitifolius
Tiarella
Tropaeolum speciosum
Waldsteinia

Perennials – for sunny positions

Acaena
Acantholimon
Achillea
Adenophora
Adonis
Aethionema
Agapanthus
Agrimonia
Agrostemma
Allium (Allium moly excluded)
Alopecurus
Alstroemeria
Alcea
Alyssum
Anacyclus
Antennaria
Anthemis
Anthericum
Anthyllis
Arabis
Arenaria
Arnebia
Artemisia
Arundo
Asclepias
Asparagus
Asphodeline
Aster amellus
– farreri
– frikartii
– linosyris
Astragalus
Aubrieta
Ballota
Baptisia
Begonia grandis
Belamcanda
Berkheya
Borago
Bouteloua
Briza
Buphthalmum
Calamagrostis
Calandrinia
Calceolaria
Camassia
Campanula
Carlina
Cassia
Catananche
Centaurium
Centranthus
Ceratostigma
Cheiranthus
Chrysanthemum
Cichorium
Cirsium
Codonopsis

Commelina
Coreopsis
Coronilla
Cortaderia
Cosmos
Crambe
Crepis
Crinum
Cyananthus
Cynara
Cynoglossum
Delosperma
Delphinium
Dianthus
Diascia
Dierama
Digitalis
Dionysia
Douglasia
Draba
Dracocephalum
Echinacea
Echinops
Edraianthus
Elymus
Eremurus
Erigeron
Erinus
Eriogonum
Eriophyllum
Erodium
Eryngium
Euryops
Festuca
Foeniculum
Frankenia
Fritillaria imperialis
Gaillardia
Galega
Galtonia
Gaura
Genista
Gentiana acaulis
Geum
Glyceria
Goniolimon
Gratiola
Gypsophila
Hakonechloa
Haplopappus
Helenium
Helianthemum
Helianthus
Helichrysum
Heliopsis
Hieracium
Hippocrepis
Iberis
Incarvillea

Inula
Iris danfordiae
– germanica
– kaempferi
– pumila
– reticulata
– setosa
Jasione
Kniphofia
Lavandula
Lavatera
Lasiagrostis
Leontopodium
Lewisia
Liatris
Libertia
Lilium
Limonium
Linum
Lobelia
Lychnis
Margyricarpus
Marrubium
Mathhiola
Mertensia
Micromeria
Milium
Mimulus
Moltkia
Moraea
Morina
Morisia
Myosotis
Nepeta
Nerine
Nierembergia
Onopordum
Onosma
Origanum
Osteospermum
Paeonia
Panicum
Papaver
Parehebe
Paronychia
Pellaea
Pennisetum
Penstemon
Perovskia
Petrorhagia
Phalaris
Phlomis
Phlox stolonifera
– subulata
Phormium
Phygelius
Phyteuma
Pimpinella
Plantago
Platycodon
Poa

Polemonium
Polygala
Potentilla
Pterocephalus
Pyrethrum
Raoulia
Reineckia
Rhazya
Romneya
Rudbeckia
Ruta
Salvia
Sanguisorba
Santolina
Saponaria
Satureja
Scabiosa
Scutellaria
Sedum
Sempervivum
Senecio
Serratula
Sesleria
Sidalcea
Silene
Sisyrinchium
Solidaster
Stipa
Stokesia
Strobilanthes
Symphyandra
Tanacetum
Teucrium
Thermopsis
Thymus
Townsendia
Trospermum
Tunica
Verbascum
Verbena
Vernonia
Veronica
Viola
Yucca
Zauschneria
Zigadenus

QUICK GUIDE
Perennials – for sunny and half-shaded positions

Perennials – for sunny and half-shaded positions

Acanthus
Aconitum
Acorus
Aegopodium
Ajuga
Alchemilla
Allium moly
Amsonia
Anagallis
Anaphalis
Anchusa
Androsace
Angelica
Aquilegia
Arisaema
Arisarum
Aristolochia
Armeria
Arnica
Arrhenatherum
Aruncus
Arundinaria
Asplenium
Aster alpinus
– cordifolius
– dumosus
– ericoides
– novi-belgii
Astilbe
Astrantia
Atropa
Avena
Azorella
Bellis
Bergenia
Bletilla
Boltonia
Boykinia
Brachycome
Bulbinella
Bupleurum
Calamintha
Caltha
Campanula latifolia
Cardamine
Cardiocrinum
Carduncellus
Cautleya
Centaurea
Cephalaria
Cerastium
Chaerophyllum
Chelone
Chiastophyllum
Chrysogonum
Cimicifuga
Clematis
Convolvulus

Cotula
Cotyledon
Crocosmia
Cymbalaria
Cystopteris
Deinanthe
Dictamnus
Diphylleia
Diplarrhena
Disporum
Doronicum
Dryas
Epilobium
Erythronium
Eupatorium
Filipendula
Fragaria
Francoa
Fritillaria meleagris
– persica
Fuchsia
Gentiana asclepiadea
– septemfida
Geranium
Gillenia
Glaucidium
Globularia
Gunnera
Hacquetia
Hebe
Helictotrichon
Hemerocallis
Heracleum
Hesperis
Heuchera
x Heucherella
Holcus
Horminum
Hosta
Houstonia
Houttuynia
Hutchinsia
Hypericum
Hyssopus
Iris foetidissima
– pseudacorus
– sanguinea
– sibirica
Jeffersonia
Lathyrus latifolius
Leucojum
Ligularia
Linaria
Lindelofia
Liriope
Lunaria
Lupinus
Lysichiton

Lysimachia
Lythrum
Macleaya
Malva
Meconopsis
Melissa
Mentha
Meum
Miscanthus
Molinia
Monarda
Myosotis palustris
Myrrhis
Oenothera
Ophiopogon
Phlox amoena
– divaricata
– douglasii
– maculata
– paniculata
Phuopsis
Physalis
Physostegia
Platycodon
Polygonum affine
Polygonum
– amplexicaule
– bistorta
Polygonum
  vaccinifolium
Primula
Prunella
Pulmonaria
Pulsatilla
Rheum
Roscoea
Sagina
Sanguinaria
Scopolia
Scrophularia
Selinum
Solidago
Stachys
Symphyandra
Symphytum
Telekia
Tradescantia
Trillium
Trollius
Valeriana
Zantedeschia

Perennials – for half-shaded and shaded positions

Aconitum
Actaea
Adiantum
Ajuga
Alchemilla
Anaphalis
Anemone
Anemonopsis
Aquilegia
Arum
Aruncus
Asarina
Asperula
Astilbe
Athyrium
Bergenia
Blechnum
Brunnera
Campanula latifolia
Carex
Chelone
Cimicifuga
Chelone
Clintonia
Convallaria
Coreopsis verticillata
Cortusa
Corydalis
Cyclamen
Cypripedium
Cyrtomium
Dentaria
Deschampsia
Dicentra
Dodecatheon
Doronicum
Dryopteris
Eomecon
Epimedium
Eupatorium
Euphorbia cyparissias
Ferns
Filipendula
Galax
Galeobdolon
Galium
Gentiana sino-ornata
Geranium
Glechoma
Haberlea
Helleborus
Hepatica
Hosta
Hylomecon
Hypericum calycinum
Hypsella
Kirengeshoma
Lamiastrum

Lamium
Lathyrus vernus
Ligularia
Luetkea
Luzula
Lysimachia
Mazus
Melittis
Mimulus
Mitella
Omphalodes
Ourisia
Oxalis
Pachysandra
Patrinia
Peltiphyllum
Phytolacca
Podophyllum
Polygonatum
Polygonum
Polypodium
Polystichum
Pratia
Primula
Pulmonaria
Pulsatilla
Ramonda
Reynoutria
Rodgersia
Romanzoffia
Saxifraga geum
Schyzostylis
Scilla campanulata
Shortia
Smilacina
Soldanella
Synthyris
Tanakea
Tellima
Thalictrum
Tiarella
Tolmiea
Trachystemon
Tricyrtis
Trollius
Uvularia
Vancouveria
Veratrum
Vinca
Viola odorata
Wulfenia

Perennials – attractive to butterflies and other insects

Achillea
Aconitum
Anchusa
Arabis
Asclepias
Aster
Astrantia
Aubrieta
Bergenia
Centaurea macrocephala
Centranthus
Dianthus
Doronicum
Echinops
Echinacea
Erigeron
Eryngium
Eupatorium
Euphorbia
Gaillardia
Helenium
Helianthus
Heliopsis
Heracleum
Lamium
Lavandula
Liatris
Ligularia
Limonium
Lupinus
Lythrum
Monarda
Nepeta
Phlox
Polemonium
Prunella
Pulmonaria
Rudbeckia
Salvia
Satureja
Scabiosa
Scutellaria
Sedum spectabile
Sedum 'Autumn Joy'
Stachys
Teucrium
Thymus

Perennials – for limy soils

Acanthus
Adonis vernalis
Ajuga
Alyssum
Anemone sylvestris
Anthemis
Asarum
Asparagus
Asperula
Aster alpinus
– amellus
– farreri
Aubrieta
Avena
Bouteloua
Campanula carpatica
– cochleariifolia
– garganica
– glomerata
– persicifolia
– portenschlagiana
– poscharskyana
– rotundifolia
Carlina
Centranthus
Cerastium
Chiastophyllum
Cichorium
Cyclamen
Cypripedium calceolus
Dianthus gratianopolitanus
Dianthus plumarius
Dictamnus
Digitalis
Draba
Dryas
Eryngium
Euphorbia
Filipendula vulgaris
Gentiana acaulis
Geranium dalmaticum
– sanguineum
– subcaulescens
Gypsophila
Helianthemum
Helictotrichon
Helleborus
Hepatica
Hypericum polyphyllum
Iberis
Inula
Iris germanica
Iris pumila
Leontopodium
Lilium candidum
Limonium
Linaria
Linum

Morina
Origanum
Papaver nudicaule
Phlox subulata
Physalis
Polygonatum
Primula auricula
– veris
Pulsatilla
Santolina
Saponaria
Scabiosa
Sedum album
Sesleria
Silene
Soldanella alpina
Stachys olympica
Stipa
Teucrium
Veronica teucrium
Yucca

Perennials – for acid soils (lime-haters)

Actaea
Adiantum
Athyrium
Blechnum
Carex
Cautleya
Chelone
Chrysogonum
Corydalis
Cyrtomium
Deinanthe
Deschampsia
Dianthus deltoides
Dodecatheon
Dryopteris
Galax
Gentiana sino-ornata
Houstonia
Iris kaempferi
Kirengeshoma

Lewisia
Lupinus
Luzula sylvatica
Matteuccia
Molinia
Osmunda
Oxalis
Polypodium
Potentilla aurea
Saxifraga cotyledon
Sedum spathulifolium
Sempervivum arachnoideum
Shortia
Soldanella
Tanakea
Thalictrum
Tricyrtis
Wulfenia

Perennials – where rabbits are a problem

Acaena
Achillea
Aconitum
Alchemilla
Alyssum
Anaphalis
Anchusa
Aquilegia
Artemisia
Aruncus
Asarum
Astilbe
Aubrieta
Bergenia
Centranthus
Cimicifuga
Convallaria
Cortaderia
Corydalis
Delphinium
Dictamnus
Digitalis
Doronicum
Echinops
Eryngium
Eupatorium
Euphorbia
Geranium
Geum
Helianthemum
Helleborus
Hemerocallis
Hosta

Hypericum
Iberis
Iris
Kniphofia
Lamium
Lavandula
Ligularia
Lupinus
Lysimachia
Macleaya
Meconopsis
Monarda
Nepeta
Pachysandra
Paeonia
Polygonum
Primula
Prunella
Ranunculus
Rodgersia
Salvia
Santolina
Saponaria
Saxifraga
Sedum
Stachys
Thymus
Tradescantia
Verbascum
Veronica
Vinca
Viola
Waldsteinia

QUICK GUIDE
Alpines – for the rock garden

Alpines – for the rockgarden

Aethionema	Polygonum affine
Alyssum	Potentilla aurea
Arabis	– tonguei
Aster alpinus	Primula juliae-hybrids
Aubrieta	Pulsatilla
Campanula	Saponaria ocymoides
Cerastium	Saxifraga
Dianthus deltoides	Scutellaria
Dodecatheon	Sedum
Draba	Sempervivum
Festuca	Silene
Geranium dalmaticum	Thymus serpyllum
– sanguineum	Veronica gentianoides
– subcaulescens	– spicata
Gypsophila repens	– incana
Hebe	
Helianthemum	
Hutchinsia	
Hypericum polyphyllum	
– repens	
Iberis	
Inula ensifolia	
Jovibarba	
Leontopodium	
Lithodora diffusa	
Lychnis Arkwrightii-hybrids	
Petrorhagia	
Phlox amoena	
– subulata	

Perennials and Alpines – on walls and between stones

Acaena	
Alyssum	
Arabis	
Aubrieta	
Campanula garganica	
– portenschlagiana	
– poscharskyana	
Centranthus	
Cerastium	
Corydalis	
Gypsophila repens	
Hutchinsia	
Iberis	
Jovibarba	
Leontopodium	
Phlox subulata	
Saponaria ocymoides	
Saxifraga	
Sedum	
Sempervivum	
Thymus drucei	
– lanuginosus	

Perennials – for dried floral use

	Harvest-month
Acanthus mollis	8
Achillea	8
Alchemilla mollis	6
Anaphalis triplinervis	8
Astilbe	7
Centaurea macrocephala	7
Lavandula officinalis	8
Echinops ritro	8
Eryngium	8
Eupatorium purpureum	9
Euphorbia	7
Gypsophila	8
Leontopodium	7
Liatris spicata	8
Limonium	7
Physalis	10
Salvia officinalis	8
Sedum spectabile	9
Solidago	9
Stachys	8
Verbascum	8

Grasses

Cortaderia	9
Pennisetum	7

Perennials – needing support

Achillea millefolium	
Aconitum	Rudbeckia laciniata
Anchusa	– nitida
Asclepias	Sanguisorba
Aster amellus	Saponaria officinalis
– novi-belgii	Sidalcea
Astrantia	Thalictrum
Campanula lactiflora	
– latifolia	
– persicifolia	
Delphinium	
Echinops	
Erigeron	
Eryngium	
Filipendula	
Helenium	
Helianthus	
Inula	
Lathyrus	
Lupinus	
Lychnis chalcedonica	
Macleaya	
Monarda	
Oenothera	
Physostegia	

Perennials – for troughs, tubs and pots

Aethionema
Agapanthus
Ajuga
Alyssum
Anaphalis triplinervis
Arabis
Armeria maritima
Artemisia ludoviciana
– stelleriana
Aubrieta
Bergenia
Bupthalmum
Campanula
Cerastium
Coreopsis lanceolata
– verticillata
Dianthus
Draba
Euphorbia polychroma
Festuca
Gypsophila repens
Hebe
Helianthemum
Hosta
Hutchinsia
Hypericum polyphyllum
– reptans
Iberis
Inula ensifolia
Jovibarba
Lamium
Leontopodium
Lithodora diffusa
Petrorhagia
Phlox amoena
– subulata
Polygonum affine
Prunella
Salvia
Santolina
Saponaria ocymoides
Saxifraga
Sedum
Sempervivum
Silene
Stachys
Teucrium
Thymus
Veronica spicata
Viola cornuta

Perennials – heavily spreading or self-seeding types

Achillea
Ajuga
Alchemilla
Anaphalis
Aquilegia
Artemisia lactiflora
Aruncus
Asarum
Astrantia
Campanula glomerata
 – persicifolia
Centranthus
Cerastium
Corydalis
Dianthus deltoides
Eupatorium
Euphorbia cyparissias
Ferns
Filipendula
Fragaria vesca
Geranium
Hepatica
Lamium
Lamiastrum
Lysimachia
Lythrum
Macleaya
Polemonium
Polygonum
Primula elatior
Prunella
Pulmonaria
Saponaria officinalis
Sedum acre
 – album
 – spurium
Solidago
Stachys
Thymus serpyllum
Tiarella
Vinca minor
Viola odorata

Perennials – for easy propagation

Increase by

Acaena: division
Acantholimon: division
Acanthus: seed/division
Achillea: division
Aconitum: seed/division
Acorus: division
Adenophora: seed/division
Adonis: seed/division
Aethionema: cuttings (Summer)
Agapanthus: division
Ajuga: air-layering/division
Alcea: seed
Alchemilla: seed
Allium: division
Alstroemeria: seed/division
Alyssum: seed
Anacyclus: seed
Anagallis: cuttings/seed/division
Anaphalis: division
Anchusa: root cuttings
Androsace: rooted rosette cuttings
Anemone sylvestris: division/seed
Anemone-hybrids: root cuttings (Spring)
Angelica: root cuttings
Antennaria: division
Anthemis: seed/division
Anthericum: seed/division
Anthyllis: seed/cuttings
Aquilegia: seed
Arabis: seed/cuttings (Summer)
Arenaria: seed/cuttings (Summer)
Aristolochia: air-layering/seed
Armeria: division/cuttings (Summer)
Arnebia: seed/cuttings (root)
Arrhenatherum: division
Artemisia: division/cuttings
Asclepias: division
Asparagus: seed
Asperula: division/cuttings
Asphodeline: division
Aster alpinus: division/cuttings/seed
Aster amellus: seed/division
Aster (other): division
Astilbe: division
Astragalus: seed
Astrantia: division
Aubrieta: seed/division/cuttings
Baptisia: seed/division
Begonia grandis: seed
Bellis perennis: seed/division
Bergenia: division/cuttings
Blechnum: division
Borago: seed
Brachycome: seed
Briza: seed
Buphthalmum: division
Calamintha: seed/cuttings

Increase by

Calceolaria: seed
Caltha palustris: division
Camassia: seed/cormlets
Campanula: division/seed
Cardamine: division
Carlina: seed
Cassia: seed
Catananche: division/seed
Centaurea: division/seed
Centaurium: seed/cuttings (Summer)
Cephalaria: seed
Cerastium: root cuttings/division
Ceratostigma: cuttings
Cheiranthus: seed/cuttings
Chelone: division/seed/cuttings (Summer)
Chrysanthemum: division/root cuttings
Cichorium: division/root cuttings
Cimicifuga: division
Codonopsis: seed/cuttings
Convallaria: division/root cuttings
Coreopsis: division
Cortaderia: division
Cortusa: seed/division
Corydalis: seed/division
Cosmos: seed
Cotyledon: cuttings
Crambe: root cuttings
Crinum: division
Crocosmia: cormlets
Cyananthus: cuttings
Cyclamen: seed
Cynara: air-layering
Cynoglossum: seed
Cypripedium: division/seed
Delphinium: division/seed
Deschampsia: division
Dianthus: cuttings/seed
Dicentra: division/cuttings
Dictamnus: seed
Digitalis: seed
Dodecatheon: seed/division
Doronicum: division:
Draba: division/cuttings
Dracocephalum: division/cuttings
Dryas: cuttings/air-layering
Dryopteris: division
Echinacea: division
Echinops: root cuttings
Edraianthus: seed
Elymus: division
Eomecon: root cuttings
Epilobium: seed/cuttings
Epimedium: air-layering
Eremurus: seed
Erigeron: division
Erinus: seed/division
Eriogonum: division
Eriophyllum: seed/division
Erodium: cuttings (Summer)

QUICK GUIDE
Perennials – for easy propagation

Increase by

Eryngium: seed
Erythronium: cormlets
Eupatorium: seed/cuttings (Summer)/division
Euphorbia: division/cuttings
Festuca: division
Filipendula: division
Fragaria: air-layering
Francoa: seed/cuttings (Summer)/division
Frankenia: division
Fritillaria: cormlets
Fuchsia: division/cuttings
Gaillardia: seed
Galega: seed/division/cuttings
Galtonia: cormlets
Genista: cuttings
Gentiana: division/seed
Geranium: division (mainly)
Geum: seed/division
Globularia: division/cuttings/seed
Glyceria: division
Gunnera: division
Gypsophila: seed/cuttings
Haberlea: seed/division/leaf cuttings
Hebe: cuttings (Summer)
Helenium: division
Helianthemum: cuttings (Summer)
Helianthus: division
Helichrysum: division/cuttings
Helictotrichon: division
Heliopsis: division
Helleborus: division
Hemerocallis: division
Hepatica: division
Heracleum: seed
Hesperis: seed
Heuchera: division
x Heucherella: division
Hieracium: seed/division
Hosta: division
Houstonia: division/seed
Hutchinsia: division/seed
Hypericum: division/cuttings/seed
Iberis: cuttings (Summer)/division
Incarvillea: seed
Inula: seed/division
Iris danfordiae: cormlets
 – germanica: division
 – pseudacorus: division
 – pumila: root cuttings with eye (July)
 – sibirica: division
Jasione: division/seed
Jeffersonia: seed/division
Kniphofia: divison
Lamiastrum: air-layering
Lamium: air-layering
Lathyrus: seed
Lavandula: seed
Lavatera: seed
Leucojum: cormlets

Increase by

Lewisia: seed
Liatris: division
Ligularia: division
Limonium: seed
Linaria: seed
Linum: seed
Lobelia: divison
Lunaria: seed
Lupinus: division/seed
Lychnis arkwrightii: seed
 – chalcedonica: division
 – coronaria: seed
Lysimachia: division
Lythrum: seed
Macleaya: air-layering/cuttings
Malva: seed
Matteuccia: division
Matthiola: seed/division
Mazus: division/seed
Meconopsis: seed
Mentha: air-layering
Mertensia: seed/division
Mimulus: cuttings
Miscanthus: division
Monarda: division
Moraea: division
Morisia: cuttings of rooted rosettes
Myosotis alpestris: seed
 – palustris: air-layering
Nepeta: division
Nerine: division of group (once in 3 years)
Nierembergia caerulea: top cuttings
Oenothera: seed/division
Omphalodes: division
Onosma: seed
Origanum: seed/cuttings/division
Ourisia: seed/division
Oxalis: seed/division
Pachysandra: division
Papaver: root cuttings
Parahebe: cuttings (Summer)
Pennisetum: division
Penstemon: seed
Phalaris: division
Phlomis: cuttings/seed
Phlox paniculata: division/root cuttings
 – subulata: division/cuttings
Physalis: root cuttings
Physostegia: division
Phyteuma: seed
Phytolacca: seed
Pimpinella: division
Platycodon: division
Polemonium: seed/division
Polygala: cuttings (Summer)
Polygonatum: division
Polygonum: cuttings (Summer)/division
Polypodium: division
Potentilla: division

Perennials – for cut flowers

Achillea
Aconitum
Agapanthus
Alchemilla
Alstroemeria
Aquilegia
Asclepias
Aster
Astilbe
Campanula
Centaurea
Chelone
Chrysanthemum
Cortaderia
Delphinum
Dianthus
Doronicum
Echinacea
Echinops
Erigeron
Gaillardia
Gypsophila
Helenium
Helianthus
Heliopsis
Iris
Kniphofia
Lathyrus
Liatris
Lupinus
Lychnis
Paeonia
Papaver
Physalis
Physostegia
Pyrethrum
Scabiosa
Solidago
Trollius
Viola

Perennials – scented

Achillea filipendulina
Anemone sylvestris
Centranthus ruber
Asperula odorata
Campanula lactiflora
Chrysanthemum
   koreanum
Convallaria majalis
Dianthus plumarius
Kitchen herbs
Iris germanica
Lupinus
Monarda
Nepeta
Paeonia
Phlox paniculata
Santolina
   chamaecyparissus
Salvia superba
Thymus
Viola cornuta
Viola odorata

Perennials – climbing

Lathyrus latifolius
Tropaeolum
   speciosum

Increase by

Primula: seed/division
Prunella: division
Pulmonaria: division
Pulsatilla: seed
Pyrethrum: seed
Ranunculus: division/seed
Raoulia: division
Reynoutria: division
Rheum: division
Rodgersia: division
Romneya: root cuttings
Roscoea: division
Rudbeckia: division
Sagina: division
Salvia: division
Santolina: cuttings (Summer)
Saponaria: cuttings (Summer)
Saxifraga: division
Scabiosa: division/cuttings/seed
Schizostylis: division
Scilla: partition of clumps
Scutellaria: cuttings (Summer)
Sedum: division/cuttings
Sempervivum: cutting of rosettes
Senecio: seed
Shortia: division/seed
Sidalcea: division
Silene: division
Sisyrinchium: seed
Soldanella: division/seed
Solidago: division/root cuttings
Solidaster: division/root cuttings
Stachys: division
Stokesia: division/seed
Strobilanthes: cuttings
Stylophorum: division
Symphyandra: seed
Teucrium: cuttings (Summer)/air-layering
Thalictrum: division/seed
Thermopsis: seed/division
Thymus lanuginosus: division
 — serpyllum: division
 — vulgaris: division/seed
Townsendia: seed
Tradescantia: division
Trifolium: seed/division
Trillium: division
Trollius: division
Tunica: seed
Uvularia: division
Veratrum: division
Verbascum: root cuttings
Verbena: seed
Veronica: division/cuttings
Viola: division
Viola cornuta: division/cuttings
Viscaria: division
Waldsteinia: division
Yucca: division

Increase by

Zantedeschia: division/cuttings
Zauschneria: cuttings/division
Zigadenus: division

Perennials – for the kitchen

Allium schoenoprasum
Artemisia abrotanum
 — absinthium
 — dracunculus
Asperula odorata
Hyssopus officinalis
Lavandula latifolia
Levisticum officinale
Melissa officinalis
Mentha piperita
Ruta graveolens
Salvia officinalis
Sanguisorba officinalis
Thymus citriodorus
 — vulgaris

INDEX
Bold figures refer to the illustrations

INDEX
Bold figures refer to the illustrations

INDEX
Bold figures refer to the illustrations

INDEX
Bold figures refer to the illustrations